THE MYSTERY OF
MARGARET BOOKER
One Woman's Triumph Over Slavery

Kathy Lynne Marshall

THE MYSTERY OF MARGARET BOOKER

One Woman's Triumph Over Slavery

Kathy Lynne Marshall

Praise for
The Mystery of Margaret Booker
One Woman's Triumph Over Slavery

Margaret Booker Asserts Her Birthright in Truth!

Falling in love with Margaret Booker the very first time I heard her exclaim, "Once upon a time in Ol' Viginny! You feel her presence while she recited the history of her lineage. In true Griot fashion, Margaret lulls her listeners into those memorable times in her life that many can relate to. The author gives us an ironclad research method within the writing, especially when geographical markers, roads and bridges are mentioned. There's a point in this work where I'm excited to read a Civil War, "Gone With the Wind" type of account from a matriarchal elder. Excellent book!

Tanisha L. Watson, Educator and Genealogist

A Striking Tale in Historical Context Not to be Missed

The author has created an important story of family and history! The Mystery of Margaret Booker surpassed my expectations. The illustrative writing pulls you into the story and you cannot put this book down. Her stories are remarkable and historically accurate told from and in her ancestor's voice. Children, there are often two sides to every story depending on who is telling it. This is a historical text not to be missed.

Robin A. Harris, M.Ed

Captivating Read! I Couldn't Put it Down.

Kathy Marshall's writing pulls you into the story from the first page. Her character development is amazing! You feel you are there in the story and that you actually could be friends, or enemies, with the characters. I am amazed at the level of research she does and she also provides guidance on how to capture and publish your own family genealogy. A great way to begin the New Year.

C.M.

Works by Kathy Lynne Marshall

Finding Marshalls: A Genealogy Trip with a Black and White Twist

The Marshall Legacy in Black and White

The Mystery of Margaret Booker: One Woman's Triumph Over Slavery

Finding Otho: The Search for Our Enslaved Williams Ancestors

Finding Daisy: From the Deep South to the Promised Land

The Ancestors Are Smiling!

Ken Anderson: Alias "Special K"

Family Harambee! How to Discuss Potentially Challenging Discoveries in Your Family Tree: A Workbook

Anthologies

"It's Storytime!" in the California Writer's Club Visions: Life Through the Eyes of Sacramento Writers

"Finally, a Priority," in Northern California Publishers and Authors Destination: The World Anthology

"A Nickel for Your Thoughts, Dad," in journalist Genoa Barrow's Daddy Issues: Black Women Speaking Truth and Healing Wounds

"Wolf Song" in the Northern California Publishers and Authors Birds of a Feather Anthology

ISBN-13: 978-1-7375733-4-0

SECOND EDITION

Cover drawing and design by Kanika Marshall Art.
Back cover artwork by Mary E. Marshall

Editor: Jean L. Cooper

Kathy Lynne Marshall Art and Books
PO Box 1202, Elk Grove, CA 95759-1202
www.KathyLynneMarshall.com

DEDICATION

Margaret Booker and her intrepid direct line descendants:

Margaret Booker
(imagined by author)
1834-1911

Joseph Lewis
Booker
1855-1952

Myrtle Booker
Williams
1881-1972

Pearl Williams
Carter
1908-1990

Mary Carter
Marshall
1934-2007

Kathy Lynne
Marshall
Author

TABLE OF CONTENTS

INTRODUCTION

Why did it take so long?

My family's most endearing tale of heroism was about my great-great-great-grandmother, Margaret Booker, and how she migrated with her children from slavery to freedom after the Emancipation Proclamation was signed by President Abraham Lincoln in 1863. Parts of her incredible story had been well-known to me for nearly four decades when, in 1976, my elders wrote to me about her bravery.

I included snippets of Margaret's fascinating journey in my first two books: The Ancestors Are Smiling! and Finding Otho: The Search for Our Enslaved Williams Ancestors. So why do I still not know the exact name of Margaret's slave owner, her parents, her siblings, or precisely where she was born? Where, exactly, did she live during her thirty years in bondage? Was she a cook, laundress, farm worker, or breeder? What did she look like? Who fathered her children? How and when did she migrate to freedom, and how did she make her living after she was free? And where did the surname "Booker" come from in the first place? The ancestors would not let me sleep until I found answers to those burning research questions and published them in a book.

For this literary nonfiction story, I scoured the usual genealogical record sources such as the US Census, marriage and death records, historical accounts of persons and events in the places my people lived, estate probate records, court minutes, land records, and newspaper clippings. I also used genetic genealogy—DNA—to prove or disprove blood relationships. Nearly every name, date, and place in this account is true. I filled in the blanks with as much heart and soul as I could to enliven the story of my ancestors, always remaining true to the data.

I helped the spirit of Margaret Booker tell her own story, which is intentionally peppered with a touch of dialect. Reading narratives from people who had been enslaved in West Virginia and then moved to Ohio, examining history books from local authors, and discovering key documents which tracked slave "Margarett" to specific owners, helped me place where she was in time and space from her birth in 1834 into the Civil War era.

For Part I, Thirty Years a Slave, I put myself in Margaret's shoes to explore her likely background, family, and daily life. She is the storyteller throughout the book, unless otherwise indicated.

Part II, Forty-Eight Years Free, describes how Margaret and her children left their enslaved status and traveled to a new life of freedom. To learn more about that phase, I drove our talented family historian, M. Lavata Williams, and my Uncle Dale Carter to Barnesville, Ohio, in October 2018. I wanted to record on video and in pictures what remained of the African-American community there.

I formed a friendly, consultative relationship with Dr. Ric Sheffield, Professor of Legal Studies and Sociology for Kenyon College, in Gambier, Ohio. We discussed the migration of formerly enslaved black folk from Maryland and West Virginia into Knox County, Ohio. I was honored to provide him with my books, which would become part of the Kenyon College Library collection of African-American research.

To help me understand where Margaret had been enslaved, I took a short genealogy trip to Beverly, Randolph County, West Virginia—a place steeped in our family lore. Dr. Chris Mielke, Executive Director of the enchanting Beverly Heritage Museum, fed my insatiable hunger about the buildings, prominent citizens, and history of Beverly, and he unknowingly helped make considerable inroads into the truth of this story.

DNA analysis was part of my exhaustive search for records. A summary of the findings is in Appendix F.

To encourage you to write a book about your family, Appendix G, "Solving Your Mystery," contains a cornucopia of hints and tips on the methodology I developed to quick-start the book-writing process. My goal is to encourage others to produce a written document they may leave as a written legacy for generations to come. Incorporating our black family stories into the American historical record will honor the fortitude and resilience of ancestors who helped us be.

It's time to introduce our brave heroine, Margaret Booker.

The Ancestors Are Smiling!

Margaret Booker's Descendants

Joseph* Booker 1855-1952	Cornelia Booker* 1856-1904	George Booker* 1858-?	May Booker* 1860-?	Ella Booker* 1863-1920	Edward Booker 1864-1919	William Booker 1869-?	Sylvester Booker 1871-?
married Sara Myers ↓	married James Anderson	married Harriet		married unknown ↓	married Minerva ↓		
Maude Ada Herbert Myrtle Booker ↓	Joseph Fred Raymond Victor Grendola Edna Leona Hazel Evelina			Clara Anna Hastings	Edward Helen Elsie Ira		
Pearl Williams ↓							
Mary Carter ↓							
Kathy Marshall (Author)							

*Children of John B. Earle

The author's Booker Family Tree, as of 2019:

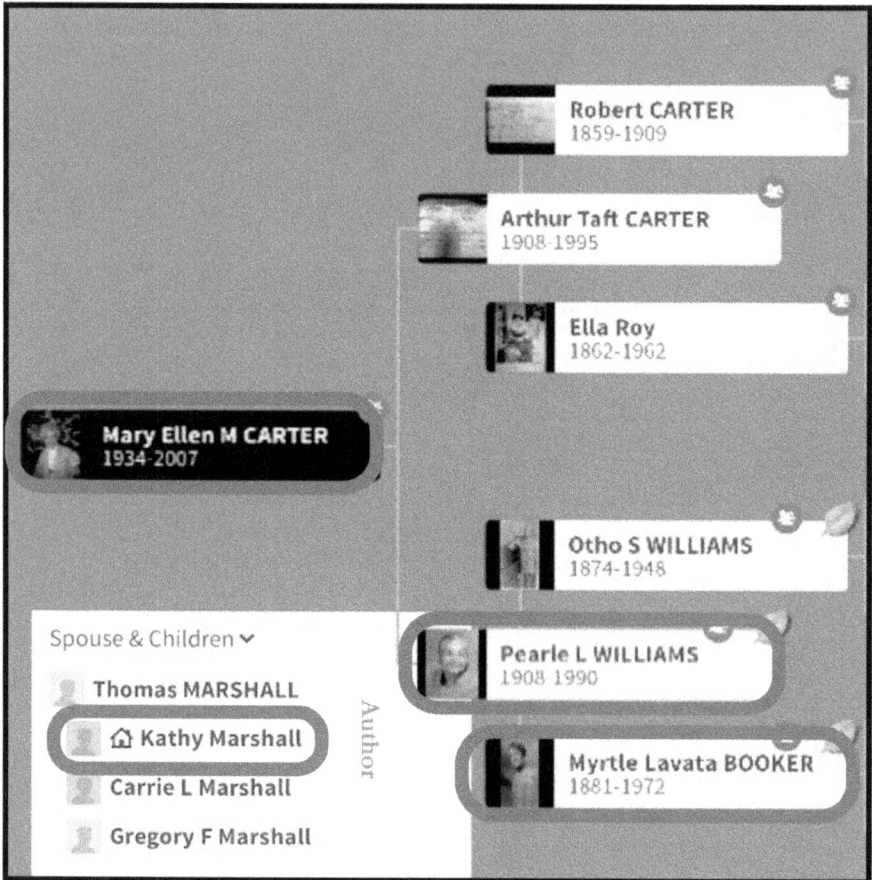

Robert CARTER
1859-1909

Arthur Taft CARTER
1908-1995

Ella Roy
1862-1962

Mary Ellen M CARTER
1934-2007

Otho S WILLIAMS
1874-1948

Pearle L WILLIAMS
1908-1990

Myrtle Lavata BOOKER
1881-1972

Spouse & Children ✓

Thomas MARSHALL

⌂ Kathy Marshall

Carrie L Marshall

Gregory F Marshall

Author

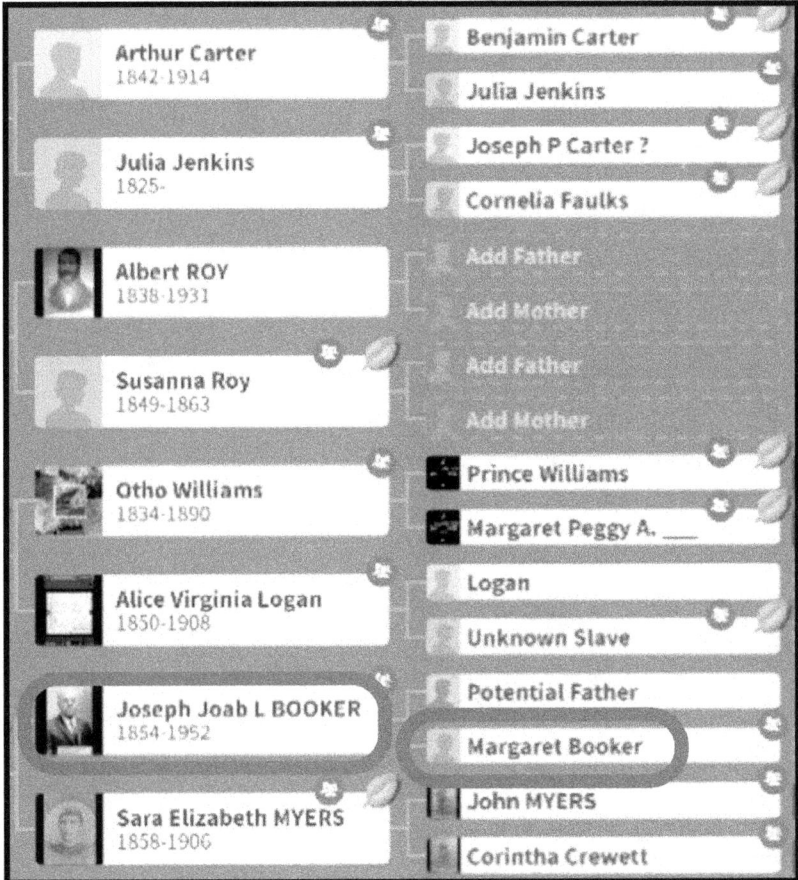

Arthur Carter
1842-1914

Julia Jenkins
1825-

Albert ROY
1838-1931

Susanna Roy
1849-1863

Otho Williams
1834-1890

Alice Virginia Logan
1850-1908

Joseph Joab L BOOKER
1854-1952

Sara Elizabeth MYERS
1858-1906

Benjamin Carter

Julia Jenkins

Joseph P Carter ?

Cornelia Faulks

Add Father

Add Mother

Add Father

Add Mother

Prince Williams

Margaret Peggy A. ___

Logan

Unknown Slave

Potential Father

Margaret Booker

John MYERS

Corintha Crewett

PART I:
THIRTY YEARS A SLAVE

Chapter 1 - The Saga Begins

A cold, boney finger poked my shoulder, rudely awakening me from a deep sleep. I had been dreaming about the magnificent forests in Appalachia. The huge maple leaves of gold and orange peppered with scarlet, detached from their lofty perches in a merry autumn breeze. The falling petals kissed my bare arms as they floated oh-so-slowly from the top branches, down, down, down to form a patchwork carpet on the moist ground. As a girl, I loved skipping through piles of those colorful stars, kicking them up into the air to see them dance anew, finally settling en pointe like ballerinas.

I loved the enchanting smell of pine needles, the loamy earth, and fresh rain in an era when children could play all day long without a care in the world, when there was no problem greater than choosing whether to play tag, or sing songs, or go fishing in Roaring Creek. Innocence was ours in the beginning, but like a fairy tale, bliss can be interrupted. Vibrant color can be reduced to black-and-white in the blink of an eye.

The Southern Cemetery was in my backyard. Spirited essences floated from their underground beds, skimming effortlessly over the sparse lawn and vegetable garden separating our properties. They slipped through my back door unannounced. Sometimes they poked me awake, demanding, "Tell our stories, speak our names, and never forget where you came from." Other times, I glimpsed shadows standing beyond my worn kitchen table, perhaps listening to the conversations I had with my children. I could feel the weight of those long dead souls pressing on me, insisting that I remember the old ones: Earle, Myers, Booker, Goins. In life, some had lived in what is now West Virginia and migrated, like me, to Barnesville, Ohio, after the Civil War. Richer folk took a stagecoach, runaways slinked on the Underground Railroad,[1] and others like me traveled by buckboard or on foot. I wasn't afraid of my other-worldly intruders for they brought a bit of home, memories I would often give to my descendants. And now, dear reader, I'm sharing the mysteries of my life story with you. Love, Margaret Booker

It's Storytime!

"Once upon a time in Ol' Virginny…

"Hush up now, children," I said, looking at my daughter Ella's youngest kids, Clara, Anna, and baby Hastings, who were making a ruckus on the porch. It was twilight on the first sweltering summer evening of the twentieth century. The Barnesville Gas and Electric Light Company started installing streetlamps in 1895, but that improvement hadn't yet reached our section of town.

Sparkling lightning bugs brightened the dark corners of my small yard, sailing on the humid air currents. Children loved catching those glowing fairies which tickled their little palms before they peered inside at the magic light that fluttered so softly in their grasp.

Everyone gathered this balmy summer evening to pay attention to me, their beloved elder, Margaret Booker. The spirits of Edward and Eve Backus stood transparent on my right side as our family's most cherished elders. My grown sons, Joseph, George, Edward, William, and Sylvester were smoking pipes, sitting on the worn porch in rickety chairs, like old men after a hard day's work. My daughter Cornelia lived in Pennsylvania with her large family, and May had died young. Granddaughter Ida was her usual prim and proper self, sitting quietly, back straight, at the edge of the stoop, her hands in the lap of her homemade cornflower blue dress, watching the younger children settling themselves on blankets on the grass.

We had a big crowd tonight. My feet began tapping to their own tune beneath the patchwork skirt I crafted from discarded clothes, excitement building. I lowered my bulk into the antique rocking chair closest to the front door of my narrow, gray clapboard house, renovated from a log cabin some years ago.

My eldest son, Joseph, and his first wife, Sara, brought their grown daughters Maude and Myrtle, teenager Ada Mae, and ten-year-old Herbert to see me. Everyone realized who saw that stylish family that Joseph was doing very well indeed in Mount Vernon, Ohio, where he worked at Cooper's[2] as a machinist.[3] Old Massa's spinster sister, Nancy, taught him to read during a time when it was illegal to do so. Being able to read and write got his foot into the door, but his dedicated work habits helped him get a good job building engines—a job rarely offered to colored folks.

Oh, that Herbert! I never seen a boy dressed in such fancy clothes. Joseph's son looked like a little soldier doll baby (Figure 1). And would you look at the amazing hat on Ada Mae's head! Seemed like it had a life of its own. Was it partially knitted, or was that actually a fluffy brown rabbit on her head? I know, it's probably just her hair puffing it out like that. All my granddaughters have such pretty hairstyles. It helps that Maude Ellen works in a beauty shop. Their granddaddy may have had some influence on the shininess of their hair …

1900: Maude Ellen, 22   Myrtle Lavata, 19   Ada Mae, 16   Herbert Euclid, 10

Figure 1: Joseph Lewis Booker (author's great-great-grandfather) and Sara Elizabeth Myer's children as of 1900.

"Grandmama, I wanted to you see our first baby, William." Maude carefully released him to my practiced arms. Cuddling the darling with just the right amount of pressure, I whispered sweet nothings into his soft ear and caressed his mop of curly black hair. I know the truth. They just wanted me to see him before I died. Little did any of us know I would see another decade before I met my maker. I handed the little dumpling back to his mother.

"You got a fine family there, Miss Margaret!" my pale next-door neighbor, Miss Eliza, called out.

"Mighty fine!" added deep-voiced Mr. Patterson from across the street, still in his blue-black work coveralls which were the same color as his skin.

"Ev'ning, y'all." I waved at the Pattersons and Littles who were watching us intently. Their observations brought the biggest smile to my lips for as fine as my family looked, you better believe I'd be the subject of gossip for many weeks to come.

"Ida Mae, bring me a cool glass of sweet tea, would ya, in case I get choked up talking about the old days."

"Okay, Grandma," Ida Mae's sweet voice replied as she jumped up, smoothed down her dress, then bounded into the narrow house through the screen door. The front room crowded with furniture led into the yellowed kitchen overwhelmed by a massive table whose chairs were currently being used outside. Waiting for her to return, I cooled myself with a stiff paper fan from the Captina African Methodist Episcopal (A.M.E.) Church. It had a blond Jesus holding a white lamb printed on the front and the church's name on the back.

"Thank you, darlin'." One sip of the purplish blackberry tea was all I needed to clear my throat. Once everyone quieted, I began the show.

"What kinds of stories do you want to hear? Do you want to learn about the man who bragged about being 'The Indian Killer'?"

The boys and men all shouted, "Yes!" and waved their arms in the air.

"When Civil War fighting came to my backyard?"

"Yes!" the same people cheered.

"When Ol' Black Jerry ran away from his master?" The younger kids shrugged their shoulders in an "I don't know" stance, but the men shouted, "Yes!"

"When a family member was sold for one dollar?" The adults looked uneasy, fidgeting in their seats.

"How about when I fell in love for the first time?"

The women and girls gushed, "Yes, ma'am!" but the males were silent.

"How about when we slept under the stars on our long trip to this house in Barnesville?" Everybody clapped and cheered.

Well, I started with myself. In a steady schoolteacher voice, I began.

For nigh on to forty years, since late 1863, I've lived right here on Vine Street, in this lovely little town of Barnesville.4 Us old codgers like to sit on the porch in our comfy chairs, just like tonight, sharing a brief look at the past with our beloved families and friends, for our present is usually much better than our past, making us feel like we're progressing as a race.

"You may not believe this, but when I look in the mirror, I see my granddaughter, Myrtle Lavata Booker, looking right back at me." One kid sniggered, not believing that I, a sixty-five-year-old woman with some wrinkles here and there, thought I looked anything like the gorgeous lady sitting next to me. I reached over and patted Myrtle's slender, high yaller5 hand. What a beauty! She was wearing a white dress with a deep-green, diagonal lattice pattern on the bodice. Her neck was completely covered with dainty white lace peeking over the top edge, a delicate cameo pin at her throat. Myrtle's posture was erect, like that of a graceful dancer or a Queen.

"Y'all know Myrtle, the second eldest daughter of my eldest son, Joseph Booker. I'm so happy they're visiting us today," I beamed.

"Amen," chimed my neighbor from her porch.

The young'uns were still laughing as they glanced from the fashionable woman called Myrtle, to me in my rundown finery.

No, really, she's the spitting image of me when I was twenty. Look. We both have a Cupid's bow mouth. See how it's indented in the middle of our top lips? We both have a full bosom. I cupped my saggy breasts—at which all the children howled. We both have shapely hips—smoothing my hands down my sides while sitting was tough, but I managed it. And look at our smooth skin—

caressing my cheek with my right hand and hers with my left. Okay, I'll admit that I may have a few more wisdom spots on my skin than she does. Even the teenagers and adults were laughing now, grabbing their tummies, tears streaming down their faces. They thought their grandma done lost her mind.

I sighed at the memory of youth, when I was thought of as a desirable woman with long, thick hair and perfectly smooth, chocolate brown skin. With a faraway look in my tired eyes, I continued speaking, almost to myself. "I was so young and pretty back then…" After a long pause, a shadow passed over my eyes. "My master thought so too," I added with a frown. "You see, I was almost thirty years a slave, from 1834 to 1863… and I was Massa's favorite," I paused.

"What's a slave, Grandma?" my four-year-old granddaughter, Anna, brought me out of my doldrums and back to the present. I gazed at her pretty, chubby face and long eyelashes, so innocent and trusting. How much of the ugliness and pain of being owned by someone else should I tell her? Maybe I should only talk about happy, nice, wonderful memories during story time, like the day I looked into the eyes of my first baby boy, or when I set foot on the free soil of Ohio. No, they need to know it all, even the time I was beaten bloody right after giving birth. Should I show them the tree6 on my back? Wait a minute, old gal, I must be careful in how I share my stories. Truth is truth, but I don't have to tell all the details every time.

Clearing my throat again, I began speaking to my audience, emphasizing each word, hoping to create the sense that they were about to hear a mystery revealed, important secrets to be shared, and something special to tell their children's children when they were old like me.

I looked closely at young Anna who had posed that simple question—"What's a slave, Grandma?" So many memories flooded back to me.

Clacking my tongue, trying to find the rights words, I finally said, "A slave was usually a black person owned by a white person, just like you own your puppy, or I own this chair right here. A slave must do whatever the owner commands."

Anna wrinkled her nose and shook her head, obviously not understanding the concept. In a way, I was delighted she did not know what slavery was because she never had to live a life of bondage.

"Honey, you asked a simple question, but the answer isn't so easy. I'll tell you 'bout my life little by little, and maybe you'll understand how most black folk lived prior to thirty-five years ago, before the end of slavery in 1865." I readjusted myself, drank another sip or two of tea, then began tonight's story.

After a pause, I said, "'Where did the time go?' I often ask myself. It seems like only yesterday when I was learning how to run like you little buggers,"—pointing at my youngest grandchildren rolling around on the grass. "But it was actually over sixty years ago when I was born near a small town called Beverly, in Randolph County, in what is now West Virginny…"

"Where's that?" Someone called out, interrupting my story before it even began.

I tapped my chin, thinking about the best way to describe the location. "My hometown was about a hundred and fifty miles away from here. Just keep traveling east from my porch toward the sunrise, across the Ohio River at Martins Ferry, then keep ongoing southeast along the Beverly-Fairmont Turnpike, past Elkins a few miles, arriving in Beverly. I'll tell you all about the exciting trip we took from there to here… on another day."

"Oh, Grandma, do we have to wait?" My stare answered her question.

The Whippersnappers

This part of the story is called, "The Whippersnappers."

"The whipper-whats?" Grandson Herbert asked, as he twirled his little soldier hat in the air.

"A whippersnapper is a kind of bratty, know-it-all kid. Do you know what I mean?" I glanced at Herbert, then resumed my story. "It's what the older folks called me and some of the other children back in the day.

Now, to begin at my beginnin'... When I was born in February 1834, only 184 people lived in the entire town of Beverly and that included sixteen slaves and two free black people.

There were a coupla boys I grew up near, named George and Hugh. I noticed the eyebrows on my sons George and Hugh raise, but they said nothing.

Oh, the fun George, Hugh, and I had when we were little! Even though they were a few years older than me, we were thick as thieves. We would climb the lower tree branches of the golden poplar tree and pick cherries and apples and play tag and make up silly songs and tap a stick on a metal pail to make music. We chased squirrels and caught tadpoles and fish in the river.

We whoop-whoop-whooped like Indians and pretended to shoot arrows at the white folks who stole our bodies. Lying on a carpet of leaves, looking up at the bluer than blue summer sky, we dreamed of being free one day.

Nothing feeds the soul like a walk in the woods during late autumn when breezes float down leaves like butterflies. There's a crisp crunch underfoot and the sound of swaying branches. My mind floated back to that pleasurable time, putting a silly girlish grin on my face when I remembered the first time we played doctor.

"Did you get to fool around all day long?" The question jerked me back to my audience. Could they read my mind about playing doctor?

Mostly, but we had a coupla chores, like feeding and cleaning up after the chickens, and bringing the eggs into the log cabin house so the Mistress of the house could fix breakfast. We slopped the pigs and sometimes brushed the horses at the end of their long workday. We helped pull weeds in the kitchen garden before I was old enough to do the cooking myself.

"What kind of garden?" someone in the audience asked. Oh, it's a little plot of land just outside the kitchen door where the Missus grew greens and carrots and corn and squash and onions and sweet pataters.

Massa would go hunting for rabbits and deer in the thick forests around the cabin. Sometimes he took the boys fishing in the Tygart River or Roaring Creek. I can still remember the mouth-watering smell of fried catfish, served with yellow corn so sweet it was like someone poured sugar all over it. Tasty greens cooked in fatback. Corn bread so light and flaky you just wanna slap yo' mama. *Old girl, you can't say that in front of the children!*

Well, what I mean is, you wanted to pat yo' mama gently on the back for a job well done." Out of the corner of my eye, I caught my sons laughing at my mistake. "We always had plenty of food to eat, 'cept during the war, when Yankees and Rebs stole everything in sight, but I'll tell you about that another day.

"Where were your parents, Grandma?" Ida Mae asked at my mention of 'mama', which brought me out of my reverie and forced me to deal with another troublesome question. Ida Mae couldn't imagine three slave kids playing all day long without parents supervising their every move, like her mama watched every step she took. You see, we din't live with our parents. We had been sold to the Massa. I ignored her question for now.

Beginnings

Today, I plan to give you a bit of history 'bout my birthplace so you can get an idea of our homeland. Is that a groan I heard? I guess I have to make this story more interesting.

West Virginny was actually part of the State of Virginny before 1863. But long before that, it was all Indian country. Just like the rest of America before the white man came and started taking all the land for theyselves, then stealing us from Africa to work the land for them, FOR FREE! Calm your emotions down, girl.

"Indians? You lived with Indians?" Herbert asked, thrilled. He was learning about them in school.

No, by the time I was born, the white folks done chased the Indians clean away. But we could play in the caves they left behind, and we sometimes climbed the large mounds of earth they built.

"What'd they do that for?" Little Anna asked.

Some of us think they mighta buried their dead in those mounds. Or maybe they were used like holy places to remember their dead ancestors. Nobody really knows.

During the early 1700s, the Indian tribes used present-day West Virginny as a hunting ground.

Just imagine waking up every morning at dawn to the piney smell of campfire smoke. Black birds with red beaks twitt'ring and squawkin'. The sky heavy with purple, turning to pinks, to oranges, then blues as the sun opens its yellow eye. Indian women with long straight black hair. Clothes made from animal hides. Babies strapped to their mama's backs. Cooking corn cakes. Making breakfast for they families, just like women everywhere. Keeping house. Grinding acorns to make flour. Raising children. Working they land. Who knows when those people first arrived? Coulda been 5,000 years ago. All I know is when folks was cutting the roads in Beverly in the 1840s, I heard some of 'em say they found the bones of gigantic animals in the ground. I wonder if that's what the Indians was huntin.'

Well, in the 1750s, some of the first white explorers come over the Allegheny Mountains from Virginny looking for a better life. The Files family built a log cabin where the creek—now called Files Creek—meets the Tygart Valley River. The Tygart family settled a short distance up the valley. Those new people started hunting and fishing in the Indians' territory. One day, a Files boy returned home to find his family being kilt by the Indians and their home being burnt. He ran away to the Tygart's; they all lef' that place real quick.

The next settlers din't come to the area 'til twenty years later. They were ready with guns to fight off the Indians who only had bows and arrows and tomahawk axes. Guess who won?

"The Indians, the Indians!" the children guessed incorrectly.

Sadly, no. They were moved off their land. The Westfalls and Stalnakers were some of those early families who built strong forts there.

The actual town of Beverly was founded in 1790. It was the first Randolph County seat. The entire area is full of thick forests: seventy-foot tall spruce trees, their prickly green needles faintly tinged with red.

Flowering blooms from pink hawthorn and the yellow and orange petals of the tulip tree. Sugar maple leaves turning from deep green to red from the crisp autumn nights. I fell into my memories, quiet.

"Uh-hem." Joseph cleared his throat. "Mother, weren't you going to tell us about Beverly?" Joseph kindly reminded me, bringing me back from the depths of my recollections.

"Oh yes, uh, thank you... Sometimes I daydream about the beauty, the freshness, the aroma of those wooded spaces of magic and possibility." After a gulp of tea, I continued.

Beverly's Main Street used to be what the Indians called "The Seneca Trail." Soon, the settlers elected a sheriff and built a courthouse to enforce the law, and a jail to lock up people who broke the law. They hired a County Clerk to handle the court paperwork and welcomed the educated attorneys who traveled to Beverly from other parts of Randolph County.

They had all sorts of stores and several hotels, since it was located smack in the middle of Maryland and Virginny on the east, and Ohio on the west. There was always wagons and stagecoaches coming and going and those travelers needed places to sleep and eat and enjoy themselves.

Beverly had a few tailors who made fancy clothes for the lawyers and other rich folk in that gov'ment town. There was even a hatmaker for ladies and gentlemen. There were a few gun shops too, and boot-makers, and a furniture builder. Like most towns that had a lot of travelers and farmers, there were a few blacksmiths too.

"What's that, Grandma? A black person named Smith?" Herbert asked innocently.

"Joseph, do you want to answer your son, since you had personal experience with this topic?"

His mellow voice started, "A blacksmith is a person who works with iron and steel. He hammers hot iron metal on an anvil[7] to change its shape into steel tools or horseshoes, bed frames, and things like that. I was trained in blacksmithing for a short time when I was your age, living in and near Beverly.

"You see, I was born a slave, just like my mama. My master owned me and George,"—pointing at his brother sitting in his chair. And these are our sisters, pointing at Cornelia, May, and Ella," who stood up and took a polite bow, her frilly blue dress flipping up to show her knees. "Cornelia lives in Pennsylvania with her Anderson family and May died some years ago."

Herbert and the rest of the kids looked at Joseph with wide eyes, their mouths open in an expression of disbelief. They never imagined the polished, dignified man wearing a sharp gray suit, white shirt, and black tie could have ever been a lowly slave. It made them proud and gave them the confidence that they, too, might become successful one day. If he could do it, so could they.

"There's one more thing you need to know about my owner," Joseph continued. "He was much more than that. He was also my daddy," pointing a finger at his chest. George and Ella also pointed their fingers at their chests.

"That's probably why we have lighter skin, thinner lips, and silkier hair than our pretty mama here." The children were slack-jawed, staring into space, processing the new knowledge of their mixed-race heritage.

Chapter 2 - The Earle Legacy

By now, a crowd of neighbors had gathered in front of my little house on Vine Street in Barnesville, Ohio. They joined my children and grandchildren on this balmy mid-summer evening in 1900. Even the stars nestled into their comfy bed of midnight blue, watching, shining, listening to every word of my memories. Many of my neighbors had similar experiences to mine and also enjoyed rekindling their lives from faraway places.

"Once upon a time in Ol' Virginny..." my stories often began.

"What do you think, Joseph? Should I continue talking about the history of Beverly where I spent my first thirty years, or should I tell 'em about the Earles who so affected this fine family of ours?" Cicadas quieted, bees stilled, owls hushed. I gazed at my eldest son for direction.

"Earles, Earles, EARLES!" the youngest children shouted, pumping their fists into the air. "We want to know about our white grandfather."

After sipping the remains of my fruity blackberry tea, I began. Now, I'm going to describe the legend exactly how I heard it from Massa John's very own lips. Well... I overheard him telling the tales to his children several times when they was young.

I pronounced every word slowly, letting the magic of anticipation build in intensity. "Recorded history of the Earle family began hundreds of years ago in Somerset, along the Bristol water channel in southwest England. Who knows where England is?" I stopped, always wanting to involve my audience in the show.

"I do, I do," said twelve-year-old Clara, raising her hand like she was in school. "It's in Europe, right?"

I beamed at my smart granddaughter. "Yes, indeed. Massa said the Earles were an ancient English family. They had stories going back to the 'Norman Conquest'—which he said was an enormous battle for land with France that took place almost 900 years ago.[8] I can't even imagine how many generations ago that was, can you?" No answer from the crowd.

He said the word 'earl' means a nobleman, someone with an estate—a house and property that's named for himself, like Earle Place or Earle Manor. Some of they folks was even knights.

"Nights? You mean dark people at night?" Herbert asked innocently, throwing his hat high in the air and catching it like a pro baseball player while I suppressed a laugh.

"No, honey, I think it's a kind of soldier who rides on a beautiful horse and wears a shiny metal suit to protect his body from swords and arrows. The King adds 'Sir' to a knight's name. Sir John Earle the First was one of Massa John's oldest ancestors, loyal to the King of England. This is Sir John Earle's story." I lowered my voice pretending to be Sir John Earle I.

Sir John Earle's Remarkable Tale

"Certainly, Sir. I shall be most pleased to represent your interests in the English colonies." I kissed the ring on the smooth hand of the new King, Charles II, soon after his father had been beheaded in January 1649.

I rushed home. "Mary, you'll never guess what just happened at Court. The King has awarded me the promise of a land grant, acknowledging my service to the Crown during our Civil War. Seventeen hundred acres will be ours once we get there."

"Where is 'there,' John?" my wife, Mary Symons, questioned, her eyes squinting with worry.

"Across the ocean to the New World, of course. The next ship leaves in three weeks and we'll be on it. Have the servants pack our bags right away. We shall briefly settle in Maryland, then on to Virginia." With much trepidation plainly written in her tight-lipped stare, my pretty wife did as I bade, ensuring that we—she, me and our young sons, Samuel and John, and daughter, Mary—were ready for the voyage.

On the appointed day, servants brought several trunks packed with our clothes and other necessities, along with crates of specialty foods, to the behemoth ship moored at Bristol Harbor, near to our manor house in Somerset, England.

After the mists cleared, it was a fine spring morning when we assembled on the main deck of our ship, Margaret of Bristol.[9] Many people were standing about, including noblemen like ourselves in fine clothing, scruffy-bearded sailors, olive-skinned Welsh wearing red scarves, men of the cloth, flame-haired Irishmen who escaped Cromwell's Army, farmers with their snot-nosed children, tradesmen, mechanics, [10] felons, and some Africans. All of humanity, nervous, chattering, dreamy. Most didn't know what to expect leaving our homeland, friends, and family. The few women on board commiserated about the future being frightening and thrilling at the same time.

Only wealthy people like us could afford the trip in relative comfort, in our separate berths. Those without money signed a contract to become indentured servants for a number of years, partially to pay for their passage, partially to get a bit of land after their service. Those people would sleep in the compact in-between, or "tween," deck.

When the ship set sail, the motion of the ocean soon separated the wheat from the chaff. Meaning, first-timers often found themselves at the side railing, depositing their meal into the roiling sea. I had already made one voyage to the New World and enjoyed the rising and falling feeling from the waves, pushing the ship up, then letting it crash down again. My wife and children took days to ease into the beautiful monotony of the six to eight-week trip, depending upon the weather. We stopped at Barbados island to refill our food and water stores. Stormy weather would require lengthier stays on shore.

The ship carried food that would keep for long periods of time without spoiling, like salted meats, dried grains, peas, and beans. We also brought along dried fruits, cheese, breads, spices, wines, ales, sweets, tea, egg-laying hens, and a few rabbits and doves to cook on board. Sometimes fresh fish from the ocean was caught with hooks or harpoons. Even water went bad, though, so we drank beer and wine instead.

"Sounds all right to me!" Sylvester jeered, pretendin' he was drinkin' from a bottle of wine. All my grown sons busted out laughin.'

"May I continue Sir John's story?" I asked sternly. Sylvester nodded with a sheepish grin.

Being on a big wooden boat with a couple hundred other people you didn't know, in the middle of an ocean, not knowing if you would survive if the boat sank, was an exciting adventure to some, but bewildering to others.

There was no land in sight for days or weeks. Nothing but water all around as far as the eye could see. Tall waves crashing into the ship. Burning hot sun rays baking our flesh. Sky, the colors of the rainbow, depending on the time of day. Wind that caught in the mighty cloth sails, pushing the boat along its course ever closer toward its destination. White sea birds dipping and soaring over the ship, pelleting unsuspecting targets below. Sparkling silver fish jumping out of the water, wagging their shiny tails at us passengers. Huge gray whales swimming alongside the ship. It was indeed an experience we passengers would never forget.

We landed in St. Marys in the new State of Maryland, settling there for a few years until the paperwork for our land grant could be secured. Then we moved to Northumberland (future Westmoreland)

County, Virginia, bordering the Potomac River. We could start our lives in the New World with land, money, position, and respect.

The land was wild in 1649 when we arrived in the New World. Forests so thick, rivers so wide, fish and game so plentiful, land so bountiful that farmers could grow just about anything. We wanted to tame the land, to mold it to our specifications, to become its masters, to civilize it. Unfortunately, there were savage Indians living there standing in the way of progress. They had to go. We wanted to build houses and roads and bring in more of our people.

My son, Samuel Noah Earle, the first, who was born in Nyland, Somerset, England in 1638, became a noted surveyor, measuring out highways for Westmoreland County. He secured land grants in the Northern Neck of Virginia, becoming a planter and merchant, hiring lots of powerful men—indentured servants and free Africans—to work his land. He and his wife, Bridget Hale, named their first-born son Samuel Noah Earle the second.

Samuel II (1670-1746) was a planter in Westmoreland. He married Phillis Bennett, who had a son named Samuel Noah Earle the third, born right before the 1700s.

Samuel III (1692-1771), like his father, was a planter, but he was also a pioneer, attorney-at-law, high sheriff, collector of tobacco for the Crown, justice, burgess, church warden, investor, soldier, and a major in the colonial regiment. Born in Westmoreland, he lived in Prince William County, then Stafford in Fauquier County, and finally in Frederick County. He was educated at William and Mary College. He owned extensive properties in six counties, including land next to that of Augustine Washington (the father of the first United States President, George Washington). Samuel III first married Anne Sorrell, who descended from a family of Huguenots from France. They received a lavish wedding present from Samuel II, including the Aquia Creek plantation, with its slaves and stock, plus 200 acres at the Yeocomico site. Anne's father was the Frederick County Clerk for many years. They had five children, one of whom was the Honorable Colonel John Baylis Earle, a well-respected judge in South Carolina. Another was Colonel Elias Earle,

25

who lived in the Winchester District of Frederick, Virginia, and had a large plantation called Mount Zion. I'll tell a story about that place later.

Mount Zion, built 1771-1772 by Reverend Charles Thurston who fought in the Revolutionary War and was known as the "Fighting Parson." Since 1842 the house has been owned by the Earle family. Barbara Frank wrote a book, *Princess Book II: Aggy of Zion*, about the slaves at Mount Zion.

After his first wife died, Samuel III married Elizabeth Holbrook. Their child was named Esias Earle (1758-1826). They lived in a plantation called "Silver Ridge" in a town called Muddy Run near the city of Front Royal in Clarke County, Virginia.

Son Esias Earle married Sarah Brownley, and they produced about ten children. Their second child, Archibald Earle, was born in 1788, the year after his brother John Baylis Earle was born.

Now it's time to pass the legacy story on to someone else.

"All right, children," (back to my normal voice), "I'll tell you about the Earles who moved from Frederick to Randolph County, which was the western part of Virginia back then."

Archibald Earle was a fearless fellow who worked a few years for his Great-uncle, the Frederick County Clerk, learning all about the duties of that important position, which included: recording documents, issuing court orders, taking depositions, making inventories, processing estates, and keeping records of births, deaths and marriages. The county clerks used to collect fees for their services, but they also began receiving a regular salary.

When he was twenty-two, Archibald struck out on his own. In 1810, he traveled about one hundred and fifty miles on horseback over old Indian trails, through the wild forests of the Shenandoah and Allegheny Mountains. After a few days of riding, he reached the little town of Beverly, in Randolph County, in what would later become West Virginny.

Archibald Earle stayed a couple of years with his family's longtime friends, Peter Buckey and his wife Christina Marteney, who had left Frederick for Beverly some years earlier. Their pretty daughter, Mary Polly Buckey, was the second of nine children. Even though she was only fourteen when Archibald started living with them, she looked grown. Their eyes met. Perhaps things happened in the wee hours of the morning, and they married in 1812.

That same year, Archibald was elected to become the Randolph County Clerk, an important job he continued to fill for almost thirty years. He had a little desk at the courthouse and made sure the court records were kept in perfect condition. He was also the town miller, grinding grains into flour and providing waterpower for other uses. Archibald had purchased the property next to Files Creek from one of the town's pioneers who left the area suddenly. In future years, he would purchase more land in the Leadsville area [now Elkins] that would be shared by his descendants.

Archibald and Mary Polly had a dozen children, starting in 1813 with the eldest, John Bayles Earle. They kept having kids every couple of years until Creed Earle was born twenty-four years later in 1837. The families in Beverly used the same names over and over when they intermarried, so you can find many people named Creed, Archibald, John Bayles, and Mary in the families of Earles, Kittles, Marteneys, and Stalnakers.

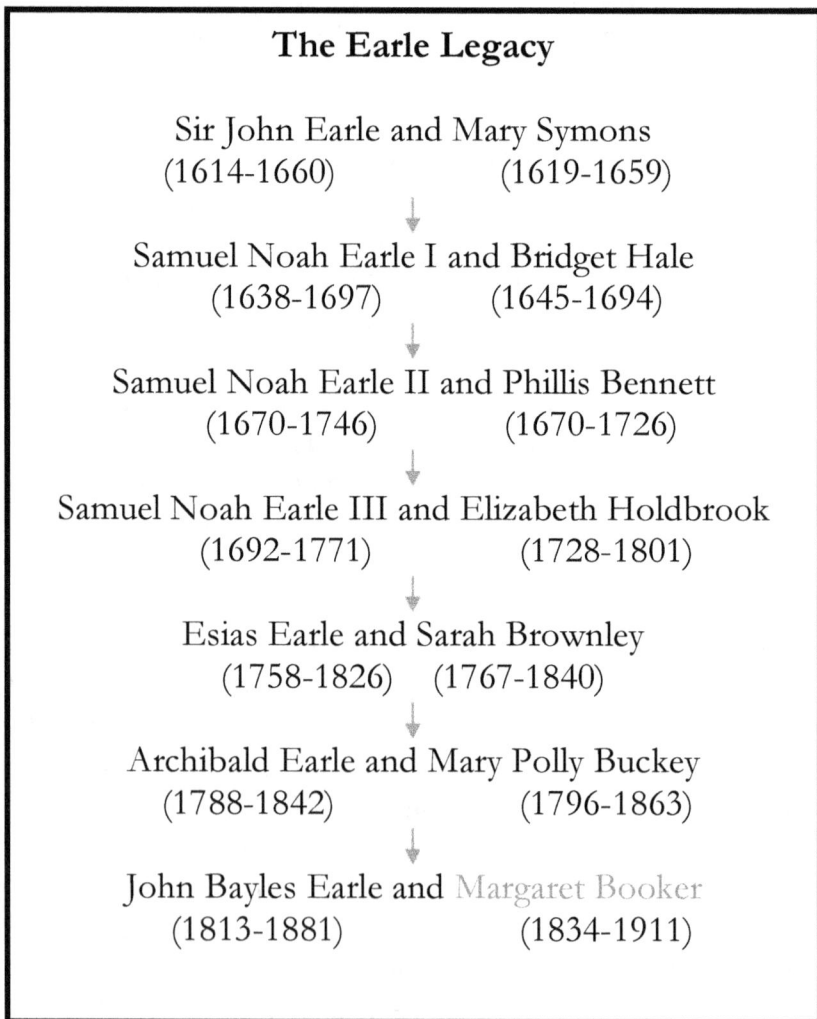

The Earle Legacy

Sir John Earle and Mary Symons
(1614-1660)   (1619-1659)

Samuel Noah Earle I and Bridget Hale
(1638-1697)   (1645-1694)

Samuel Noah Earle II and Phillis Bennett
(1670-1746)   (1670-1726)

Samuel Noah Earle III and Elizabeth Holdbrook
(1692-1771)   (1728-1801)

Esias Earle and Sarah Brownley
(1758-1826)   (1767-1840)

Archibald Earle and Mary Polly Buckey
(1788-1842)   (1796-1863)

John Bayles Earle and Margaret Booker
(1813-1881)   (1834-1911)

"Archibald and Mary's first child, John Bayles Earle, was my slaveowner and yo' daddy," pointing to Joseph, George, and Ella, three of our five children present that evening. I put my hands in my lap. "So that's the saga of the Earles, your blood relatives. What do you think of all that?"

"I had no idea anybody could trace their family back that far. Many hundreds of years of history? It was really fascinating, Grandma. Thank you."

"That's a lot of names and places, Grandma. You may have to repeat the story a bunch of times, so we don't forget the details," Myrtle said.

"I'll be glad to. Anytime. I promise to write the family lines down for you one day."

"Promise?"

I nodded. "Wanting to hear my stories again will encourage y'all to come back and visit me while I'm still on this good Earth." My girls gathered around and showered me with hugs and kisses while the boys cheered.

Unfortunately, I never made good on my promise and most of my stories were lost and forgotten as the years passed.

Chapter 3 - The Indian Scout

Awakening to the sound of doves cooing got me thinking about how to describe my earliest childhood memories for tonight's crowd. I needed to ease into this story for it would contain an unexpected revelation. Imagining I am now back home in West Virginia, the memories flood forth.

Seasons of My Childhood

Springtime awakening in the mountains brings purple and white crocuses reaching up from the snowy ground, tiny orange narcissus, yellow daffodils, baby leaves peeking out from once-bare tree limbs. New emerald-hued grasses pop up from winter's embrace, covering the rolling hills like a mossy green blanket. Active, billowy clouds of white, pearl, dove gray, and light blue float across my vision. Is that a dog above the highest mountain or a sheep?

Teams of tan horses with yellow manes yoked together, pull plows directed by farmers in blue coveralls, hats and leather gloves.

They dig the sleepy ground for spring planting. The ancient, earthy smell of dirt and sod and dung fill my nose. The sparkling water of nearby Stalnaker Run courses fast and cold.

Summer black Hereford cows with white faces stand under shady trees, selecting the tastiest turf, jaws chewing side to side, slowly, watching, munching, spying another tasty morsel, nibbling, growing big for the inevitable. Sweaty horses finish their day's work, relaxing inside a logged fence near the water trough, with straight rows of cornstalks covering the hillside beyond.

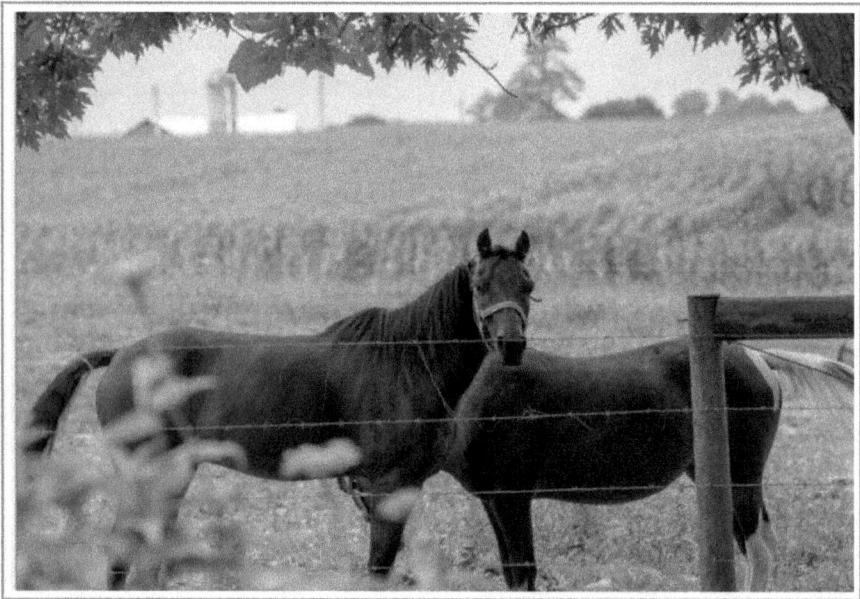

Fall is my favorite season for its vivid contrasts. Grassy greens and brilliant autumn leaves: red, golden, bright yellow-to-orange-to dusty rust. Within my vision, one color layers another surrounding a little shack, shed, or house of weathered gray-brown boards.

Turkeys standing stock-still as I come near, reddish feathers covering tiny heads, curved necks cascading over a heavy oval of dark chocolate feathers. Long, flat tails of light and dark chevrons trail over the ground like a bride's train. Deer alert, staring at me, silent, still, safely blending into gold and brown grasses, avoiding the hunter's gun. Emerald-headed male Mallard ducks dip their bright orange feet into the river, safely leading their drab mottled mates to the other side.

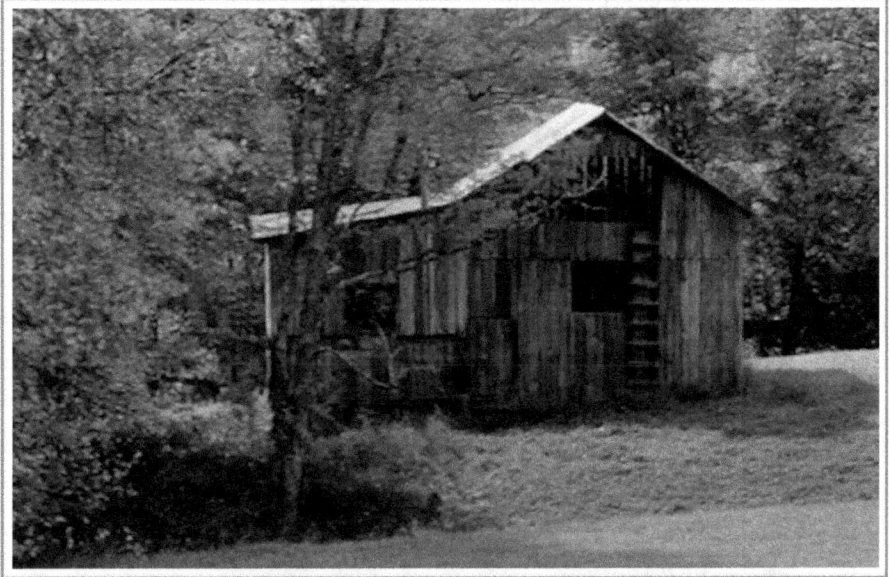

In mid-October, the apple crop is ready for picking. I join other slaves grasping, then twisting the scarlet and yellow-green treasures from their branches, depositing the jewels into boxes or crates to be shouldered onto wagons for transport to the market. Me, learning from the Missus how to thinly slice the shiny fruit for her famous apple pie, dropping dabs of freshly churned butter and a sprinkle of cinnamon and sugar on top. She, sharing her secrets for making a flaky crust, the delicate crisscross lattice laying like a lacy shroud over the fruity morsels. The smell of baking apples follows me from the kitchen to the front room, up the stairs, everywhere. Slicing a warm piece, mouth-watering aromas filling the nose as my mouth clamps around the sweet chunks, each chew releasing more flavor, happiness cascading to my fingertips and big toes.

Winter, stark snow tinged with blue undertones, blankets bare tree limbs. Blood-colored berries on spiky holly bushes gleam next to barren trees. The dark Tygart River races clear and cold between snowbanks, rising higher as rains fall through the season. Bloated rivers run faster with a warm spring breath. Orange-beaked birds fat with extra down perch on snowy pine branches, stealthy, waiting for a special worm invited for dinner. Puffy red cardinals hop on bare branches, made brighter still against a pristine new snow.

Following the path, little more than an animal trail, gigantic oaks and sycamores grow near the water, trunks wider than the rumps of the biggest plow horses. Naked trees hold up their barren arms like so many graceful ladies forming an archway for river dancers. Leathery wet bark in winter dress shines bright in the afternoon light.

Down the stream a ways, I stop for a moment at a low waterfall, admiring, listening to the brisk rush of foaming water over rocks in its path. A large log laid as a footbridge across the creek beckons me to cross and explore the other side. I never want to leave this Heaven.

Winter and summer storms are magnificent and thoroughly frightening. They start far away, sky darkening, clouds rolling through the heavens, approaching closer, darker, windier. Then a low growl prowls toward my ears, then suddenly CRACK! The sharp sound of thunder is followed by blinding white swords of lightning that God himself throws from the sky toward the Earth. Shattering. Scary. Beautiful in its way, but dangerous. The sooner the bolts follow the clap of thunder, the sooner the storm hits this spot. Guessing when the first raindrops will appear, I run home as fast as I can before getting soaked.

Sunsets and sunrises send my heart to flutter. Lime to apple to olive to jade to dark green pastures extend far into the distance, forests at the farthest corners of my vision. A few houses here or there, gardens, farms, and cattle dot the landscape. But most of what I see in front of me are spectacular clouds billowing from afar, coming toward the sky just over my head. Purples, deep pinks, light peach, the barely yellow rising sun peeking through the far clouds, me feeling tiny in that splendid picture before me.

The sun setting. More yellow, merging orange, blending pink to violet, as the day disappears beyond the horizon. The sky slowly turns to blueberry. Stars twinkle bright white above our insignificant heads. This is indeed God's work.

In the night's cool, I lie on the grass, back against the spongy turf, looking upward into the navy blue depths. "There's the Big Dipper and there's the North Star," I say to nobody in particular. I heard tales that slaves running away from their masters followed the North Star to freedom in Ohio or Pennsylvania or Canada. Would I dare do that one day? No, I am treated well here, with enough food to eat and clothes to wear, a bed, and people who are usually kind to me. But if my situation changes in the future, who knows what I might do?

Native Rule

"Once upon a time in Ol' Virginny..."

Remember, folks, that this entire country was inhabited by Indian tribes for maybe thousands of years before the white man came from Europe to colonize this land.

Let's imagine you're one of those white settlers, getting off a ship from Europe at a seaport in New York. The land looks wild. There are no neatly clipped bushes or mansions with white Roman columns like back home. No, there are swamps, small huts made of logs, and can't-see-through thick forests.

The spirit of ancient trees is all around, beckoning you to come closer into the wood. The piney air smells so fresh after a recent rain. Trunks are mossy wet, encouraging you to touch the spongy bark. Straight prickly pine needles, dried to varying shades of brown, cover narrow walking trails made by deer and wild pigs. Unusual reddish orange and deep purple flowers pop out of deep green shrubs along the path. A few trunks were blackened from lightning that bolted from a cloudy sky, fire-kissing specific trees.

You imagine what the winter will be like, frost and snow falling through the thick canopy blanketing everything in white. But now, as you walk, the piney scent pulls you forward, deeper into the thicket. You meander along the quiet path, exploring, regarding, deep in the peacefulness of nature.

The shadow light of the forest plays with colors between the trees, like a game of cat and mouse. You see things in the shadows— a red-and-black striped snake crawling along a limb, furry brown squirrels hopping from one branch to higher hideouts in the tree. Black crows peer wisely at you. Fat rats run past your feet.

The forest is getting thicker still. It's harder to see where the trail leads. You felt trapped, wondering whether you can find your way back to the shore. By and by you notice a sound coming from behind your back. A dead leaf crunches. A dove cries its mournful song above your head. You look up. A twig snaps. Someone or something is definitely following you. You walk faster, but the thing behind you speeds up too. More noise. Is it a person or a pig or a bear following you? Faster you walk, now at a slow jog, turning into a run for your life. You are scared out of your wits. Why did I leave my family on the shore?

It's not your imagination. Twigs are breaking as someone or something tries to catch you. Sweat appears on your upper lip. Your underarms smell like fear.

There's a split in the narrow path in front of you, going off into two directions. Which one should you take? Which will lead you to safety? Go right. Right is always right, right? You try to convince yourself. Diving into the right trail you break into a full run, trying to remember how to get back to the mouth of the forest. But the trees are so thick, and every tree looks the same after a while. A labyrinth. Panic sets in as you try to escape from… well, you don't know. Looking from side to side, concentrating on finding the correct path, you don't notice what's right in front of you, until…

"Hau!" A nearly naked brown man stands in the path right in front of you. You stop as quickly as though you hit a brick wall, almost running into him. You're so startled you fall to the ground. He has a long pointy spear in his left hand, or is it just a long walking stick? There's a strip of leather circling his head with a long feather sticking straight up in the back. His old face is chiseled, lined, wrinkled maybe, but he stands tall and strong. His upper body bare, muscular, slim, his waist and hips covered with some kind of cloth.

His feet are encased in an unusual leather shoe with fringe at the edges. He stands still, looking down at you. Somehow you scramble into a bush at the side of the path, trying to hide. He's already seen you, though. Your brain knocks you awake. If he planned to do you harm, silly, he would have done it already, right? Slowly, you come out of the bush and stand, staring at his plain but dignified person.

Again, he says, "Hau!" but this time he raises his right hand, palm toward you.

"What would you do?" I looked up at my audience, most sitting at the edge of their chairs.

"Kick him!" George cheers.

"Shoot him!" Sylvester shouts.

"Run the other way!" Ella whimpers.

"Say 'hau' back and raise right hand too," Clara offers.

I asked, "Which of those answers do you think the settlers chose most often?" I think most Europeans were afraid of all people who looked different from them. I think their fears usually encouraged them to do the natives harm instead of trying to communicate and live peacefully with them. Yes, there were some kind settlers who tried to be friendly, but I think they were few and far between.

The native people who had lived in what Europeans called the "New World" comprised different tribes of Indians, just like there are different countries in Europe, and different customs in the various parts of the United States. Before the white man came, some tribes lived in the tidewater and oceanside areas along the east coast, in what we now call New York, Virginia, Massachusetts, Maryland, the Carolinas, and Florida. Other tribes lived mostly peaceful lives in the lush woodlands.

Indians hunted animals, making use of the skin, meat, claws and teeth—all parts of the animal. They fished the mighty rivers and creeks, made canoes and boats out of trees. They built round teepee huts from straight branches covered in waterproof animal hides. The natives discovered which plants were safe to eat, which ones could heal the sick, and which ones could kill. They lived simply on the land. They were one with nature. They believed in the spirits of animals.

Disagreements between tribes were rare. Many preferred to compromise and come to an agreement in a dispute. Sometimes there were deadly exchanges of bows and arrows, or tomahawk axes.

Indians were a community-oriented people who did not believe in owning anything, not land or houses or animals. They shared everything with one another. Mostly, Indians lived simply with what nature provided. They wasted nothing. So, they weren't thrilled when Europeans started coming into the land, cutting down whole forests for their big houses, burning trees for charcoal for ironworking, killing animals to near extinction, disrespecting Indian culture and customs, and forcing the native peoples to move from their longtime homes.

How would you feel if people came here and moved you out of the place you had lived for hundreds of years, without a word of explanation or regret?

Sylvester said, "That's what guns are for, protecting our property. They shoulda kicked their pale butts back to Europe." The crowd laughed. Sylvester stood, took a solemn bow, then sat back down to sip his spirited beverage. I cut him a disapproving glance.

Some tribes attempted to fight back and protect their homeland and families. But Europeans had horses and guns and were much more warlike. And… they kept coming, by the shiploads from England, Ireland, Scotland, France, Germany, and elsewhere. Natives living along the east coast, especially, were the first to be pushed farther west into the wilderness. And as soon as they resettled in the new place, new settlers hungry for land pushed them farther west, and on and on. The land was being gobbled up by these immigrants, taken for their own purposes.

Some tribes made a stand and attacked the settlements. That's what happened to the Files family who, in 1754, had settled in what became Randolph County, Virginia. It's possible the Indians thought the white-skinned people were blue-eyed devils, destroying whatever they saw. Perhaps the Indians were afraid of those immigrants and meant to remove the intruders. Children, there are often two sides to every story, depending on who's telling it.

Figure 2: A typical frontier dwelling in western Virginia.

Just imagine coming home (Figure 2) after a day fishing to find your family being killed by Indians and your house aflame. Your parents are screaming in agony. Your possessions are burning before your eyes. Well, that actually happened to a young Files boy. He ran up the hill to their only neighbors, the Tygarts, and told them what was happening to his family down below. They all fled the area.

No other settlers came until Captain Wilson, known to be a famous Indian fighter, arrived in 1772 to build a strong fort from thick tree trunks. They would protect their investment, using guns or any other means necessary. This second Caucasian settlement wave consisted of nine families, including the Westfalls and Stalnakers.

The Indian Scout

Take a deep breath old girl. "Folks, I've been keeping a little secret." They looked at one another, perhaps wondering what it was.

The truth is… before the age of twelve, I was the slave of a widow who had been married to an Indian Scout named Herbert—I glanced at Joseph's son of the same name—"Richard" Kittle.

"What's an Indian Scout?"

I responded a Scout was kind of like a hunter who tracks and kills deer, or ducks, or squirrels. The difference was that Richard Kittle was an Indian Scout whose prey was Native American Indians.

"What? He stalked and killed Indians? Why? What did they do to him?"

Nothing to him personally, but some Indians had killed the Files family twenty years earlier, and Richard was bound and determined to avenge their deaths.

Richard was born in New York in 1761, the son of Abraham Kittle and Christina Westfall. They migrated to the Tygart Valley in what eventually became Randolph County, Virginia. People like the Kittles and Westfalls came from New York, and the Stalnakers, Marteneys and Earles came from Frederick, Virginia. All of them came seeking to possess land. Some immigrants from the east coast traveled even farther south and west to establish coal and salt mines, which needed considerable slave labor.

Richard Kittle became a well-known Indian Scout in the Tygart Valley where Beverly is now located. The sad story of the Files family's fate was on twenty-year-old Richard's mind and he vowed to do something about the Indian "problem."

The story goes that Richard was with four other men when a complete band of Indians, living at a nearby settlement called Bulltown, were destroyed by "Indian Scouts" during a time of peace. Richard denied that he and his friends murdered them all.

"I just threatened them a bit. They ran away on their own," Richard maintained throughout his life. However, on the deathbed of one of the four Indian Scouts, it was confirmed that Richard and his buddies had killed an entire band of Indians in cold blood—men, women, and children. After the grisly deed, Richard and the other killers reportedly dipped their moccasins in bear fat to remove the smell of blood, and then burned the buildings. Those Native Americans were a peaceful tribe who had been "removed" from New York State and settled in Bulltown, which was named after their Chief Bull.[11]

Many white folk deemed this type of "Indian Scout" in a positive light and Richard capitalized on it for the rest of his life. Later, the term "Indian Scout" was used differently, to describe a soldier who operates in the bush, or of a Native American population skilled in tracking.

In 1785, Richard married Margaret Elizabeth White. She was a widow whose first husband, John Stalnaker, was reportedly killed by Indians in 1784, after the births of their children, Rebecca and John White Stalnaker.

Richard and Margaret Elizabeth Stalnaker were married for forty-five years in the Leading Creek area, which became Elkins, a few miles north of Beverly. Both towns were bounded by Roaring Creek and connected by the Old Seneca Indian Trail. [Author: This trail is presently called Highway 250.]

Richard Kittle died in 1831, leaving one-third of his estate to his wife—including a Negro woman named Peg valued at $150— and two-thirds of his land and property to his five children. Their daughter Jane was willed a Negro girl named Phebe valued at , who was Peg's daughter. After Richard died, Margaret Elizabeth continued to live in their family home, which was surrounded by the homes of several other Kittle families.

Are they all awake? I know this is a lot of dates and names, but listen up, I nearly shouted. In February 1834, the cries of a newborn girl echoed through the snow-covered valley in Leadsville. That baby girl was me. I think Peg was my mother and Richard Kittle, the Indian Scout, was Peg's father. I believe that Indian Scout was my grandfather and, therefore, your ancestor. Silence.

MARGARET BOOKER'S POSSIBLE LINEAGE:

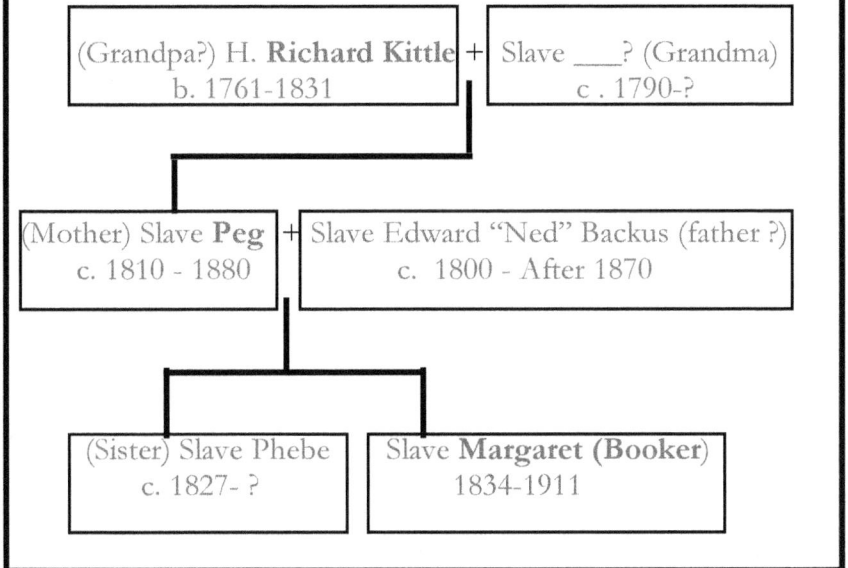

(Grandpa?) H. **Richard Kittle** + b. 1761-1831	Slave ___? (Grandma) c . 1790-?

(Mother) Slave **Peg** + c. 1810 - 1880	Slave Edward "Ned" Backus (father ?) c. 1800 - After 1870

(Sister) Slave Phebe c. 1827- ?	Slave **Margaret (Booker)** 1834-1911

Margaret Booker's Possible Lineage, based on an 1832 Richard Kittle Will leaving Negro woman Peg to his wife, Margaret Elizabeth White Stalnaker Kittle, and Negro girl Phebe to his daughter, Jane Kittle.

Chapter 4 - What a Dollar Buys

"Once upon a time in Ol' Virginny…"

Last time, I told you I was born in February 1834, but I remember little about my first three years of life. Every now and then, in my mind's eye, I can sort of see a very tall chocolate woman bending over me.

Mostly, though, I remember an old white woman, Miz Margaret Elizabeth, during my first years of life. She fed me and clothed me and braided my thick hair every week. She made me special birthday cakes, and when I fell on the back porch and skinned my knee, she bandaged it. She taught me the difference between which greens were good to eat and which were weeds to pluck. She showed me how to feed the chickens, retrieve their eggs, and clean their henhouse. Most importantly, Miz Margaret Elizabeth let me play and run and jump and be happy in a safe, loving place.

John White Stalnaker

"You know I don't mean any disrespect, mother, but you are way too old to be taking care of a young girl by yourself."

I heard Miz Margaret Elizabeth's son, John White Stalnaker, whom I called Massa John White, say this one time when he was visiting. I was jabbering with my doll baby in the front room, throwing her up in the air and catching her, and dancing around the room with my dolly, pretending not to listen to the grownups.

He said, "Just look at her, mother. She's a wild child. She needs to learn her place in the world now that Peg is living with Jane Crouch, and my sister Jane is a married woman with Phebe as her charge. Why don't you let me take little Margaret? My wife can begin teaching her what she needs to know to become a good handmaid."

"But John White, my little namesake, Margaret, is my joy. She's the reason I want to wake up in the morning. Just look at her, so cute, so precocious, such a ball of energy. I watch her play for hours. She's no trouble at all. She's so loyal, so loving, just like a pet dog." Miz Margaret Elizabeth smiled my way. I felt warm inside at what I thought were kind words. Truly, she was like a mama to me. I didn't learn until later that she was actually my owner.

Massa John White said, "Mother, you can come visit her anytime. Better still, why don't you move in with us? We have plenty of room since many of the kids have moved out on their own. We'd be more than happy to take care of you in your eighth decade. Come live with us, the both of you."

"Only if your wife agrees."

"Mary has mentioned several times her desire that you and little Margaret live with us. She can use the help. I can have Hugh and George get you packed and moved in the next few weeks. We will all enjoy helping you be more comfortable. It looks like you've been limping lately."

"Oh yes, my hip bothers me something fierce, especially during the coldest part of winter. Well... if you're sure. I'll be glad to move in."

Little Slave Margaret

Sometime after I was a few years old, Miz Margaret Elizabeth and I moved in with her son, John White Stalnaker, and his wife, Mary Chenowith Stalnaker. I slept in Miz Margaret Elizabeth's room so I could help her out of bed, get her dressed, bring her breakfast, and do whatever else she needed.

I was glad to move into the large Stalnaker house, a two-story log cabin (Figure 3) at Stalnaker's Run, which was a five-acre parcel of meadow land with Leading Creek running through it. We lived few miles north of the town of Beverly in Randolph County, which was still in Virginia back then. Chinking made from clay, lime, and sand wedged between the logs kept the icy wind and rain out during the snowy winter months.

Massa John White's house was full of interesting objects that made it a home. He had a spinning wheel in the corner of the common room downstairs, as well as a loom for weaving cloth or floor rugs. They had a butter churner in one kitchen corner and a tall, hardwood grandfather clock chiming every hour in another space. A coffee mill was used to make a strong bitter brew for folks who arose early in the morning to start a day of hard work.

I fondly remember sitting in front of the stone fireplace in the main room, working on some sewing or tatting or knitting, feeling the warmth on my skin, watching the orange and red flames dance around their airy bluish partners. The fireplace was big enough to heat the entire house in the wintertime. Hugh and George made sure they cut enough firewood before the snow fell in November so we could always have a warm fire in the hearth."

Figure 3: Stalnaker Log Cabin, circa 1795. Might be similar to John B. Earle's original log home which would have been located at Main and Crawford Streets. He sold the property in 1879 to Isaac Baker who rebuilt the house. Source: Randolph County Historical Society. The small structure next to the house may have housed slaves, like Margaret Booker and her children.

"Grandma, who's Hugh and George?" Ada Mae asked.

"I'll tell you that in a few minutes, honey."

The house had a wooden side chair for each of the family members living there in 1840. They ate their meals around an enormous table near the kitchen or at one of the side tables scattered around the house. Hugh, George and my six-year-old stomach ate after the family finished.

We got to eat their leavings and the less desirable parts of meats and fish.

A hutch, diagonally placed in a corner, housed the pewter plates, cups, bowls, knives, spoons, and forks. There was a small desk under the side window to write letters and pay bills.

A metal chandelier with four candles hung from the living room ceiling and oil lamps encased in glass were placed on the mantle and attached to the walls to provide a dim yellowish glow at night.

Thick, colorful, oval floor rugs made from rags kept the floors from freezing our feet in the cold winters. The women of the house created many rugs that were used all over the cabin. Those carpets were knitted, crocheted, or sewed. Working on projects together while talking and laughing made our jobs more fun. Oh, the funny stories I overheard when the men were gone working in the fields or pastures!

There were three bedrooms upstairs, each with two windows or more. A rocking cradle made from dried reeds was next to mamas' beds. They didn't have to leave the room to nurse an infant at night. Each room had brass bedwarmers that were filled with coal and heated in the hearth, then placed between the sheets to warm the double-wide tick mattress,[12] filled with soft feathers, before a person got into bed. Chamber pots were placed underneath the bed so people didn't have to trudge outside to the outhouse at night. Each bedroom had at least one bureau with four drawers for storing folded clothes. (Figure 4)

Figure 4: Inside of Stalnaker home, restored, moved to Beverly.

Outside the house were deep, covered porches on two sides of the house. Benches on the porch allowed the owner's family and friends to relax outside after dinner, watching the kids play, enjoying their lush surroundings. The view was especially memorable at sunset when sky painting flowed from light blue to yellow to orange to red as the ball of light descended below the horizon. The most brilliant part of the sky show was saved until the very end.

The Stalnaker house was built on the brow of a hill. It was a hewed log cabin and was still standing when Mr. Daniel Baker built a mansion a little back of it before the Civil War. I came to live there with Massa John White, his wife, Miz Margaret Elizabeth, and two enslaved servants named Hugh and George, who were a few years older than me.

Massa John White's Grandpappy, Jacob, was the first Stalnaker to come to Randolph County, and he built this house before 1800. Jacob Stalnaker owned hundreds of acres which he passed to his children when he died, and they passed the lots down to their children. Jacob's parents came from Germany and his daddy was a Captain who fought in the American Revolution.

As the Stalnaker children grew older, they married and left their parents with us three slaves to take care of them. The small cabin in back of the Big House was officially the slave quarters. It was a single twelve by fourteen foot room with a large open stone hearth, an earthen floor, and windows stuffed with rags and paper. Beside the chimney stood a ladder leading to the sleeping loft, where the boys' pallets would be in the summer. Sometimes they were invited to sleep in the warmer attic in the Big House during the freezing winters.

"Where did Hugh and George come from?" my son who was also named George asked.

"Yeah, who were their parents?" my other son, Edward, wanted to know. He was born free in Ohio in 1864. I had told him his daddy's name was Hugh Booker.

Well, I don't know for sure, but I always wondered if Massa John White Stalnaker was the father of Hugh and George. They were his trusted servants until he freed them in 1863 and wrote his Will to give them some of his estate when he died. It indicated a blood relationship if the owner freed his slaves, left them money or property in their will, and if they were described as "mulatto" or "mixed." So, it's possible they were blood kin of the Stalnakers.

Massa John's family planted the orchard long before I came along. Apples and peaches, especially, grew well in Randolph County. It was George's, Hugh's and my job to pick the fruit when it was perfectly ripe. Then I helped Miz Margaret Elizabeth, Missus Mary and her daughter, Miss Labana, do the canning and preserving. Those sweet fruits were especially delicious during the freezing winter months.

The Missus also taught me to spin yarn from sheep's wool and to sew blankets and clothes. They taught me how to cook, wash and iron clothes without burning them, and how to clean every aspect of the house to make it beautiful.

Lots of Kittle families lived nearby, as did Crouches and Stalnakers. I never knew for sure whether we were blood kin to all of 'em. We lived next to the Old Earle home, which stood on the same side of the road, but back on the hill. Our house overlooked the river and bottom land owned by the Earle family. Theirs was a brick house of considerable size, owned and occupied by Mrs. Mary Polly Earle, widow of Archibald Earle who died in 1842. They had six slaves in 1840 to work their grist mill. Some of her children were married, but Archibald Jr., Elias, and Creed were still living at home with their mother.

The Suiters' home was next to the Earles at the foot of the hill. A blacksmith's shop was in the upper corner of their lot. When Hugh and George had some time off from their duties, they liked to go by the smithy and learn how to make horseshoes and keys and hooks and such.

Crossing the creek using a footbridge reached the mill race on the right side as you went into the town of Beverly. Mr. Keesy lived in a long, low building, running back from the street. He was a tailor who had an extremely long nose, and his wife liked to wear bustles that made her bottom look huge. That was the style back then, don't you know? We black women didn't have to pad our bottoms to look big.

"Yes, Precious Lord!" the man exclaimed; others snickered.

Down a ways, across the street from Mr. Logan's place, was a two-story log house, which was occupied by Mr. John B. Earle and his large family.

On Christmas Day in 1845 I got my bleeding. That meant I was ripe, now a woman who could have a baby. I didn't know that last fact but Massa John White evidently did. I heard him and his mother talking one night, worried that I could have a baby by George or Hugh, us being so close together all the time. I didn't realize the importance of that conversation.

On February 2, 1846, right before my birthday, Massa John White Stalnaker done sold me to Elizabeth S. Earle. (Figure 5) She was his niece, I think. The following month Miz Margaret Elizabeth died from old age and from missing me.

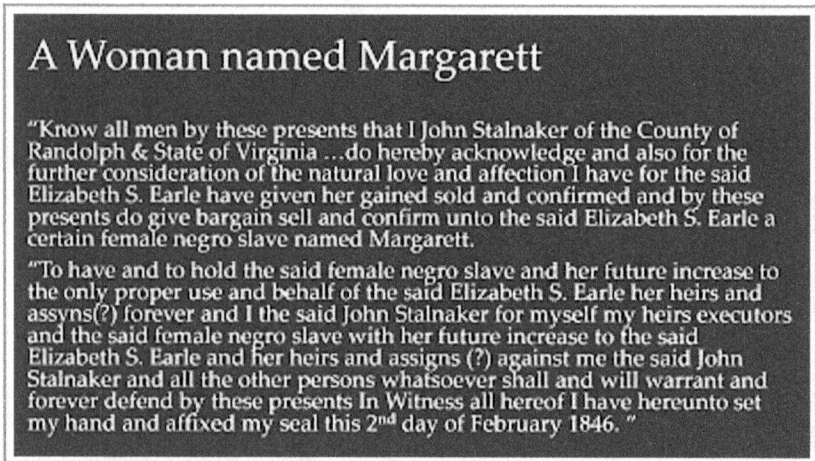

A Woman named Margarett

"Know all men by these presents that I John Stalnaker of the County of Randolph & State of Virginia ...do hereby acknowledge and also for the further consideration of the natural love and affection I have for the said Elizabeth S. Earle have given her gained sold and confirmed and by these presents do give bargain sell and confirm unto the said Elizabeth S. Earle a certain female negro slave named Margarett.

"To have and to hold the said female negro slave and her future increase to the only proper use and behalf of the said Elizabeth S. Earle her heirs and assyns(?) forever and I the said John Stalnaker for myself my heirs executors and the said female negro slave with her future increase to the said Elizabeth S. Earle and her heirs and assigns (?) against me the said John Stalnaker and all the other persons whatsoever shall and will warrant and forever defend by these presents In Witness all hereof I have hereunto set my hand and affixed my seal this 2nd day of February 1846. "

Figure 5: 1846 Bill of Sale found in the Randolph County, Virginia, Oaths and Licenses Book, indicated that Slave Margarett was sold by John Stalnaker to Elizabeth "Betty" Earle.

Massa John White wrote on my bill of sale something like: "For the natural love and affection I have for Elizabeth S. Earle, I have sold to her a certain female Negro slave named Margaret. To have and to hold the said female Negro slave and her future increase"—

which meant any children I might have in the future—"to be used on behalf of Elizabeth S. Earle and her heirs, forever."

I'd been with the Kittle and Stalnaker families all my young life, but Massa John White sold me for one dollar. I couldn't believe it. Is that all I was worth to him? One measly dollar? All those years working for him, helping with his elderly mama, helping with the cooking, helping with the cleaning, helping with the laundry, and helping with the farming. That's all I was worth? It sure didn't make a girl feel good about herself.

Yep, I was sold just like a one dollar sack of flour from one white person to another. I had to live with and do whatever my new Massa wanted me to do. If I had a family and friends I grew up with, or loved, or needed, so what? It didn't matter. I couldn't walk to the store to buy candy without Massa's say so. I had no money no ways. I couldn't go nowhere my Massa didn't know about and approve. All that mattered was what the slave master wanted and paid for.

My saucy grandson Herbert piped up, "It sounds just like being a child now. We can't do whatever we want, whenever we want either, unless an adult says we can." Even though some heads laughed or nodded in agreement, every child now fully understood that being a slave was more, much more.

Chapter 5 - The Handmaid #1

"Once upon a time in Ol' Virginny…"

"Margaret!" yelled an agitated female voice from somewhere upstairs.

"Yes, Miz Betty, I am comin' up," I responded. My white apron flapped against my legs as I rushed up the wooden stairs that smelled of pine trees. I held a tall glass of freshly made apple juice, the fruit picked from Massa Hart's apple orchard up a ways on Rich Mountain. That's where an important Civil War Battle occurred in 1861 with young David Hart leading the Yankees through the forests. They captured the Confederate stronghold and took over the town of county seat of Beverly.

Massa Hart's people was one of the first families to settle in the Beverly area before 1800. They come on horseback from New Jersey, then bought lots of property in these parts, eventually planting apple and peach orchards on the hillsides. Oh, the pretty pink and white petals in the spring that float through the scented air. My favorite apples are the tart, kind of sweet green ones with a sun-kissed middle, perfect for apple pies and cobblers.

We lived on the Earle property at the corner of Main and Crawford Street in little downtown Beverly (Figure 6). It was my fifteenth birthday. I hurried to deliver the sweet drink to my mistress with the hope she might have a little present for me. Miz Betty was waiting impatiently in her bedroom at the end of the second-floor hallway.

"Now, Margaret, how many times do I have to tell you to have my juice on the bed stand before I wake up?"

Elizabeth "Betty" Stalnaker Vinyard Earle—I called her Miz Betty—affectionately scolded me on that chilly February morning in 1849. Her husband, Massa John, already been up and dressed, getting ready for a long day at his mill down the road a piece.

"I sorry, Miz Betty. I din't hear the wakeup bell this morning, so I woke up a might late. I dressed quick as lightning, then got the fire going, brewed coffee for Massa and made bacon and eggs and porridge for him and the older children." The unmistakably delicious smell of sizzling meaty pork clung to the folds of my checkered dress and white apron.

"I boilt some sweet yeller apples and a lil bit of the tart green ones last night, then mashed 'em really good this morning with water. I hope you like the juice, ma'am."

Figure 6: John B. Earle's home from 1838 to 1879, at Crawford and Main Streets, Beverly, West Virginia.

"Well, thank you for removing all the seeds this time," Miz Betty said, gulping the last of the pulpy liquid and wiping her chin with the towel I handed her.

"You want me to help ya git dressed now?"

Missus ordered, "Get me that white shirt with the pretty lace on the collar and... let's see, the dark gray skirt. I've lost so much weight since Page's birth, and now I've got another little bugger in my belly."

Frowning, she wondered, "Why are people always asking how I'm feeling, or saying I look tired, or that I need to eat more?"

Like everybody else, I knew something was wrong with my mistress. I pretended to be so busy looking through her closet that I din't answer. "Oh, here they are," bringing the clothes to her and

56

placing them on the foot of the bed. At her nod, I turned back the covers and offered my hand to help her up. Her pale face looked a little shaded, eyes rimmed with dark circles like she hadn't slept good, hair thinner than usual, cheeks sagging, forehead damp, skin so white you could see the blue veins underneath. She was no longer the lovely woman I met a few years ago, no longer the woman who sang in the church choir, baked the most heavenly berry pies. She was no longer the woman who taught me how to sew clothes and quilt blankets and use the spinning wheel to make yarn from lamb's wool. That woman was disappearing day by day, replaced with the shell of her old self.

I helped Miz Betty take off her sleeping gown, then sat her onto the wooden commode in the corner of the room, holding her arms to keep her balance. After my mistress finished her business, I directed her to the vanity chair, washed her face, neck and underarms with a damp washcloth. I handed her some clean white drawers,[13] helped her slide up the cotton stockin's and wrestle on a maternity corset that made room for the growing baby.[14] I then helped her into a black crinoline petticoat[15] that had six hoops from just below the waist to the floor. The cream-colored, puffy-sleeved shirt with a deep V-necked bodice allowed for easy nursing (Figure 7).

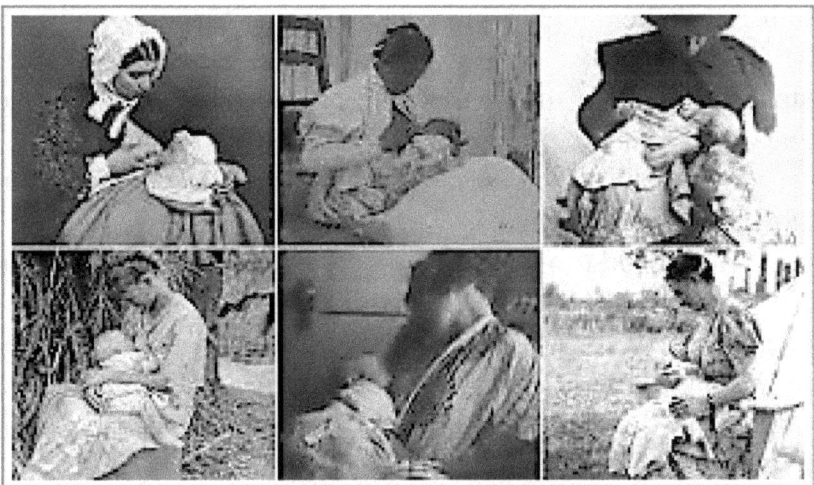

Figure 7: Samples of women breast feeding.

With her arms up to the sky, I draped the gray skirt over Miz Betty's head down her body and clasped it at her waist. Last, I inserted her stockinged feet into ankle-high button-down shoes.

There weren't any wet nurses[16] in Beverly, and not enough black women available to perform the task. White women actually had to feed their own babies, at least until they had another one, which seemed to happen every two years.

"Why don't you bring me Page now so I can nurse him while you do my hair?"

"Of course, ma'am. I'll be right back." I retrieved the squirming toddler from his crib in the children's nursery down the hall. He shared the room with three-year-old brother Burns S. Earle who slept in a small bed, and now ate the same food as the rest of the household. Sometimes I slept there on a pallet to make sure the youngest children were safe at night. If they awoke, it was my job to get them back to sleep. Usually rubbing their backs did the trick. Their three older sisters slept in another bedroom across the hall from the boys.

Miz Betty sat calmly on the chair before her mirror, the one-year-old's mouth clamped onto her thin, saggy breast. His toddler fingers played with a toy while he ate greedily. I combed her once-thick, sandy-colored hair, then wrapped it into a tight bun at the back of her neck, holding it in place with hairpins. Since the baby's birth, Miz Betty had lost more than just a little baby weight. Her hair started falling out, and her cheeks seemed to cave in. She looked ill and weak. Everybody noticed it, especially her husband.

"Miz Betty, I gots to check on the breakfast warming on the stove. I'll be back soon."

I did my best to keep up with the house cleaning and cooking, but it was tough. When Miz Betty was feeling good last fall, she taught me how to "put up" juicy, sweet blackberries that we picked every August from the bushes around the house. We also picked tart red cherries and juicy dark-blue plums from the backyard orchard, to become delicious jams and jellies.

We pickled cucumbers and canned dill and sweet pickles. Root vegetables like carrots, potatoes, parsnips, and beets were stored in the cold cellar for eating throughout the winter and spring. Cabbages were eaten fresh, usually in coleslaw, from June through September, and sauerkraut was canned for winter and spring meals. Beans and peas were harvested and canned before mid-September every year. Squash and pumpkins were harvested through November. Miz Betty would send me to Blackman's Store early in the fall to buy crates of apples and we would store 'em in the cellar during the freezing winter months so we could have juice in the spring.

That meant in March 1849 there were apples for Miz Betty's juice, seasoned link sausages, sunny-side-up eggs, warm, buttered biscuits with plum and peach jam, and oatmeal porridge that I made for the day's morning breakfast. All these tasks were performed before I came upstairs to see to my mistress. I was her handmaiden first and foremost, but when she began feeling poorly, I had to do her cooking and cleaning jobs too.

"Margaret!" The familiar voice called from upstairs. She musta finished feeding Page.

I trudged up the stairs wondering what she would ask me to do this time. When I entered her bedroom, I was happily surprised to see her old smile again. Her fingers signaled for me to come to her vanity table. "Happy birthday!" she wished me in her sweetest voice. "You didn't think I forgot, did you?" My warm chocolate cheeks blushed because yes, I had thought she forgot all about my special day. "Open it," she encouraged, as I stepped forward.

A small black velvet box sat on the vanity, wrapped with a red ribbon. I picked it up, turning it carefully in my hands, enjoying the feel of the soft velvet against my coarse skin, still not believing it was for me. I gently pulled one end of ribbon, watching the bow slide apart, falling beside the box, calling me to release the surprise. I lifted the lid and spied inside. "Oh my!" I gasped out loud. "It's beautiful. For me?" I looked at my mistress and she nodded. I reached my trembling fingers inside the container, grasping a gold locket attached to a delicate gold chain.

"My mother left that to me and I want to give it to you on this important day, as thanks for always taking such good care of me and my babies. Do you like it?"

"Do I like it? No, ma'am. I love it!" I responded, never having owned anything this valuable in my whole life. "I will always remember your kindness, Miz Betty." Tears welled in my eyes and my lips began to quiver nervously. I felt emotional. I suspected Miz Betty would not be with us for much longer. Reaching my hand to my throat, I fingered the little gold locket that I still wore fifty some-odd years later.

The Master Disappeared

One day, in late spring of 1850 after school was out, Massa John told us to pack our clothes and favorite possessions. We were going to visit the White's house during his children's summer vacation. The Whites were Miz Betty's parents. We all were excited to have an adventure in the country, but my ailing Missus was especially happy. We packed our bags, closed up the house on Main and Crawford Street in Beverly, got into the carriage—me in the back with the suitcases, and them up front—then we bumped along the turnpike for an hour, reaching the White's house by lunchtime.

I grew up in this area with the Stalnakers, Kittles, and Westfalls, all some of the first families who settled there in the late 1700s. Most people in the country were farmers, of course, but there were ranchers herding cattle, plenty of carpenters to build houses and outbuildings, a blacksmith or two, and saddle makers. Most homes had five or six people in their household to work their own plots of land. A few had enough land to hire laborers or have a few slaves to do the work.

The White's house was much like most cabins built in the county at that time. There were three bedrooms upstairs, a front room and kitchen and dining area downstairs, one big hearth for cooking and heating, a wide porch outside, and at least one window on each side of the house downstairs and upstairs. The Whites did not own slaves, so there was no separate cabin for me. I would sleep on a pallet on the floor in the bedroom with the young children.

As soon as I got my leave from Miz Betty, I ran into the forest. It was as if I was in a different world. The "living green" of fresh new ferns peeked out from dark green undergrowth. The moss-covered floor looked soft enough to walk on barefoot, so I took off my shoes and let my feet luxuriate in the thick carpet. Giant spruce trees towered above, and the smell—oh the fresh pine scent that made my lungs feel free. Familiar. Home. I wept.

It had been four years since being sold to the Earles and while city life was interesting, I missed my forest something' fierce. Then I suddenly remembered that my life was no longer my own. Wiping my teary face with the long sleeve of my shirt, I sprinted back to the White's house, just in time for a scolding.

Massa John was gone when I got back to the house. Nobody would say where he went, but there was obviously something wrong. Lips were shut tight. There was no laughter. People looked like they were sleep-walking, in a daze. Well, I couldn't worry about white folk's problems. I had to go to work, taking care of the children while Miz Betty's step-mama and daddy watched over her.

Day by day, my mistress looked sicker and sicker, poor thing. She was carrying Massa's sixth child when her body hadn't recovered from the fifth. It was a blessing, really, that he brought us to a place where my mistress could be taken take of better than my sixteen-year-old self could. But where did Massa John go?

During the dinner service, I heard all sorts of clues about why he left. You see, a proper servant—they liked to call us slaves "servants"—brings food out on big platters and goes around the table letting the diners dish out what they want, or we did the dishing. A proper servant stands silently behind the table, like a statue, in case a diner needs something else: "Refresh my beverage. Bring me the saltshaker. (It's right next to you, get it yourself!) Bring me a clean napkin. Get me another fork. Take away my dirty plate."

"Yessum," is all we supposed to say in response, a perky smile on our faces no matter how tired our feet are, or how hot we feel, or whether we must use the outhouse. That is our lot, until the last plate is cleared away.

It's not all bad, though. While a fly on the wall, as they say, we servants get an ear full of the happenings in the house, our town, our state, and the wide world beyond. Some diners said Massa John went plum crazy, drinking gin from the fine crystal decanter all day long. Some said he was having money trouble. Others said it was trouble at the mill with his workers and the equipment, so his brother Elias had to take over operations. Mr. White said he been playing in the wrong sandbox when his wife was too sick to... well, they didn't say because the children would hear. We all knew what they meant. Massa John liked to make babies.

Some admitted he'd always been a bit "teched in the head."[17]

Days later, I learned the truth when someone whispered that Massa John had been admitted to the Western Lunatic Asylum in Augusta, Virginia. They said, "In its early days, the facility was a resort-style place with pretty terraced gardens where patients could plant flowers and take walks or even mosey along the roof garden to see the mighty mountains. They said the building itself had many architectural details that created an atmosphere that would aid in the healing process. However, they also talked about horrifying ankle and wrist restraints, and straitjackets. I felt kinda bad for Massa John.

But he was back in a few months, as good as new. We all stayed with the Whites until Miz Betty died on May 11, 1851.

It was so strange returning to our house in Beverly without Miz Betty. I was soon to find out what the full functions of a handmaid were.[18]

Chapter 6 - The Handmaid #2

"What happened next, Grandma?" Ada Mae asked, as she pulled on her fluffy pigtails wrapped in blue ribbons.

I threw my head back and laughed, my shoulders heaving up and down in merriment. I was thrilled she was so excited to learn about our ancestors. I began the story in the old familiar way.

"Once upon a time in Ol' Virginny..."

With Miz Betty gone to Heaven, I had to become the mama and the maid in the Earle household. I was tall for my age and strong enough to carry a young child in each arm up the stairs, plow the kitchen garden, and do the laundry. Miz Betty taught me well and I felt comfortable handling my increased responsibilities. Tasty meals were prepared on time, kids readied for school, clothes washed and ironed, and the kitchen garden thrived. The household was running smoothly. The children asked about their mama and I told 'em all sorts of wonderful stories about her. Sadly, they mentioned her less and less as time went on. Even Mary Elizabeth who was thirteen and Nannie who was eleven hardly mentioned their mother anymore.

Massa John took back control of the mill after his stay at that lunatic place in 1850. He was kinder and more interested in his children, even playing ball with them on occasion. He was even nicer to me. Women felt sorry for him. "Oh, the poor man, with no wife and five motherless children," they said in a pitiful voice as they boldly dropped off pie after casserole for the widow. You can guess what happened next.

"He got a girlfriend?" Clara perked up.

Better than that. He married Miss Labana Stalnaker on Thanksgiving Day in 1852, roughly a year after his first wife died. Labana was the daughter of my former master, John White Stalnaker. I was happy Massa chose someone I knew and liked. In fact, Missus Labana was almost like a mama to me, being sixteen years older than I was. She watched out for me when I was a youngster living in her parents' house near the Earles' original property at Leadsville. I was more than happy to become her handmaid number two.

We did everything together: spinning yarn from sheep's wool, weaving rugs, getting fabric from Crawford's Store and sewing clothes for the kids and ourselves. We sometimes tried new cooking recipes. Buckwheat, peaches, and apples were the most important food products, so we often made pies and cakes with those ingredients.

Our family favorite was stewed squirrel cooked with onions, garlic, thyme and bacon. Yum! Bear meat was also prized back in the day. Wild greens were a staple of the earliest settlers, but we also planted corn, beans, and potatoes.[19] Most families kept a few pigs and chickens too. Massa's youngest children loved toddling around after the hens. They squealed with delight at the oink-oink of the pinkish piggies. Yes, there was lots of laughter in the Earle household once again.

We were over-the-moon happy when Missus Labana started getting big with her first child. Neither one of us had ever had a baby before, but I helped Miz Betty when Page was born. I knew what to expect. I was in the room when Miz Betty birthed her sixth baby… and I watched, horrified, when they both ascended through the pearly gates that same day.

"Oh Margaret, my left side is paining me something fierce," my new Missus would moan. "It goes away for a while, then it moves to another part of my belly minutes later. What do you think's wrong?"

I'd press my hand where she directed and felt the strong movement of a foot or elbow pushing against her side, moving itself to the front of her belly. "Oh, that's just your young'un turning hisself over. Maybe we should loosen your maternity corset so it doesn't hurt you so much," I'd suggest. Slave women was lucky in that respect because we wasn't expected to wear a corset or enhance our figure in any way.

Some days she'd sigh, "Margaret, I am especially hungry today. I have a taste for pork. Would you fix me something please?"

"Surely, Missus, anything you want." I would cut up a tater, boil it with some salt pork and greens from the garden, then add some dried pork I had in the larder. Maybe fifteen or twenty minutes later, I'd bring her a bowl of whatever she craved. She was my special lady and I'd do anything for her.

It's Time

Screams pierced the quiet of the mid-January morning at the corner of Crawford and Main Streets. "Look into my eyes, Missus, and breathe, breathe," I encouraged as her hand gripped my arm. It was showtime. Sweating, writhing, panting, moaning, gasping at yet another sharp pain rippling through her belly. My mistress said she didn't think she could survive another minute.

Milder contractions had started during the middle of the night, but now the squeezing, gripping pains in her stomach came every seven minutes or so, then every six. Massa John went to get Doc Bosworth when the sun stretched yellow rays from their night blanket.

Fluffy feather pillows propped behind the laboring woman's back helped her sit upright in the marriage bed, letting gravity help the straining baby inch downward little by little as the hours passed oh-so-slowly. I was told that squatting was the old African way, to encourage the birth canal to open for a speedier delivery.

Missus Labana's mother, Mary, was staying with us for a couple of weeks. She placed damp washcloths on her daughter's forehead and I replaced them often to cool the mama-to-be's heated efforts. Mother Mary kept up a steady stream of conversation to keep her daughter's mind off the incessant, uncomfortable, rhythmic tightening inside her belly, as the baby's head began to wedge lower into the birth canal.

This was her first baby, even though she was old to be having her first at the age of thirty-seven. She had no idea how long the birthing process would be. None of us women ever do. Two hours of agony stretched into four, the contractions getting stronger and stronger every few minutes. The doctor told me to boil water and have clean cloths handy. He inserted a finger in the birth canal to get a better idea of how things were progressing.

"It should be quite soon now, Labana," he said with a practiced calm.

Towards noon, the moans and screams stopped altogether. It was rather surreal not to hear them anymore. Now it was too quiet. Massa John hoped everything was all right but he didn't dare go inside the birthing room to check. What if the baby had died? What if his beloved Labana had passed like his first wife after birth... no, he couldn't, he wouldn't imagine that.

Just then, a high piercing sound, like a bird strangled in the talons of an eagle, or a sickly tomcat, came from the room down the hall. Then everything was quiet again, followed soon by another wailing sound, then another beautiful cry. They were alive!

A few moments later, the doctor came to the front room where Massa John was pretending to read a book. "You have a strong son and your wife will be just fine with a little rest. We've cleaned the baby up for you in case to want to visit your wife and new son."

Massa John ran inside, kissed his wife, and marveled at his strong new son. Missus Labana smiled weakly as she gazed at her first born nestled on her chest, like a new, hairless baby mouse attempting to suckle.

Stop Bothering Me!

Massa John was so happy when Baylis A. Earle was born. It was his sixth child, five by Miz Betty and this first one by Missus Labana. As with most babies, especially the first, the new mother was indescribably sore everywhere, but especially "down there."

Generally, all her energy is focused on healing, breastfeeding, sleeping, and learning how to read her baby's signals. A new mother is not usually interested in resuming randy activities right away. The new father, on the other hand, has no such constraints.

The male desire does not turn off easily, especially during the winter months when snuggling to keep warm often leads to "stimulating" experiences. So even though the new mama may close the store for a while, the male is still ready to shop. I looked up at my audience, winking at the men who snickered their agreement.

The new father may instead go to the next best thing... a female slave who is not at liberty to deny her master's wishes. That not-so-lucky female was me.

After Missus Labana gave birth, Massa John started hanging around wherever I was working. Smiling, winking, letting his arm brush across my bottom when I passed by, and putting his arm around my shoulders when he spoke to me. His attentions were all too obvious. I was nineteen, fully grown. My smooth coppery skin gleamed in the sunlight and I sewed clothes that complemented my skin tone—blues and whites, especially. My shoulder-length hair was black as coal and usually braided from my forehead down each side of my face, clasped in the back. A colorful kerchief often covered my head. I did not want to betray my mistress. She was my friend, but I had no choice.

The next day, Massa John told me to go to the barn and feed the horses. It was an odd request because that was not one of my normal tasks. I did as I was told, though, opening the barn door and walking toward the feed bin. Startled, I heard a raspy, "Come on over here, gal." It was Massa, standing at the far end of the barn near where the horse whips and leather gloves were hanging from a hook on the wall. As I approached, I noticed his pants were loosened. I knew what he wanted, even though I hadn't been touched yet. Innocently playing doctor with Hugh and George those many years ago as children was nothing like what this man had in mind.

"Massa, Missus Labana is my mistress and my friend. I cain't do that to her."

"Gal, I'm not telling you to do anything to her, I want you to do something to me. Get on over here right now. I hesitated, then started walking slowly toward the last stall. He had spread hay on the floor and a horse blanket on top to make a more comfortable pallet. He looked me in the eyes, licking his lips as he lowered his gaze to my chest, the way men do. Then he started breathing more heavily, his eyes looking farther down my body. His hand reached toward my private areas. I jumped back, automatically.

"Massa, please, no!" I pleaded without success.

He grabbed me by the arms, then lowered me onto the scratchy blanket. Quickly, he raised my dress, freeing my stockinged legs. He looked like a salivating dog wanting to chew on my meaty bone. He began taking off his shoes, his belt, his pants. He got down on his knees, straddled my legs, strong fingers pushing my tense limbs apart. He found what he was feeling around for, then jammed what felt like a broom handle inside me. I screamed, the white hot pain extending from the entry point racing to my feet and fingertips, then to my brain. I moaned in extreme discomfort, but Massa John just pushed himself farther in, then out, over and over again, faster and faster, his face crazed like he was in some other world.

Stuttering, he ordered, "B-b-be quiet, gal!" as he continued his push-pull exercises. Oh, when will he stop bothering me?

Finally, he made a low, animal grunting sound, then fell on top of me, chest surging, breathing even more heavily than before. After a minute or two, he stilled, got up, put his pants on, tied his shoes, then readjusted his shirt.

His voice stern, he said, "Get yourself cleaned up and get back in the house, and if you tell anyone about this, I'll beat you senseless with this horse whip. Do you understand me?" He finished the warning at the same time he finished dressing.

I nodded, wincing, trying not to cry. After he left, I slowly pushed myself up and smoothed down my dress. I felt an icky wetness between my sore legs as I picked straw out of my hair and gown. I would wash myself when I got back into the house. I hoped this would never happen again but suspected that it would. And it did, just about every day. When Massa John pointed toward the barn, I had to do my duty without comment, without complaint. I lay there like a rag doll, which was fine with him. I had now learned the full scope of what being a handmaid was.

Eventually, the inevitable happened. When did my monthly bleeding stop? I noticed that my titties had become very sore and seemed larger than before. I noticed that my dresses felt tighter as my waist expanded… just like Missus Labana's. You see, she was pregnant again too. I felt so bad lying to her about who the father was, but I couldn't hurt her by spilling the beans about her lecherous husband. Plus, I didn't want a whupping from him.

Believe it or not, the Missus and I gave birth on almost the same day. I named my son Joab at Massa's insistence. He named his wife's son, John Baylis Earle, after himself. From that point on Massa John continued to put babies in his wife's and my wombs. My Joab was born in 1855, Cornelia in 1856, George in 1858, May in 1860, and Ella in 1863. His wife, Labana, gave birth to Baylis in 1853, John in 1855, Lenora in 1856, Floyd in 1858, and Louida in 1861, after which my friend, my mistress, died the following year. That's ten children in eight years, in addition to the five he had with his first wife, Miz Betty. Massa John B. Earle proved to everyone that he like to make babies. Fifteen of 'em! Whew!

My Town

My life had settled into a routine of sorts: canning, cleaning, cooking, dressing Missus number two and her children, laundering, milking, sewing, shopping, weaving, breeding, nursing, caring for my children, hoeing, planting, and harvesting the kitchen garden. I feel tired just thinking about all the responsibilities I had in my twenties.

What I looked forward to most was being sent to pick up something from the store a half a mile away. To be by myself for an hour or two was pure Heaven! I'd wrap my head in a beautiful scarf and wear my prettiest blue dress and my best shoes. A basket over my arm and I was off. No orders, no questions, no requests, just me and my basket. It was lovely. Once downtown, I began my favorite game: listening. I used this opportunity to learn what was going on in our town, our county, our state, and even the world beyond.

When we "servants"—as they preferred to call house slaves—walked into Bosworth's store to get sugar or Crawford's shop for hair ribbons, we studied white folks outta the sides of our downcast eyes. That's how we knew the history of the town, who was powerful, who was in trouble, who had a baby and by which man, who was friends and who wasn't. Whatever we found out we passed to our chocolate friends at church and at the market. We paid attention, grasping interesting tidbits outta the mouths of visitors stopping for lunch on the way to Phillipi, or Huttonsville up the road.

In addition to the news, my town contained a lot of interesting buildings and history that I want to tell you about. The Blackman-Bosworth Store on Main Street was the first all-brick commercial building west of the Allegheny Mountains. Over the years, it served as a county courthouse, post office, meeting place, and a store. Check this out. When Mr. Blackman married, his father-in-law gave him several slaves as a wedding gift. While Mr. Blackman said he didn't like the concept of slavery, he sure did use his human gifts to mold and burn them red bricks to build the storehouse and other buildings around town.[20]

"Would you have stuck to your morals or done exactly what he did?" I asked the crowd who provided many different responses:

"I'd do the same thing if I was white and had the power to control others."

"No, my conscience wouldn't allow me to have slaves, even if they fell into my lap."

"I'd be stupid not to use the gift, but I would treat the slaves well to justify to myself using them that way."

"I would free 'em, then pay them to work for me," another answered.

I replied, "See, it's not so easy to keep to what you know is right and what you want, is it?" Heads shook, shoulders shrugged, and "Amen!" was what someone added.

Believe it or not, there was only one doctor in all of Randolph County for nearly fifty years. Everyone, black and white, liked and respected Dr. Squire Bosworth. He married Hannah Buckey, daughter of one of Beverly's founding fathers and the auntie of my Massa John Earle.

"Grandma, didn't you say Archibald Earle lived with the Buckeys when he first came to Beverly?" my granddaughter Maude asked.

"You have a great memory! Indeed, Archibald stayed with them for a couple of years before he married their daughter Mary Polly, and the year after that Massa John was born. Maude, that means Archibald is your grandfather... Ella, honey, bring me some more tea before I continue?"

"No problem, Mom, I'll be right back."

The younger kids took this opportunity to jump up from the grass and stretch their legs. Some twirled around with their arms stretched out wide, spinning like tops until they fell over dizzy, laughing, then doing it again and again. Ah, the bliss of youth.

"Thank you, darlin'," I sipped at the tea, then gulped, then placed the glass on the tiny wooden table next to my chair.

Let's see. What else should I tell you? The early roads in the Tygart Valley were nothin' more than horse bridle paths before 1800.[21] Then the court recommended those trails be kept at an eight-foot width so wagons could use the roads too. As business increased and people kept a-comin', better roadways were needed. In 1835, the population of Beverly was 184 residents, including me and fifteen other slaves, and two free Negroes.[22] By 1847, the important Staunton-Parkersburg Turnpike was completed, connecting the Shenandoah Valley with the Ohio River. Beverly served as a major crossroads and stopping-off point, encouraging the town to grow even more to accommodate the increased traffic.

Resident Lemuel Chenoweth was a respected carpenter and bridge builder who constructed many of the covered bridges on the turnpike, including the one in Beverly, and the Philippi Covered Bridge. He also built a sawmill and his own house, both overlooking his Beverly Bridge. They say he was brilliant, using many of the construction techniques in his home that he used for bridge building. Massa John's house was next to the bridge.

[Author's note: The map in Figure 8 shows where John B. Earle's saw and flour mill, and his house, were located in 1854 when Margaret was his only slave. The author's great-great-grandfather, Joab/Joseph Booker, was born in the slave cabin behind that house in 1855. A photograph of the house is shown in Figure 6.]

More transportation improvements were made. The Beverly-Fairmont Turnpike was completed in 1852, partly from travelers' fees collected at tollgates. Our residents now had access to the new railroad fifty miles away in Grafton. Beverly was the county's center of commerce, at least until my family fled during the Civil War, but I'll talk about that thrilling adventure on another day.

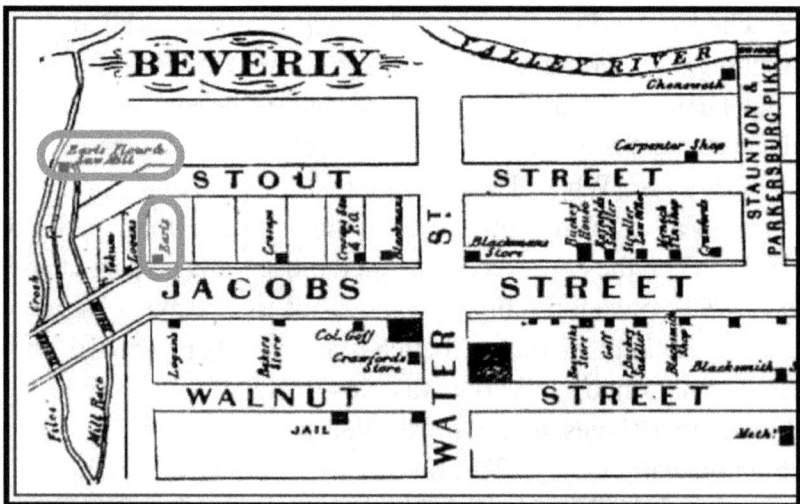

Figure 8: Map of downtown Beverly as of 1854, part 1.

I heard Herbert sucking his teeth. That spoiled boy always wants to hear all my stories at once, which is flattering, but he'll just have to wait until I'm ready to tell 'em.

Mr. Rowan's hat factory had all sorts of fascinating head ware in the front window. Regular ladies wore simple bonnets on their heads, maybe with silk string ties or colorful ribbons. At home they wore white caps. Colored women wore head scarves wrapped and twisted in interesting designs around their heads. Rich ladies kept up with the fashion styles they saw in catalogs and on travelers passing through Beverly from Baltimore and Richmond on their way to Ohio. There were woven hats, brims decorated with colorful silk flowers and bows and trims. There were long tails of lace or brocade hanging down the back of some hats. My favorites had turquoise and purple peacock feathers poking straight up. Mr. Rowan made all manner of hats for the bigwig lawyers and gov'ment men in town. Tall top hats, felt bowlers, small "Nattie" straw hats with wide ribbons, casual wide-brimmed hats, as well as typical canvas work hats with brims that shielded the eyes and neck from the sun.[23]

There were two boot and shoe shops that were indispensable, as most men wore boots in those days. There were two tailor shops, each having several men cleverly crafting men's and boys' suits and casual clothes. There were three saddlery shops making saddles and bridles from cattle hides. Two blacksmith shops were miserable places to be in the summertime with the extreme heat from the hearth and furnace helping the smiths create and fix all manner of metal tools, wheels, and such.

The two gunsmith shops made excellent guns, many of them ornamented with silver mountings, beautifully engraved. You better believe the blacksmiths and gun shops were especially busy during the Civil War!

Two carpenter shops in town created basic furniture like beds and cabinets and chairs, but they also constructed wagons, which were in high demand by farmers and city folk alike.

Beverly also had a toy factory with toys, train sets, blocks, and ornaments made of plaster of Paris by two Italian men. They were among the first local volunteers in the Confederate army.

There were usually at least two hotels in town; the largest was owned and managed by Massa John's sister, Lucinda Leonard. (Figure 9) I'll tell you an interesting story about it…"

"On another day…" Herbert sighed. I had to chuckle.

Ahem, clearing my throat to continue—Stagecoaches drawn by four horses traveled between Staunton, Weston, and Fairmont three times each week. People could make good time on the turnpike, with horses being changed every ten or twelve miles, night and day. Approaching the town, the driver would blow on a trumpet. Toot-doodle-loo-TOOT! The loud noise would signal citizens to gather at hotel stops to see who was arriving, as well as get the latest news from big cities in Maryland, Virginia, and Ohio. Those coaches could carry nine passengers inside and could take two on the top seat with the driver. There was a big area at the back of the coach to hold baggage. Well-to-do passengers traveled in private carriages.

So, as you can see, there was a lot going on in Beverly, the seat of government in Randolph County where I grew into a woman.

"Grandma, where did you go to church when you were little?" Myrtle asked.

Well, my first twelve years was with the Stalnakers. There was a traveling preacher that came around, but most folks rode in their wagons a few miles to Beverly. The Methodist Church had deep roots there from the time of its settlement, built from logs at the western end of Court Street. It was used for almost eighty years until the Civil War, when Union troops dismantled the building, using the logs for huts for their commanders. Most Negroes were of the Methodist faith, but I heard they built an African Methodist Episcopal church after slavery, somewhere around Fountain Street, a block or so from the jail.

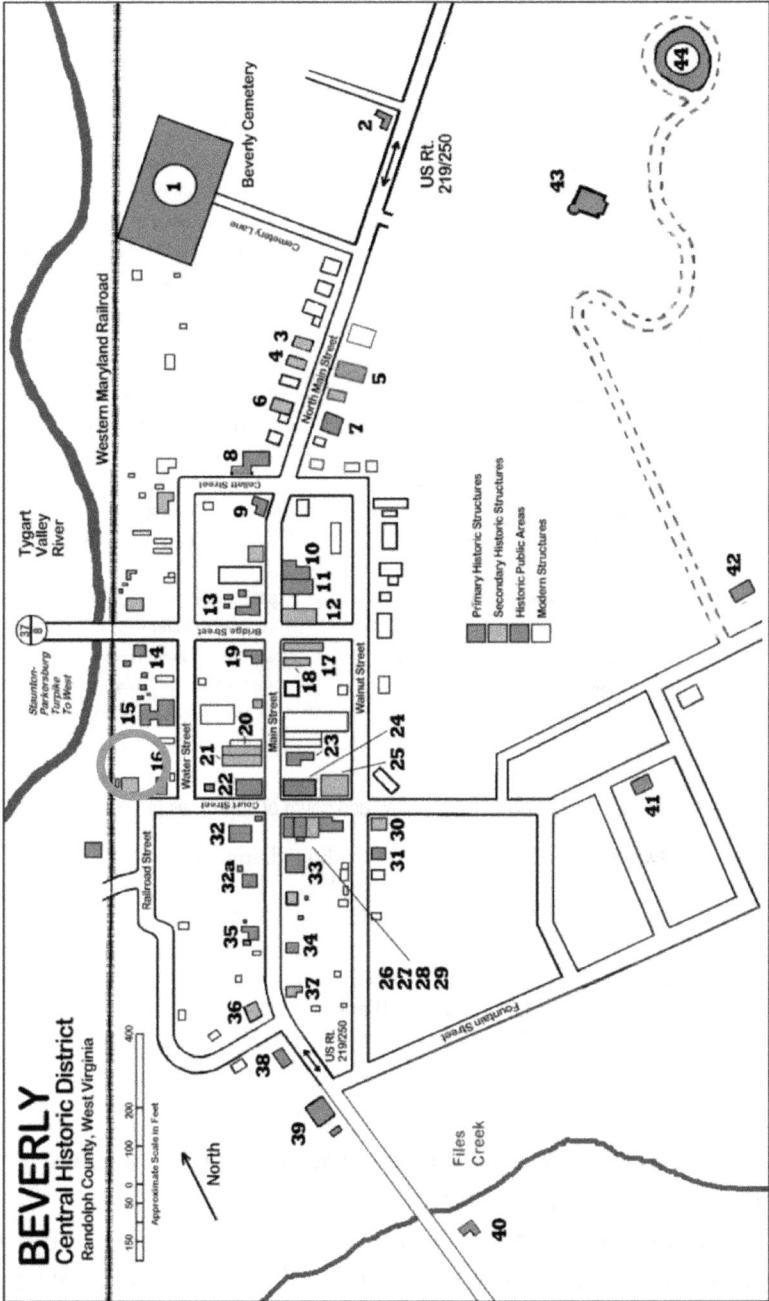

Figure 9a: Map of downtown Beverly as of 1854, part 1.

Beverly Features

1. **Beverly Cemetery** -- *ca. 1768*
2. **Calvin Collett House** -- *ca. 1869*
3. **Dreppard House** -- *ca. 1895*
4. **Curry House** -- *ca. 1897*
5. **The Pines** -- *1800?* (Demolished June, 2010)
6. **Willa Hill House** -- *ca. 1910*
7. **Beverly Methodist Church** -- *1890*
8. **Beverly Presbyterian Church** -- *1869*
9. **Montgomery Hart / Andrew Collett House** -- *pre-1840*
10. **Peter Buckey House and Hotel** --*pre-1791*
11. **Enterprise Building** -- *ca. Early 1800's*
12. **Bosworth Property** -- *early 1800's*
13. **Jonathan Arnold House** -- *ca 1820's*
14. **Lemuel Chenoweth House** -- *1856*
15. **Rowan House** · John Earle after 1838.
16. **Louisa Gilmore House** -- *ca 1890* (Demolished May, 1996)
17. **Masonic Lodge Hall** -- *ca 1907*
18. **Channel Store** -- *ca 1903*
19. **Adam Crawford House** -- *early 1800's*
20. **Beverly Market** -- *ca. 1900*
21. **I.O.O.F. Lodge Hall** -- *1914*
22. **Blackman - Bosworth Store** -- *1827-28*
23. **1813 Randolph County Jail** - *1813*
24. **Beverly Public Square** -- *1813*
25. **Rohrbaugh's Store** -- *ca 1915*
26. **Beverly Bank** -- *1900*
27. **Randolph County Court House** --*1808-1815*
28. **Hill Building** -- *ca 1907*
29. **Bushrod Crawford House** -- *ca. 1850*
30. **Scott House** -- *ca 1893*
31. **1841 Randolph County Jail** -- *1841*
32. **Blackman - Strader House** -- *1861-66*

32a. **Staggers House** -- *1921*

33. **David Goff House** -- *1835*
34. **Eli Baker House** -- *1873*
35. **Birkett House** -- *1867*
36. **Baker House** -- *ca. 1900*
37. **Logan House** -- *1810?*
38. **Edward Hart / George Yokum House** -- *ca 1855*
39. **Humbolt Yokum House** -- *ca 1890*
40. **Henry Suiter House** -- *pre-1850*
41. **Cunningham House** -- *ca 1894*
42. **Eli Butcher House** -- *ca. 1778*
43. **Ward House** -- *1890-1895*
44. **Mt. Iser Cemetery** -- *ca. 1860's*

Figure 9b: Map key of downtown Beverly, and count of slaves, as of 1854, part 2.

Slaves Owned in Beverly in 1852 (excluding children)

Samuel Crane	1	George Buckey	1
Bushrod Crawford.	1	John B. Earle	1 (Margaret Booker)
John Crawford	2	Lucinda Leonard	1
Adam Crawford	1	Jonathan Arnold	3
David Goff	2	David Blackman	6
Rev. Enoch Thomas	1	Dr. Squire Bosworth	1

"So, what's the most important thing I've wanted you to understand from today's stories?"

"We shoulda been born a free white person?" Young Ira spoke a painful truth all right, and I burst out laughing, uncontrollably, pitifully, so hard that tears dropped down my cheeks and I had to wipe them away.

"No, darlin'. Since we weren't born white and free, we had to keep our eyes and ears open. At home, we heard the owner's children practicing their spelling and numbers. We picked up some learnin' from them. Standing still as bored statues, we actually paid attention to what our owners said at the dinner table, hearing about the news of the day. Understand that we've never been the dumb-as-stone idiots that white folks always made us out to be. It is painfully true that it was against the law to teach us to read and write, because that would give us too much power. But we understood that staying quiet about what we knew sho' nuff kept us alive and informed. That's how I survived thirty years a slave."

The Slave Auction

The full moon cast a warm glow on the grass and clover turf in front of my house. Most of my children, grandchildren, and several neighbors were waiting patiently on our long slatted porch for me to begin tonight's history lesson. The stars were as bright as the faces of my children in the vast of night. Us old codgers sat on flattened cushions in wooden chairs, fanning ourselves to create a breeze in the still, humid evening.

"Once upon a time in Ol' Virginny…"
Probably the thing that put the most fear into a slave's heart was the thought of being sold away from our families. Some owners threatened us with the possibility of the "auction block" if we didn't work hard enough or do what they asked when they asked. Women were especially at the master's mercy. My high yellow[24] mulatto children were a living testament to that.

"What's an auction block?" I had asked my son, George, to ask so I could ease into the subject for the younger children.

An auction block is usually a movable wooden platform or a large flat-topped stone set in the town's marketplace or town hall. There's a confident, quick-talking fellow with a loud voice called an auctioneer. Crowds of people surround the block once the slave auction begins.

The auctioneer shouts, "How much am I offered for this good servant wench? It's true she's a little old, but there's lots of work left in her. How much am I offered? Speak quick, for she's going to sell. How much am I offered?"

A well-dressed man walked up to the platform. In a rough manner he caught the lips of the woman and pulling them apart, took a thorough look at her teeth and mouth. He ran his finger into her mouth to feel her "back grinders." He ripped open her blouse to look at her private areas. The slave's eyes opened wide and her cheeks turned red at this indignity, but soon her face gave way to the sad look of resignation.

Another man took hold of her arms and punched her in the side and back to see how solid she was, then he looked at her hands. If they seemed soft and tender, it signaled she probably worked as a house servant and would not be a good field worker.

"Can you imagine anyone treating you like that?" I looked into the horrified eyes of each person listening to my story.

"No, ma'am. I woulda run clean off that platform," one of my grandsons replied.

"With all the buyers standing there, someone woulda catched you right away and whupped you good in front of everybody. For sure, somebody like you would be deemed a troublemaker. You would be sold to a master who would work you the hardest and treat you the worst," I replied, shaking my head.

The auctioneer cried, "I am offered fifty dollars. Going and going at fifty dollars, who'll give more?"

"Seventy-five," came from another bidder, whose voice had a strong Southern twang.

"I'm out," said the first bidder as the auctioneer turned toward the second bidder, asking for a higher bid.

"And going, going, gone at seventy-five dollars!" the auctioneer rapped his gavel on the wooden speaker box.

The winning bidder was a thin man with a large black mustache. He walked up to the sheriff, handed him the money and said, "Give me a bill of sale for this wench." This was promptly done, as bills of sale were prepared in advance, leaving nothing to fill in except the purchase price, name of the purchaser, date of sale, and usually the name of the slave purchased. The children were riveted to this story, leaning forward, attentive, quiet, transfixed on the words coming out of my mouth.

"Now, children, a strong male slave in the prime of his life could be sold for as high as $1,500."

All eyes widened. "Wow! That's a whole lotta money!" one child exclaimed.

"You better believe it! That's more money than I could make in ten years. Now don't you feel lucky to be living here, in this time and place?" I finished. Heads nodded, but everyone was quiet, I imagine thinking about what it was like for so many of our people in America, the "Home of the Brave and Land of the Free."

"Were you ever on the auction block?" Edward asked.

"Thankfully no, not me, but one of my friends saw a slave auction in Wheeling, Virginia, and she described the horror to me. A milk chocolate woman, maybe forty, was standing on the platform, her head held low, tears streaming from her eyes. She had a full face and grayish hair peeking out from the front of her checkered bandana. Her whimpering was heart-breaking, for those who had a heart, that is. Two young coffee-colored boys were standing next to her on the platform, likely her children who probably would be sold off to different masters. That was the most awful, frightful, scary part of a slave auction: splitting up families."

"Why did they sell those poor people, Grandma?"

"I don't know. Maybe the owner needed to pay his debts or needed workers for his fields or to work in his house."

"What did they do with them, Grandma, after they bought them?"

"They'd probably be taken to the Deep South in Alabama or Mississippi and worked like beasts, just as farmers work their horses and mules."

"Will their owners beat them like farmers strike their oxen?"

"Some may be beaten. Some may be hired out to work for other people. But the worst thing is that they'll most likely be sold away from their families, never to be heard from again."

I wanted to change the negative energy of that important story. I told them I was actually lucky in a way. Even though I didn't live with my parents and was sold by Massa John White Stalnaker to Miz Betty Earle, I didn't have to stand on a box with a bunch of strangers touching my body and bidding for me like a sack of potatoes. I lived in safety the thirty years I was a slave, even though my life was not my own. I had five babies in a home that usually was peaceful and more pleasant than some others experienced. I lived in a small town that had very few slaves.

They generally called us "servants" instead of slaves, almost elevating our lot in life. Still, many of us longed to be in charge of ourselves. Tomorrow's story will reveal how one of my closest relatives took the life of his family into his own hands.

Herbert whined as usual. "Not again. Can't you just tell it to us right now, Grandma? You're such an excellent storyteller and I hate waiting to hear more."

My widest smile betrayed my inner joy. My descendants love hearing about their ancestors as much as I love telling their tales. A friend of mine once said, "Speak their names and they will live again.[25]" That's what I intend to do, as long as this old body will let me.

Chapter 7 - Ned's Incredible Adventure

"Once upon a time in Ol' Virginny, and many other places in the United States of America…"

The following sad tale happened to many a free person of color after the Fugitive Slave Act of 1850 was passed by Congress. It was part of the Compromise of 1850 which would allow California to enter the union as the 16th free state, but there would be no restrictions on slavery for Utah and New Mexico, among other concessions.[26] The Fugitive Slave Act required that runaways be returned to their owners, even if they were in a free state. It also made the federal government responsible for finding, returning, and trying escaped slaves.

One famous case concerned Solomon Northup, a freeborn black musician who was kidnapped in Washington, D.C. He would spend twelve years enslaved in Louisiana before winning back his freedom in 1853.[27]

My Pappy, Edward "Ned" Backus, had an unbelievable adventure, stranger than what the most creative storyteller could ever make up. For you see, my Pappy was an old slave of a farmer named Abraham Crouch. They lived a few miles north of Beverly. Born about 1791, he may have originally been the slave of Abraham's father, Major John Crouch, who was the first white child born in Randolph County, in 1773. But who knows how many times Pappy mighta been sold to different masters? I heard tell that Massa John's Great-Uncle Elias had a slave named Ned in Frederick County, Virginia, but I don't know if that's where my daddy was actually born.

Who knows whether Pappy was allowed to marry the person he loved or whether his masters forced him to breed with someone's slave to have children? All I know is that I was born in 1834 in the home of Massa John White Stalnaker and his momma, Margaret Elizabeth White Stalnaker Kittle; most people called her Miz Margaret Elizabeth cuz her name was so long.

Anyway, Pappy married a woman named Eve after I was born. They had two daughters and a son. Abraham's Will was supposed to free Pappy and his family in March 1854 after the master died. However, Massa Crouch's sons would not free Eve or the children. The sons knew Eve's pretty girls could breed them some fine babies if'n they was kept under the Crouch's control. It didn't matter what the Will said. When you're the boss and the law, you kin do whatever you want.

Pappy was fit to be tied. He didn't know what to do to, but he was bound and determined to get his family back, by pleading, paying for their freedom, or by hook or by crook, whatever it took.

You see, Pappy "Ned" was a Negro in good standing because of his skills as a blacksmith. He had helped many a neighbor with their smithy needs from decades of being rented out to his master's neighbors. Ned demonstrated his expertise by forging plows, hoes, pots, chains, locks, and other tools needed for the operation of a plantation farm. He sometimes even made fancy designs out of metal for fences. Some owners gave their enslaved blacksmiths a share of the profits earned from work performed, allowing the talented slave to save up a bit of money. Those savings could be used to buy his enslaved family.[28]

Pappy started talking with customers he knew was anti-slavery, explaining his situation, asking for their help. One customer got him an attorney who submitted numerous petitions through the Randolph County court asking for Ned's family to be released. Those pleas were always "continued" to the next day, then the day after that, then to the next term. The jury never decided one way or the other. After a year of barking up every tree trying to find a solution, Pappy was desperate.

Now I'm gunna tell you the most amazing story I know, just the way my Pappy told it to me. Are you ready to hear the impossible? I had everybody's attention.

I pretended to go into a trance, my head circling around my neck, eyes closed, moaning softly, hands limp in my lap. Then my head sprang up, my eyes focused on the crowd, and my voice lowered considerably as I began to speak.

Ned Takes a Stand

"Now here's what I think you need to do, Ned. You need to travel to the town of Ravenna, located in Portage County, Ohio. Go to the Methodist Church there and seek out the Reverend J.R. Locke. He knows an attorney named Ezra Barnard Tyler who might be able to weed through this legal mess you've got here in Randolph County. I've done all I can do for you. Take your Freedom Paper with you and all the money you've saved to buy your family from the Crouches. I'll be happy to write a letter on your behalf explaining that Crouch's sons won't let your wife and children join your free status. I think Mr. Tyler will know just what to do. He's a lawyer and a judge. If you agree with my suggestion, I'll send this letter right away to Reverend Locke to get the ball rolling. I'll write a Letter of Introduction that you can take with you on the trip in case you get questioned along the way."

Extremely interested in what my lawyer had to say, I responded, "Who is this Mr. Tyler that you speak so highly of?"

"Ned, how much do you know about politics?"

"Well, I do keep my ears open when I'm working with folks at the smithy and going to the general store and such. Of course, I know there's a big divide in the country about slavery. The South wants to keep my people in bondage, but the North does not."

"Yes, and the North does not want that heinous practice to keep spreading like wildfire into new states. There's a movement coming, Ned, my friend, that will change everything about our country. It will eventually be for the better, but it will take time, energy, persuasion, and luck to make it happen. Mr. Tyler is one of the movers and shakers in this new way of thinking. He's a part of what's called The Fusion Party."[29]

"Never heard of them. What do they stand for?" I asked.

"Anti-slavery parties have been forming in many Northern states in opposition to the Kansas-Nebraska Act of 1854.[30] Our Northern Democrat President, Franklin Pierce, signed the Act into law because he believes abolitionists are a danger to the country. That law created the states of Kansas and Nebraska and will open up more lands in the West for an eventual transcontinental railroad extending from one end of the United States to the other. It would also allow the popular vote, not Congress, to determine whether a new state could have slaves or not. This has made anti-slavery groups angrier than a hornet's nest.

"Many of the Northern political parties adopted the name 'Republican' Party. However, the Ohio convention adopted the name 'Fusion Party,' which they felt more accurately described the fusion, or melding, of persons from a variety of political backgrounds, including members of the Republican Party, Free Soil Party, the Whig Party, and the Know-Nothing Party.[31] The Fusion Party would also include the few members in the Southern Democratic Party who are opposed to slavery.

"Ned, my friend, I think you are the perfect person to plead your case at the upcoming Fusion Convention in Ravenna, Ohio, this July 4th. You'll get plenty of supporters, I'm sure, and maybe Mr. Tyler, or someone else, will put up the money to free your family once and for all."

I had to sit down. It was almost too much to think about. I was delighted there might be a good chance someone would help me. At the same time, I was uncomfortable at the thought of leaving my family here, not knowing whether they might be sold out of state while I was gone to plead my case in Ohio. Most of all, though, I was terrified at traveling to an unfamiliar place.

I replied, "This is a lot to take in, but know this, I will do whatever it takes to get my family back. But I've never been outside of Randolph County for I've been a slave for over fifty years. That means I was never allowed to do much on my own that wasn't related to blacksmithing. I have no idea where Ravenna is, how to

84

get there, how to find Reverend Locke or Mr. Tyler, where to stay, where to eat, nothing."

My attorney said, "I know it won't be easy for you, but here's what I'll do. Let me see if I can find a Quaker[32] who has a small private carriage and will take you to Ravenna. It will probably be a three- or four-day trip just to get there. Maybe we can find some colored families you can overnight with along the route. Let me check around and get back to you soon."

I gushed, "Thank you so much for the uplift. You have given me hope. I'll be working over at Henry Sutter's this week. Looking forward to hearing from you soon. Again, many thanks." I reached out my hand and we shook, man to man.

"Oh, uh, and Ned, it's best not to tell anyone about your possible plans until the day you leave. We don't want to sabotage anything, do we?"

"No, sir," I confirmed.

The days passed way too slowly. I went through the motions, trying to work in the smithy like normal, but my mind was racing. I couldn't tell anybody about my exciting news, not Mr. Sutter, not the church, not even my wife. I couldn't imagine what kind of plan could successfully get me to Ohio, but I kept the faith that everything would all work out in my favor.

The Road to Ravenna

BAM! My eyes opened wide as I shook myself awake. Did someone just shoot at me? Or was it a crack of thunder? I felt a rumbling underneath my feet. Where am I? Slowly the fog lifted and I remembered. I was in a private carriage which was carrying me north on the Beverly-Fairmont Turnpike, the graveled roadway recently completed in 1852.[33] The driver suggested I leave the curtains closed to reduce the chance that slave-catching patrollers would stop us and cause trouble along the road to Ravenna.

What an amazing dream I had been having! I was wearing my best church suit, navy blue, black tie, white shirt, respectable shiny black shoes. Folded into a small brown suitcase on the floor next to my feet was a change of shirts, socks, and undergarments. I brought all the money I had saved over the past year—$180 in gold and silver coins—and my precious Freedom Paper.

I began the biggest adventure of my life the twenty-eighth morning of June in 1855. The rhythm of the road soon lulled me into a deep sleep. My overworked brain dreamed about the upcoming Fusion Convention: me flying onto the stage on the back of a black-and-white-striped horse.

Me with bulging muscles on my nine-foot-tall brown body. Me standing in front of a crowd of hundreds. Me with educated words booming out of my mouth. The crowd cheered and threw money onto the stage. Soon I was standing in a pool of gold coins. I not only had enough money to buy my family's freedom, but also enough to purchase a stone castle sitting next to a wide river, full of sparkling fish that jumped right onto my plate, fully cooked. I had shiny black horses that my fancy-dressed children could ride after their private school lessons. I had many servants who cooked and cleaned the castle, leaving my beautiful wife, Eve, to do as she pleased every day. My large, successful farm was worked by white employees who took orders from me…

Far too suddenly, though, my perfect dream vanished in a blur when one of the carriage wheels drove over a large rock, bumping me awake to my stark reality.

The Letter of Introduction from my attorney, which I carried in my breast pocket, had been most helpful on the trip. People who might normally cause trouble for a black man traveling on his own in a carriage in Virginia, turned gracious when they read the letter. I had the added security of riding with the same Quaker carriage driver the whole trip to Ravenna. He would also drive me back home again. Mr. Roberts—he told me to call him "Friend"—was a happy round-faced fellow with sunburned cheeks. He promised to deposit me every night at a safe house and pick me up the next morning to continue our trip to the Fusion Convention about 150 miles away.

The frumpy driver had been instructed to take me that first night to the Marshes' house. They were a free black family in Fairmont, a city along the Monongahela River, which was the last major hub on the Beverly-Fairmont Turnpike. We arrived at dusk, secretly, so fewer people might see my brown-skinned personage exit the carriage.

Thomas and Mary Marsh graciously provided me with a room, dinner, and most importantly, information. We stayed up nearly all night long. They recommended the safest Ohio communities for freed people of color, as well as contacts who might aid my family in the future. They described the Underground Railroad and where the stations were in Martin's Ferry, Barnesville, Flushing, Mount Pleasant, and Massillon in Starks County... just in case something backfired with my plan and I became separated from my driver. They urged me to be extremely careful at all times, reminding me that patrollers could easily pick up free people of color and drag them back into the depths of bondage. Most of all, they gushed about how wonderful it was to be responsible for their own lives, instead of being forced to do another's bidding. My head was about to burst with the delicious possibilities for our future happiness, once my family joined me in the Promised Land of Ohio.

After only a couple hours of sleep, I washed the dust of the road and cobwebs from my head in a basin of water Thomas had provided in the guest room. I dressed; ate a quick but hearty breakfast of hotcakes, toast, bacon, and eggs; shook hands with my new friends; then exited the house. Mr. Roberts was waiting for me, having already secured fresh horses for today's grueling drive to carry us northwest, alongside the B&O Railroad line. If all went well, we would spend the night in a free land—the town of Martin's Ferry, at the far side of the mighty Ohio River.

Yesterday, I dutifully kept the curtains closed as instructed, but my dreams last night were so uplifting that I took a chance and lifted the curtain just enough to peek outside.

The sun's rays momentarily blinded my vision, but after my eyes adjusted to the brightness, I gasped at the terrain passing by. I'm used to the green rolling hills and forests in Randolph County, but before me were farms with rows and rows of corn fields or wheat fields or tobacco fields or cotton fields, all with my brethren working the soil. This was still the South, after all. We road past lovely green canopies of apple and peach orchards dotted with red and orange fruits. Familiar pasture lands for grazing cattle extended far into view, bordered with tall trees in the distance. We passed grand plantation homes, shacks for blacks, and everything in between. Trains tooted by, as the turnpike was parallel to the train tracks for much of this segment of our route. We took breaks every couple of hours to relieve ourselves and water the horses.

Farmington, Mannington, Littleton, Cameron, Sherrard, all towns came into view, then retreated just as quickly, until we reached Wheeling, the easternmost town in Virginia along this turnpike. That important town at the Ohio River state border became a major regional hub for hiring or selling slaves to the salt industry, and to markets in the lower South. Weekly slave auctions were held there, usually at the county courthouse.[34]

My driver made sure we crossed the wide Ohio River before nightfall. A ferry boat took our carriage and fresh horses across the brisk current, since the bridge that had been built in 1847 was destroyed in a storm the year before my journey.

Martin's Ferry was the oldest city in Ohio, settled in 1785.[35] I felt so much better once we crossed the river, not just because swimming was not my strength, but also because we had crossed into the free State of Ohio where so many slaves yearned to be. I actually felt myself breathing easier because the air smelled sweeter there, being home to one of the most important Underground Railroad stops in the country.

"I'll pick you up at eight a.m. with fresh horses," Mr. Roberts said as he dropped me off with the Crater family at the edge of town. I waved goodbye, not really thinking about where he would sleep.

Isaac and Jamila Crater told me the most extraordinary stories about the runaway slaves they helped escape from Maryland and Virginia. I enjoyed Jamila's home-cooked meal of black-eyed peas, rice, and fall-off-the-bone ham hocks. I shared details of my situation with them, and they responded with advice about jobs, housing, churches, and organizations for free people of color. Once again pumped full of information, I slept a few precious hours before readying myself for another day.

Jamila had thoughtfully prepared a lunchbox of tasty fried chicken, biscuits so buttery and flakey they rivaled my mama's. The huge slice of gingerbread made the carriage smell sweet the entire day.

Northward to Cadiz, we traveled through Carrollton, Minerva, then Hometown, stopping at Mount Union in Starks County, Ohio. Mr. Roberts indicated we would be spending the night there, because the horse couldn't comfortably travel the entire ninety mile distance from Martin's Ferry to Ravenna in one day.[36]

Our last stop was at the Williamson's house. My driver said he would be knocking on the door at eight a.m.

After a sincere welcome full of hugs, Charles and Margie asked how my trip had been. Like the last family, I told them my sob story. They toasted to my success, supplying me with a marvelous meal of fried catfish, okra, and corn bread, with a generous helping of sweet potato pie for dessert. They tried to persuade me to bring my family to live in Mount Union.

"Our small community of colored folk is growing. Most of us belong to the Methodist Episcopal Church, but we're talking about starting our own African Methodist Episcopal church."

"Why?" I asked.

"Because some of the white members don't feel Negroes should play an equal role in church functions," Charles scowled.

"Wait!" I blurted out. "Do you know of a Methodist Reverend named Mr. Locke?" I asked, daring to have the good fortune that my new friends knew of the fellow who agreed to help me.

"Of course. He's from the First Methodist Episcopal Church in Ravenna. He sometimes preaches here."

Stay calm, old boy. "My attorney said Reverend Locke may be the key to my finding an attorney named Ezra Barnard Tyler, who may have enough power to help release my family."

"Sounds like you've got an angel watching out for you. Well, we all bes' get to sleep now. You got a busy day ahead of you."

Relieved, I retired to the small room they gave me in back of their comfortable home. It was perfect for a one-night traveler: wash basin and towel in one corner, white enamel chamber pot under the single-sized bed, colorful quilt Margie probably made from scraps, and a chair on which to hang my day clothes. I slept quite soundly and awoke refreshed. I dressed quickly, then enjoyed a filling breakfast of flapjacks, bacon, and eggs.

At the appointed pickup time, Mr. Roberts was waiting outside to take me the last twenty miles to my destination: Ravenna, in Portage County. Our first stop was at the church. My stomach was churning, as we rapped on the carved wooden door, hoping Reverend Locke was there on a Monday. We were in luck, but he was not what I expected. He was short, balding, youngish, maybe in his thirties, sturdy of frame, with a rather high voice for a minister, I thought. Looks don't mean a thing, though. It's what's inside that counts.

I was happily surprised to learn the reverend had been in contact with my attorney and with Mr. Tyler—many times—in fact. I wonder why nobody let me know that. Maybe they didn't want me to be disappointed if their plans didn't work out? Reverend Locke was prepared to take us to Mr. Tyler's home, not four blocks away. Could I stand the excitement? Would I present myself well to these men who seemed willing to help a black man they didn't even know?

"It's good to finally meet you," Mr. Tyler said, shaking my hand with vigor. He asked about my trip, then we sat down in his luxurious front room, full of fine mahogany furniture, stately paintings of landscapes and his family, I imagined. There was a large crystal chandelier over the sofa where we sat. I showed him my Freedom Paper and was prepared to give him the $180 in coin I had saved to buy my family's freedom.

"Not so fast," my potential savior said, shooing my money away. "Let's sit down and talk about our options first." Again, you can't judge a book by its cover. Lanky and fresh-faced, Mr. Tyler said he was born on a farm in Portage County but went to the big City of Cleveland to become a lawyer. He came back home to serve his community as a prosecuting attorney and had plans to become a judge. He enjoyed helping people like me who'd been harmed by unscrupulous people. I thanked my lucky stars he chose to use his lawyer skills on me.

Mr. Tyler carefully revealed his "game plan," as he called it. "You will ride with me to the July 4th convention here in Ravenna. Right before lunch, we'll go up to the stage, I'll introduce you, then you'll give a two-minute speech about your problem and what you want them to do for you. Simple. Then you'll sit with me in the lunch hall afterward, in case people want to talk with, and give you money personally. Your driver will pick you up at three p.m. and take you to the Andersons' house. Later that night, I will stop by and tell you how much money was collected. We will make a final plan on how to force the Crouches to free your family. We must ensure they join you here in Ohio, safe and sound, so you may make a free life together."

Not wanting to doubt him, I mustered my enthusiasm and said, "You make it sound so simple. It encourages me to think positive thoughts that your plan will work." A breath of pure relief escaped my lips. The plan was so far-fetched... but it was an idea Mr. Tyler had carefully thought about.

The night before my speech, I practiced and practiced what I was going to say in the Andersons' safe house, even asking my hosts, Matthew and Lavata, for their opinions.

The next morning, I felt ready when a two-person, open-air gig carriage[37] picked me up and drove me to the brick building that housed the Fusion Convention. There were hundreds of people walking about, all white except for the servants who were passing out drinks and sandwiches. I was escorted to sit next to Mr. Tyler in the front row with the other speakers. Soon enough, it was our turn to walk up the stairs onto the stage. But this is where the plan changed. Mr. Tyler not only introduced me but actually told my story for me, then turned to me and asked, "Is that about right, Ned?"

All I had time to do was smile and say, "Yes, it is. I'd appreciate any help you could give me and my family." Done. We both walked off the stage and Mr. Tyler clapped me on the back exclaiming, "You were great, Ned!"

During the lunch break, only two people came to our table. They donated a total of 82 1/2 cents to my cause—nowhere near the pile of gold coins I had dreamed about days before. I wasn't sure what to make of it all. Was my performance that bad, or my story that uninteresting, or was it something else entirely? Was I supposed to be a clown for them, something to laugh at?

A young, fast-talking newspaper reporter from the Portage Sentinel interrupted my thoughts. Pencil in right hand, pad of paper in the left, he smirked, "So, how much financial help did you get, Mr. Edward 'Ned' Backus?"

"Eighty-two-and-half cents," I replied, trying hard to keep myself from knocking that smirk off his pock-marked face.

"And how long did it take for you to get to this convention from… Virginia, wasn't it?" he scoffed.

"Altogether, about five days," I forced my voice to sound cheery.

"Hmm, doesn't sound like the trip was worth it to me," the smart-aleck reporter replied.

Realizing that he was going to print my response for the world to read, I muscled myself to say, "Absolutely! I met so many great people, got to see a part of the world I'd never be able to experience as a slave, got to attend an important convention and speak before hundreds of people, and I got to get my story in your newspaper," I put on the biggest fake smile I could muster. "I'd say it was worth it. What about you?" I dared to stare at that white man in the eye until he blinked.

"That's the spirit, Ned," Mr. Tyler whispered, as the reporter left in a huff. "I think he wanted you to shout or break down in tears, or something. You've got real character, Ned. Impressive." I felt Mr. Tyler watching me, measuring me. "Well, we'll see if anyone else offers to help. I'll stop by tonight at the Andersons' to talk about your options, OK?"

Trying not to explode from anger, I merely nodded. Shaking Mr. Tyler's hand, I managed to say, "Thanks for all you've attempted to do for me, Sir." Frustrated, fuming, and furious, I made my way to the appointed pickup spot, where the arranged carriage was waiting. Heavy sigh. I won't know our fate for hours…

All afternoon, I enjoyed talking with my hosts, learning about their lives and family, job opportunities, Negro organizations, churches, and what kind of people lived nearby. The same topics all my hosts spoke about. I was formulating a plan in my head about what I wanted to do with the rest of my life. I knew I could never live in Virginia again. Everyone with sense could smell trouble brewing in this country. I wanted to be as far away from Southern states as possible… with all of my family, including my eldest daughter Margaret.

The nighttime deadline for Mr. Tyler's appearance came and went. He didn't show. I had been wondering as the day went on whether he had used me in some way, to get himself on that stage perhaps. After all, he did most of the talking, not me. I began to pity myself for being so stupid as to think white strangers were going to help a former slave. They're probably all having a big laugh at my expense. Joy left. Anger and hurt consumed me.

In the middle of my souring attitude, the doorbell rang. My heart skipped a beat, hoping it was Mr. Tyler, just an hour late. No, it was a messenger delivering a letter for me.

"I can read plain writing," I informed my hosts, "but I'd sure appreciate if you'd read this fancy letter to me."

"Oh, of course." Ahem. Matthew cleared his throat.

"My apologies, Ned, for not meeting with you this evening as planned. An emergency came up at the convention that I had to take care of. The lackluster results of our request were disappointing. There's no other way to put it. We got 82 1/2 cents from the entire Fusion Party. I'm embarrassed, ashamed, and quite frankly, angry by the lack of financial response from a group that claims to hate slavery.

But worry not, Ned. I've decided to take it upon myself to work with Reverend Locke—with whom I have already exchanged many letters—to take care of your issue myself. I know your local attorney had been several times unsuccessful to petition the Randolph County jury to grant freedom to your family. With my expert help, though, I expect us to win the case this time. Soon. Your family is in good hands. Trust me.

Ned, I'm very impressed with you so I'm going to offer you an option for your consideration. I can get you a position as a blacksmith's assistant near my home. If you agree, give yourself no more trouble about your children. I will personally be responsible for bringing them and your wife to you here in Ravenna, should you choose to accept my offer. I'll visit tomorrow morning after a good night's sleep to hear your decision. Yours,

Ezra Barnard Tyler, Esq.

"Did somebody hit me in the head with a rock, or am I just dreaming right now?" I asked my astounded hosts. None of us could believe my good fortune. "Would you mind reading me the letter again?" After a second reading, it was clear. Hope restored, we all danced around the front room, jabbering at once. And yes, I shed tears of joy.

The rest of the story was a whirlwind of activity. The same fresh newspaper man came to interview me at Mr. Tyler's home a few weeks after we returned from the convention. On August 18, 1855, he filed a news article entitled:

"Abolition Philanthropy—Edward Backus."[38] They said, "A Virginia slave, who wished to redeem himself and family, made application to the grand Nebraska Fusion Convention which assembled in Ravenna, Portage County, Ohio, on the 4th of July, for aid…Subsequently, a man named Tyler made himself individually responsible for the amount asked, and the slave has gone on his way rejoicing." ·

Mr. Tyler said the lengthy, complete story was plastered in numerous newspapers east of the Mississippi River.

A New Life

I'm happy to say that Mr. Tyler was able to add another "win" to his list of successful cases.

I wrote him a letter wanting to place my hard-earned money in his hands, but he refused, and suggested I put it in a bank. In fact, he accompanied me to the bank in Ravenna to deposit the gold and silver coins I'd been carrying around since I left Randolph County. Mr. Esbert, the bank cashier, even gave me a premium of one percent on the money I deposited. I never knew such things could happen, especially not to a black man who had been a slave for over fifty years.

All the details about what Mr. Tyler and Reverend Locke did for my family drifted above my head like birds in flight: a certificate of deposit in Mr. Locke's name stated the money was to pay a bond for the freedom of my wife to the tune of $221, and $206 for the children, even $50 for my outstanding debts.

My children, who were living with a different Crouch family member than my wife, would be sent through Wheeling by Mr. Locke's agents to freedom. They would carry letters explaining their situation and where they were to be sent along the line until they reached me in Ravenna.[39] Other arrangements were made for my wife's safe passage.

A miracle on Earth was granted to my family. My wife and our children joined me in Ravenna and as promised, Mr. Tyler secured work for me at a smithy in Mount Union, where we lived for a few years.

My only sadness was not being able to free my daughter, Margaret, who by then was the slave of John B. Earle in Beverly. She was always in my thoughts and prayers though. Once I learned more about the best communities for Negroes, I set my sights on Barnesville, Ohio, where I moved my family in 1861. Yes, I got a nice little place in a mostly white neighborhood on Vine Street, which had the Southern Cemetery in its backyard...

"You mean this house, Grandma? This is where your Pappy and Mama lived with your sisters and brother?" Grandson Hastings asked.

I replied, "Well, not exactly. Eve was not my mother, and I didn't live here growing up, but the rest was true. You can look at newspapers dated July and August 1855. It's all there, every detail. Well, not about how Pappy got from Randolph County to Ravenna."

"So, who was your mother? Did she die when you were born? Was she sold to someone else? Why won't you tell us?" Herbert demanded.

I responded calmly, "I wanted to wait for the right time. I wanted you to really understand the answer to Clara's 'What's a slave?' question she asked me some time ago. I wanted you to know how my life started and how I was fortunate to end up here in this house."

"Not again!" Herbert fumed, strutting around like a mad rooster. "I know what you're about to say. Always got to wait. Darn! I'll be so glad to be a grownup and do what I want!" [Note: See Chapter 18 for more about devil-may-care Herbert Booker].

"Tomorrow, honey. I promise. Now, that's enough of your nonsense, mister." I had enough of his latest tantrum. We ended the night with raisin cookies. Even Herbert smiled.

Loose Ends

"I heard Massa John talking about his ancestors one day. While researching the Earle family who came from England in 1649, he found an interesting document from his Great-grandfather, Samuel Noah Earle III. Written in 1770 in Frederick County, Virginia, it said:

"I give and bequeath unto my son Elias one negro man named Ned." Additionally, "...I desire at my death sons Joseph, Stricklin, Pres and Fase, take Ned."

I wondered whether that Ned was the father of my Pappy, Edward "Ned" Backus? Was my family linked to the Crouches and the Earles who lived in Frederick, VA, before Archibald Earle migrated to Beverly in 1810?

Was Edward's and Eve's son, Adam Backus, named for Adam Stalnaker? Was Adam a private who fought in the 99th Regiment of the US Colored Infantry in the US Colored Troops?

Was daughter Sophie Backus named for Sophia Stalnaker or another slaveowner's daughter?

Was daughter Angina Elizabeth named after Anzina Earle, who was likely one of Margaret's close playmates during her carefree days of youth?

I've left so many clues with these stories that it should be easy for you, my blessed descendants, to take it upon yourselves to find out more details about our family from West Virginia.

My audience looked at each other, shrugged their shoulders, and said in unison, "Who, me?"

Chapter 8 - Peg & the Ginger Cake

The heavenly smell of spiced gingerbread filled the kitchen and my clothes, so that wherever I walked, I carried my favorite aroma with me. Daughter Ella glanced outside and counted how many people were gathered for tonight's show. She then sliced enough pieces of gingerbread—plus a few extra for stragglers who might appear later—so everyone would have a piece before I began.

"Good evening, everybody. Tonight is a very special story, near and dear to my heart. I want you to not only hear my words, but also smell and taste and touch this story. Ella, pass out the star of the show, would ya?"

"Certainly, mother," as she started with the eldest in the crowd, giving them a napkin with a slice of fragrant gingerbread, until she finished with the youngest.

"Once upon a time in Ol' Virginny…"

There was a young slave girl who grew up not truly knowing who her mother was. For all she knew, the slaveowner, Margaret Elizabeth White Stalnaker Kittle (Miz Margaret Elizabeth) was her mama, for when the infant girl was hungry, it was Miz Margaret Elizabeth who fed her from a bottle. When the girl was a few months older, Miz Margaret Elizabeth and her daughters fed her solid food from a tiny spoon.

When the girl had her first birthday, it was Miz Margaret Elizabeth who baked her the sweetest little birthday cake and taught her to use a fork to feed herself.

When the girl was a toddler and fell down and skinned her knee, it was Miz Margaret Elizabeth who kissed her boo-boo, cleaned it, and put a bandage on it.

When the girl was three, it was Miz Margaret Elizabeth who taught her the difference between greens to eat and weeds to pluck. They spent an hour everyday tending to the kitchen garden, teaching the girl to love the feel of soil on her hands and rejoice in the wonder of nature in all its forms.

When the girl was four, it was Miz Margaret Elizabeth who taught her how to feed the chickens by flinging their seedy feed around their feet, so it didn't all land in a clump. The girl learned how to gently search under the hens' fluffy feathers to carefully retrieve the eggs they laid, putting them in a basket and carrying them inside the kitchen, unbroken, for the morning breakfast.

"When the girl was five and lost her first baby tooth, it was Miz Margaret Elizabeth who put a bit of cold rag on the sore spot.

When the girl was six, it was Miz Margaret Elizabeth who taught her to sit on a seat facing the side of the spinning wheel, to fit the big bobbin onto the flyer and screw it in place with a whorl, then insert the flyer into the Mother of Awl. She pressed her tiny feet alternatively on two foot pedals underneath which caused the big wheel to spin around and around. Holding lamb's wool in her right hand, the girl pulled thin strands of wool with her left onto the spinning bobbin. They could sit for hours in the calm of turning wool into twisted thread and yarn.

When the girl was seven, it was Miz Margaret Elizabeth who made sure she knew how to make flapjacks by whisking together flour, sugar, baking powder, salt, and nutmeg. In another bowl, they beat the eggs until they were foamy, then whisked in the milk. They stirred the wet and dry ingredients until they were just mixed, then poured about one-quarter cup of batter into a hot buttered skillet. After bubbles appeared on the top of each flapjack, Miz Margaret Elizabeth taught the girl to slide a spatula underneath and in one movement, lift the jack and flip it over so it landed back into the pan to cook on the other side. The girl got so she could lift and flip dozens of perfectly round pancakes for Sunday breakfast for the large families she served.

When the girl was eight, it was Miz Margaret Elizabeth who taught her how to wash clothes by separating them into piles by color, putting the white clothes first into the bucket of sudsy warm water, wringing them out, rinsing them in clean water, wringing them again, then standing on a step stool to affix the clean clothes on a clothesline to dry in the fresh air.

When the girl was nine, it was Miz Margaret Elizabeth who showed her how to iron clothes without burning them.

When the girl was ten, it was Miz Margaret Elizabeth who had her help cook all the meals.

When the girl was eleven, it was Miz Margaret Elizabeth who had her doing most of the cleaning around the house.

When the girl was twelve, it was Miz Margaret Elizabeth who died of old age, at ninety, leaving the girl to feel like she lost her very own mama. That was the same year the girl got her bleeding, indicating her body was now that of a woman able to have children.

There were two male teenagers working in the house. The fear they might create a baby with the girl-turned-woman made the new master nervous. In February 1846, the son of the deceased Miz Margaret Elizabeth sold the girl away from the only home she had ever known, for one dollar, to his beloved niece named Mrs. Elizabeth S. Earle.

Silence. Everyone was staring at me. The older kids had heard the story before, but the younger kids now understood why I never mentioned my mother in stories.

"I never really knew who my mother was until…" The words caught in my throat.

"Ella," I whispered, "would you mind refreshing my drink?" My daughter got up from her seat, momentarily putting her hand on my shoulder before she went inside the house. I was quiet the whole time she was away, eyes closed, gone inside myself reliving the pain of losing my best friend, the only mother I ever knew.

All of a sudden, I felt arms around my neck. Opening my eyes, Herbert was sobbing. "Oh, Grandma, please forgive me for being mad at you yesterday, pouting because you wouldn't answer my question about your mama. I didn't know…"

"That's all right, honey," I patted his back. "It is what it is. I've lived with this feeling of loss since I was twelve."

Ella returned with my glass full of sweet peach juice. I drank it all down, took a deep breath, then blew out the painful memory.

Years later, my master, John Bayles Earle, was really mad at me. Something terrible happened that day that I would never forget, and on that day he enjoyed telling me who my birth mother was.

He sneered, "You know that woman I send you to buy the ginger cake from, Big Peg? Well, she's your natural-born mother! HUH! Yep, she dumped you with the Stalnakers when you were a little baby!" Then Massa John laughed, turned around, and left me to my thoughts.

Big Peg is my mama? I couldn't believe it. All those years, I been seeing her around Beverly. She was really something, taller than most men, at least six feet and dark as her molasses ginger cake. She baked great squares of the spicy treat—the best in the town. She would put the pieces on a large flat board carried on her head, like the Old Africans. She also carried a jug of beer in one hand and a cup in the other. On public days she sallied forth, her ample hips gliding smoothly from side to side, to sell her spicy cakes at the market. She charged ten cents for each ginger cake and I don't know how much for the beer.[40] They say she made quite a bit of money.

Big Peg is my mama? Is that why she always gave me free pieces of ginger cake for myself when I saw her at the market? Is that why she always made a point of saying hello when I was near? Is that why so many times when I felt eyes on me and turned around, there she was, watching me? Is that why she sometimes gave me birthday presents of dolls or other knickknacks she made?

Big Peg was Miss Jane Crouch's servant. Miss Jane was the schoolteacher in Beverly. As far as I knew, only white kids was allowed to learn to read and write. Big Peg probably knew her letters and numbers because she was living with a teacher. As bold as people said she was, she probably demanded to be taught. If I had only known earlier she was my mama, I coulda asked her to teach me to read. Now that I'm thinking on it, there was one day at the market right before the war started when she pulled me aside and whispered, "You make sure that boy of yours, Joab, pays attention when he's with Mr. John's sister. I heard tell she likes to teach him things. Reading and writing are the most important things black folks can learn to do. You mind me now, d'you hear?"

I thought it was strange at the time that she knew about Miss Nannie liking to bring Joab into her room and teaching him to read and write and talk proper, in secret. In a small town, everybody knows everybody's business. Looking at my neighbors who were listening to the story, I asked, "Isn't that right?" and they chuckled.

"You better believe it, sister! It takes a village to raise a child."

I often regret I never took the opportunity to ask Big Peg why she left me to be raised by Miz Margaret Elizabeth. Events happened so quickly at that time in my life, though, that I never had a chance before we left Beverly for good. When we came here to Barnesville, I asked Pappy why he never told me who my true mother was.

"Well, Darlin' Girl"—that's what Pappy always called me, "I thought it would be more painful to tell you the truth. You see, your mama and me... Well, what I mean to say is that we, uh, we had a fun evening one night. You might remember that Big Peg always had a mug of beer with her on market days. Well, one night, I shared that mug and *other* things with her. It was a year or two after her Master-maybe-daddy, Richard Kittle, died. You know John White Stalnaker's mamayour Miz Margaret Elizabeth she was Richard Kittle's wife, right? Well, Big Peg was valued at $150 as part of his estate in about 1832. Peg was *given* to Miz Margaret Elizabeth. Your sister, Phebe, was *given* to his daughter, Jane Kittle." (Figure 10).

I cried to Pappy, "So there were two important things that I didn't know—who my mama was and that I had a blood sister? My life woulda been so much better knowing I had family. I hardly knew about you until you left in 1854. Oh, the helpless life of a slave."

Pappy took me in his arms and continued, "Well, months after Peg and me had that crazy night together, we found out you were on the way. Her owner was fit to be tied. She was pretty religious, you know, and she didn't cotton to her female slave having a baby without a husband. After you were past the nursing stage, I think she sold Peg to Jane Crouch, the schoolteacher. Your mama had no choice. She had to leave you. That's just how our life was. Family could be sold or rented out whenever the master wanted, for whatever the reason. You of all people should know that." I looked at my Joab, now called Joseph, who had been rented out away from us that time Massa was so mad at me.

Will book number 2, page 259-260, Randolph County Courthouse records Richard's will. It names wife Margaret; daughters: Jane Kittle, Ann Wilmoth and Mary Phillips; grandchildren: Nestor, Martin D., Clarissa (children of his son Isaac Kittle, he died in 1816), John, Richard and Ann Scott (children of his daughter Agnes [Kittle] Scott). Richard willed a Negro slave woman named Peg to his wife Margaret and a Negro slave girl named Phebe to his daughter Jane Kittle. Executors: Isaac White signed October 8, 1830, probated January 1831. Witnesses: Jacob Kittle and Elijah Kittle.

Figure 10: Herbert "Richard" Kittle's Will leaving Slave woman Peg to his wife and girl Phebe to his daughter.

Pappy said, "I know for sure Big Peg felt bad about the whole thing. I know for sure she was always watching out for you, in her unusual way. I know for sure that she loved you from afar. So, Darlin' Girl, don't you ever think she didn't want to be your mama."

Tears flooded my eyes and when I looked up, I noticed many in the audience were wiping their eyes too. "I tried to find out what happened to Big Peg after we settled down here in Barnesville, but by that time, Miss Jane Crouch had married a Union soldier and she and Peg disappeared from Beverly.[41] One of my old friends said she died of typhoid fever in 1880 at the age of seventy-nine, somewhere in Randolph County. I never got the chance to speak with her, daughter to mother. But I feel proud to carry the name Margaret. After all, 'Peg' is a nickname for 'Margaret,' don'cha know?"

What all this means is that we are blood-related to the slave-owning Earles, Stalnakers, Kittles, and Crouches, and lots of other Beverly families. They intermarried with each other all the time and didn't mind "sharing themselves" with their servants.

Chapter 9 - The Goddess Worshippers

It was frightfully warm and muggy that summer evening. The crowd gathered on sheets, waving paper fans to create a cooling breeze. I sat on my makeshift throne on the porch stoop, sipping some sweet tea, pinning my hair on top of my head, damp flowered house dress sticking to my legs. After a few deep breaths, I began one of my favorite stories, about the Goddess Worshippers.

"Once upon a time in Ol' Virginny…"

"Now I don't know if all of this story is true, but I choose to believe most of it is grounded in fact. I cain't even remember who told me this story, but it's mighty fascinating, I think. So, here's how it goes. There was a girl named Aggy[42] who got her training on how to be a good housemaid at Virginia Governor John White Page's Whitehall Plantation in Frederick County, Virginia. That area of Virginia is where some of the people living in Beverly originally came from.

Aggy's mama, Betty Ann, told her they came from a long line of African princesses who worshipped the Goddess.

"What's a Goddess, Grandma?"

"Near as I can tell, it's kind of like in church when you say your prayers to the Lord, or you study the ways of Jesus Christ. Instead, you would pray to a woman, called a Goddess."

You all know that our ancestors were brought from Africa to become slaves in America, right? (Heads nodded) Slave traders from Europe and America sailed their ships across the wide Atlantic Ocean to Africa. They brought stolen Africans away from their families long, long ago. Those slavers filled the bottom of their ships with Africans and left them to suffer in the dark stink no-air little-food cramped area below deck, for weeks, or months. Some died on the way, but the ones who made it to America were strong of body and faith in their Gods and Goddesses, African holy people who were different from what the white folks teach us to pray for here.

"I don't know what you're talking about, Grandma. There's only one God and that's Jesus Christ. That's what we learn in Sunday school. Everybody knows that." Herbert replied with a righteousness our pastor would be proud of.

Well, that is true for us here, but there are many different religions around the world, and I guess they believe different things. Just like all the different types of churches we have here in Barnesville—Catholics, Baptists, African Methodists, Jewish—they're all a little bit different from one another. Each one of them believes theirs is the only true religion. Anyway, I'm talking about this story that I was told when I was little. You make up your own mind whether it's true or not.

Aggy was told she came from a long line of African princesses: her mother Betty Ann, grandmother Libet, and great-grandmother Annyliz who was the first generation brought to Gloucester County, Virginia, straight off the boat from Africa. Annyliz was sold to the powerful Robert Carter family who were granted 50,000 acres of land on the Shenandoah River in 1730. They acquired hundreds of African slaves to work that land.[43]

The Governor's children were Aggy's playmates. She went to school and learned her letters and numbers with them. In the afternoons, Aggy helped her mother work in the big house, while the older white children stayed in class learning Latin and French or took dancing lessons. Aggy was her mother's housekeeping assistant, learning everything there was to know about keeping a mansion spotless. She also helped in the kitchen.

She and her mother even went to church with the owner's family at Stone Chapel near Cunningham's Tavern, climbing the stairs to the balcony to sit among the other servants. Aggy learned passages from the Bible by heart and when she was twelve. She was confirmed and allowed to take Holy Communion at the altar beside her mother.

But her mother had a secret. She learned that her African grandmother, Annyliz, possessed powerful, even magical abilities. Their family ruled kingdoms in Africa, and she would have become their Queen had she not been captured by slavers to become a servant in the Carter household."

"What's the secret, Grandma?" Ida Mae whispered.

Holding my hand to the side of my mouth like I was whispering, I revealed, "Annyliz worshipped the Goddess. Whenever she was in trouble, she would call on the Goddess from the full light of the moon. Once, on her annual midnight swim on Christmas Eve in the winter-cold York River, Annyliz got caught in the tide which pulled her farther and farther out to sea. The ship of a slaver was waiting to catch her! Annyliz called on the Goddess for help. All of a sudden, a great light in the black sky shone down onto the path of the riverbed where her friends waited to help her up and out, wrapping her in a warm blanket. She was saved by the Goddess.

In another story, Annyliz flew up and out of the water onto the back of a winged horse which carried her away to safety. Do you think these are true stories, children?"

"Yes, and I bet it was a pretty horse with pink hair," Clara voiced innocently.

Well, what was certain to Aggy was that the grandmother from Africa was a remarkable woman, capable of anything. It gave Aggy the belief that she too could do anything if she believed in the Goddess of the Moon. After all, she carried the Goddess sign on her backside, like her mother and her mother's mother.

"What sign is that?"

It was the African grandmother, Annyliz, who brought the sign with her when she travelled over the ocean. It was the mark of every first-born daughter in their family line. The sign of the Goddess is a half-moon shape carved into their left butt cheek, with three little dots above it. It was a sign representing the mother of all living, the Goddess of birth, love and death who shows herself in the phases of the moon. The mark signals that the woman bearing it is next in line to be Queen of the kingdom.

They also had a ritual, a ceremony, they performed. There were chants and prayers to the Goddess, like the verses and songs we learn in church every Sunday. In the evening, after supper, they made a small altar at the edge of the hearth in their cabin, pulling together a few of the stones kept there for that purpose. They put dishes of sweet oil and bits of food and herbs before the stone tower. A cup of elderberry wine sat beside the plates. They lit a wick of string that had been coated with grease and placed it in the dish so the sweet scent of smoky incense filled the room. Then they sat before the altar and began to chant special words. One of the prayers asked the Goddess for strength and protection, but they had many more that stood for: giving them the power to enhance life, to bring truth and harmony, to exercise good wisdom and counsel, to reign with principle and justice, to have an eternal soul that never dies, and to have her spirit reborn every time she is reincarnated.

"Ree-encar-what, Grandma?"

Kind of like when Jesus died on the cross and they put him in that cave and days later he was resurrected. It means you live a new life after you die, or something like that. I'm not sure I exactly understand it myself. I'm just telling you the story I heard.

One day, when Aggy was about fourteen years old, she was sent away to work for a few weeks at Colonel John Baylis Earle's Mount Zion plantation in Warren County, Virginia. You might remember I mentioned Mount Zion during the story about the Earle family who migrated from England (Chapter 2). Their large plantation was located about seven miles from the area called White Post where Aggy grew up.

Mount Zion was one of the few structures constructed entirely of stone. Inside were four bedrooms and two bathrooms and a grand center door. There was extraordinary woodwork and carving in the main parlor and dining room. The property also contained a stone meat house, summer kitchen, and part of a slave's quarters.[44] Guests at their many parties admired the great ceiling height and large scale.[45] And you know what all that means, right?

"They had a lot of slaves to do the work!" half of my audience shouted in unison. Of course, they were correct.

I nodded. At times there were from fifteen to fifty slaves working and some of those souls coulda been our family members.

You see, my Massa John was the nephew of Colonel John B. Earle. His grandfather, Samuel Earle III, had a slave named Ned in 1770.

"Like your Pappy, Edward 'Ned' Backus?" son George asked, eyebrows raised in shock.

Anything is possible until proven otherwise. Those Earles and Stalnakers and Crouches and Whites all spent time in Frederick and Warren and Clark County, Virginia, at some point. Who knows if my Pappy's father was also named Ned and was sold to the Crouches who moved to Randolph County?

The truth of this story was that Aggy had been sold away from her beloved family forever—to pay off some of her master's debts—not just for a few weeks like she was promised. Her story reminded me of mine when I was sold away from the Stalnaker family in 1846, losing touch with Hugh and George, my childhood friends who seemed like brothers. They also lived about seven miles away from where I grew up.

I had to wait a moment to compose myself. Every time I think about the generations of African people removed from their families forever, I get a hitch in my throat and my blood boils.

Fourteen-year-old Aggy was bought to eventually take the place of Maude, the ancient head housekeeper at Colonel John Earle's Mount Zion mansion.

"You mean I was named for the elder housekeeper?" My beautiful, cultured granddaughter, Maude Ellen, asked, surprised.

I looked at my son Joseph—Maude Ellen's father—waiting for him to answer.

He replied matter-of-factly, "Maude is not a common name. It is possible that name was deep in my subconscious having heard these stories before. Sara—bless her eternal soul—is no longer with us to remind me why we selected the name Maude."

I continued, "Well, the story goes that Aggy grew to be over six feet tall, which was very unusual for anyone, let alone a woman, back then. She came from a long line of extremely tall African women, warriors, leaders. Now children, what was the story I told you about last time?

"About Ginger Cake Peg?" Clara questioned.

"Yes, and what was special, so unusual, about Peg?" I asked.

"She was really tall," Clara replied.

"Exactly. So, do you think Aggy was Peg's blood cousin? And, if so, was she my and your blood cousin too?"

"YES!" the children screamed, delighted that they might be part of this fantastical story.

"Does that mean you have the magic in you too, like Aggy and the African princesses? The magic to protect yourself from bad people? The ability to make good decisions and be kind to Mother Earth and to each other?"

"YES!" they answered confidently. Lesson learned.

Chapter 10 - 1863: The Pivotal Year

Most people can identify one year in particular which changed their life forever, whether it is their wedding day, the birth of their first child, or the death of a loved one. My pivotal year was 1863.

❦

It began on January 1st with President Abraham Lincoln freeing all the slaves in Confederate states—may God eternally bless his soul. Of course, we weren't told about that decision and were kept working just like always. If we didn't hear white folks talking about events outside our little world, we didn't know a thing. Most of us couldn't read newspapers, after all. Thankfully, we overheard Yankee soldiers walking around Beverly who spoke about this remarkable news.

After learning we was supposed to be free, all bets were off. It was harder to pretend to be ignorant and play our lowly slave roles without questioning our owners. They soon started calling us "uppity" and saying we "needed to remember our place." But we now knew that at least on paper we was FREE and that put an inner smile on our lips and a little gitty-up in our step.

❦

In February 1863, ol' Massa John White Stalnaker—the son of the only mama I knew, the one who sold me to the Earles for $1 in 1846—did something totally unexpected. He wrote a Will which not only freed his slaves George and Hugh, but also gave them part of his estate. Can you believe that? It made some of us wonder if George and Hugh were more than just his slaves. Could John White Stalnaker have been their daddy too? Hmm...

❦

In March 1863, Massa John's mother, Mary Polly Buckey Earle, died, but she left no Will so her three slaves was split up among her sons. I think Rachel, the cook, went to Massa John's brothers named Creed and Elias, who lived together. Between you and me, I always wondered if she was more than their cook. My old brain forgets right now where Moses and Miz Mary's other slave went.

❧

In April 1863, I birthed Massa John's fifth child and I named her Ella. (I pointed to my daughter who curtsied to the crowd.) She and her eventual children, Clara and Hastings, live with me in Barnesville, taking real good care of me in my old age. Thank you, darlin'.

❧

On June 20, 1863, the western part of Virginia where we lived, split off from the slave-loving part of Virginia to become "West Virginia," the 35th State in the United States of America. Technically, slavery was outlawed everywhere in West Virginia, so ALL OF US IN BEVERLY WAS FREE! Sort of. The truth was that emancipation would be eventual, not immediate.

❧

In July 1863, I saw Glory for the first time in my life and nothing could top that.

Chapter 11 - War in My Back Yard

The stars twinkled overhead in their broad bed of midnight. Katydids[46] played their crusty winged violins. An owl hooted in the cemetery behind my yard. It was a typical balmy summer night in 1910. I hoped the crowd was ready to be shocked that night with a passel of stories about the Civil War, some horrifying, some hilarious, some hopeful, some happy, some heroic, all historic, all true.

"Go ahead and grab those blankets to lay out on the grass, y'all," I suggested. My dutiful daughter, Ella, and her kids Clara and Hastings who were still living with me on Vine Street in Barnesville, helped our visitors get comfortable.

My sixth child, Edward, his wife Minerva, and their three young children, Edward Jr., Helen, and Elsie came all the way from New Jersey to visit me.

My eldest son, Joseph, and his family were visiting from Mount Vernon, Ohio. This time, he brought his now twenty-one-year-old son Herbert as well as his newest granddaughters, Reba and Pearl Williams for me to bless. Joseph's first wife, Sara, had died in 1906. He remarried, bringing his new, much younger wife, Viola, for the first time to my family legacy show.

1910: Reba Mae, three, and Pearl Lavata Williams, two, were the author's maternal great-aunt and grandmother.

I felt like a Queen whose subjects gathered 'round at my feet on the porch, or sat cross-legged on blankets, listening with attention to my every word. I had to make this a very special night indeed. Frankly, I didn't know how many more years I had in me.

A cool breeze tickled my neck below the red, white, and blue head scarf that wrapped my frizzy gray hair. The pleasurable feeling reminded me of when Miz Betty would tickle my neck to bring me out of a sad mood. It helped the difficult memories began to flow like a spring river unleashed from the deep freeze of winter.

Clearing my throat, I began.

"Once upon a time in Ol' Virginny..." The familiar words dripped off my tongue.

Even though I'm getting up there in age—a wise seventy-six—I can still remember many scary days and nights when the Civil War came to the little town of Beverly, in Randolph County, in what is now called West Virginny.

Let's see, by the start of 1861, there were thirteen people, living in Massa John's house at Main and Crawford Street in tiny downtown Beverly. He was a miller by trade who also was elected County Clerk—a position of responsibility that his daddy held for thirty years. Massa John's land and property was worth $7,000, which was a decent sum of money back then.

His daughter Matilda was eighteen and keeping house, Burns was a sixteen-year-old farmer, and Page was thirteen years old. They were the children by Massa's first wife, my beloved Miz Betty, who died about 1851. Boy, did I miss her something fierce. Miz Betty, like Miz Margaret Elizabeth before her, taught me all about taking care of a household, how to cook tasty food, and how to wash and iron clothes properly. She was always kind and gentle and never made me feel stupid like her husband sometimes did. It was so hard to watch her get weaker and weaker after that last baby. Both of 'em died within a few days of each other. I was silent for a few moments of grief.

Like a wind-up toy, I started talking again, pulling up stories from my way-back memory.

Massa John's second wife, Missus Labana Stalnaker Earle, was keeping house—with my considerable assistance. She had three young children by Massa John. He already put four children in my belly by then: Joab, who calls himself Joseph now, Cornelia, George, and sweet May, my newest baby, just born in 1860.

Missus Labana called out from the colonial-style chair in the front room, "Margaret, come feed Floyd. He's been fussy all morning. Another tooth must be coming in." Missus Labana sighed, as she put her needlework down for a moment. She shushed her plump toddler who was whining at her feet, telling him to be quiet.

"Yes, Missus Labana. I just started feeding my little girl in the kitchen." May was still latched on, with a lace napkin covering my open blouse when I walked to the mistress. "I kin put Floyd on the other titty at the same time, if'n I sit in that big chair over there."

"Please do. That will keep him quiet for a little while," she said, bringing her son to me after I sat down.

Soon, I had two-year-old Floyd suckling on one titty, while my newborn May latched onto the other. It was kind of cute, really, Massa's pale son holding his slightly darker half-sister's tiny hand. I saw Missus Labana frowning outta the corner of my eye. She musta known Massa was the daddy of both our babies. I couldn't worry 'bout how she felt knowing her husband was sleeping with the both of us. There was nothing us women could do about it anyway. I had to make sure I ate enough food in order to have milk for her and my babies, along with all my other responsibilities in the house. It was tough on me some days, I won't lie.

After the children finished eating breakfast at my place—the older folks listening to my story smiled, knowing what I meant—I went outside. There was something strange in the air. Maybe it was the sly north wind that brought bad luck. Maybe it was the grassy odor of fresh cow dung mixed with skunk in the close pasture. I don't know how to describe the feeling. It wasn't really a smell or nothing we could see or hear but still, everybody was nervous. I suppose it was because different folks was riding into town telling all sorts of scary stories.

One afternoon in early April 1861, I walked toward Blackman-Bosworth's Store to pick up some thread for Missus Labana. As I approached, I notice a bunch of men standing outside the store.

A funny-looking short guy cursed, "Well, I want to buy some land and move my family and slaves to Kansas, but those damn Yankees won't let me."

A tall, sunburnt man with a brown hat low over his forehead said, "I think California should stay a free state. There's plenty of gold in them thar hills for ever'body to get rich." I wondered if he was part-Negro by the shape of his nose and full lips.

I came closer to the store when a scruffy loudmouth fellow with a long mustache was bragging in a heavy Southern accent, "It's about states' rights to keep our slaves workin' however and whenever we wanna work them." Seeing me, Mustache spat a lug of tobacco juice onto the ground near my feet. The men around him howled like a pack of dang coyotes. I looked Mustache square in the eye, bold, defiant, daring. I felt the urge to spit right back at his pasty face. Who did I think I was? He grabbed me by my titties, then pulled me tight to his body, wrapping his stinky arms around my waist, then wiggled his hips against mine in a nasty sort of way. The other male creatures laughed and egged him on.

Mustache sneered, "You think I cain't take you right here, right now in front of these fine fellows if'n I wants to? You think I cain't cut out your eyes for looking a white man in the face? You aint' nuthin' but a nigger bitch." He let me go and I thought I could get away. Slap! My hands automatically went to my face, cheek stinging where he hit me. "You see that, fellows? That"—pointing at me— "is what we gunna fight for: keeping those monkeys in line and workin' them 'xactly as we want. We are the master race and they will always be our property, to do with as we please."

As he was boasting, swinging his arms around in excitement, I made my escape, scurrying around the corner of the building to catch my breath. Instead of going right home, though, I stood behind a tall bush and continued listening to the news.

I heard clapping as Mustache ranted about us no good niggers thinking we were better than we are, assuming we's as good as them. On and on be blathered.

116

A low-voiced man interrupted Mustache, "No, our new President wants the states to get along and stay together as one strong Union."

Back and forth, forth and back, hotter and hotter. It seemed half the white folks wanted to keep us Negroes as property and let new states own slaves. The other townsfolk thought owning people was un-Christian, that Negroes should be free, and that the states should stick together as one Union. Voices got louder and louder as each side pleaded its case. Alcohol on top of that produced many a fistfight, which sometimes lead to gunfire, and death.

Someone said, "We's done arguing about it. We gunna break away from the Union to make our own country. Yessir, we gunna call it the Confed'ret States of Amurica." Some folks cheered and clapped their hands. Others scowled, muttering under their breath. That's when I got my wits about me and hurried home to safety.

Ever'body started whispering, gossiping, guessing what was about to happen to our town, our state, and our country. Some people was yelling about getting rid of slavery and others swore to keep it. People wondered if the country would break apart in a war of the states."

Soon, the Southern sympathizers—Rebels, or Rebs, they was called—did what they promised. The Civil War officially began on April 12, 1861, when the Confed'rets shot at Union soldiers somewhere in South Carolina. Most of the slaveowner's sons living in Beverly signed up as Confed'ret Rebels, but some signed with the Yankee northerners. It would become a war of brother against brother, father against son, neighbor against neighbor. Families were split down the middle over their beliefs about the war. There mighta been more Union troops enlisted in West Virginia, but there was a lot of southern sympathizers from Beverly who fought in militias and such.[47]

Oooh, chil'! I still cain't believe the incredible noise from all that fighting and death right in our backyard. You remember last year when the train ran off the tracks and crashed into the brick building?" Heads nodded. "Everybody could hear the crash from a mile away, it was so frighteningly loud. Well, the sound of gunfire and cannonballs was ten times louder than that train—Pow! Pow! echoed over the mountains. Crash! Powww!—it lasted for hours.

When the ruckus started, I was twenty-seven years old. Joab—uh, Joseph here—was 'bout six, Cordelia was four, George two, and May was just a little bitty baby.

People who was friends before the War now became enemies, not trusting each other a lick. Even some of us slaves wanted to keep things as they was, prob'ly cuz they didn't know what to do with theyselves without a master. Others, like me, always dreamed of being free—free to do what I wanted, when I wanted, wherever I wanted, with whoever I wanted. So, behind Massa's back, I always bestowed my prettiest smiles for the Feds in town, because they were the key to me being free.

Y'all children might laugh at me, but I was serious as a heart attack. I wanted those Yankees to know they had my full support and gratitude.

My Massa's brother, Archibald Earle Jr., was a Confed'ret soldier in the nineteenth Virginia cavalry. Massa John sort of sided with the Union, even though he kept me and our children as slaves. He stayed in Beverly as the County Clerk during the war years. That was sure helpful for his white family and us. We felt a little more protected with him around, unlike many of the women who were living alone when they men went to war.

More and more slaves was running away along the Underground Railroad, many joining the Union Army to ensure they won the war.

"A railroad cain't be underground, Grandma," Edward Jr. smirked.

Oh, yes, it can and I've got a great story about… I started to reply.

"I know, Grandma," interrupted Herbert, speaking dramatically. "You'll tell that us that great story on another day." Herbert's lower lip pumped out like a balloon as he pouted. He was used to getting his way at home, but I rule this roost and I'll tell the story when I want to tell it.

Laughing, I said, "Honey hush, you know me so well. Yes, you'll just have to come back and see me again real soon. But seriously, there really was an Underground Railroad and the station is close by this house. I'll take you to see it after…"

"You tell us the story." Herbert finished my sentence and pouted anew.

May I continue, Mr. Herbert?" He bowed; the spoiled boy satisfied he was getting the attention he craved.

Getting back to the Civil War in our backyard, I heard Massa John say: "By 1861, there was every indication the Federal Army would arrive at any moment. There would be fighting through our Beverly streets and probably a battle, and people might be killed. I told my mother to take the Negro servants to the Whites' house in the country where they might be safer."

Some of the white folks gathered their families and left town altogether. Most of them were going to stay nearby with friends in the country. There were probably not more than half a dozen white families who remained in town. Those who had, or could hire transportation, continued southward to Virginia with the retreating Confederates.

From the very beginning of the War, Beverly served as a staging and supply point for Rebel troops from eastern Virginia, Georgia, and Tennessee. In May of 1861, General Robert E. Lee ordered some Colonel to transport a thousand muskets for the volunteer companies from Staunton, Virginia to Beverly—which was 'bout 100 miles away over the mountains. That fellow only made it about twenty miles to the town of Philippi before being routed by Yankees. All those muskets became Union property.[48]

Boom! Crash! Pow! Pow! Pow! The Battle for Rich Mountain started at three in the afternoon on July 11, 1861. The fearsome noise continued until about six thirty that evening. The pungent smell of gunfire was carried to Beverly by the crisp spring wind, as was smoke from Rich Mountain and screams in the air. Crack! Silence.

Pow! Shouts coming closer. Boom! Quiet. Crack! Boom! Smells. Pow! Eerie calm.

Naturally there was great fear and excitement in Beverly at this sudden and continuous sound of musket and cannonball fire, even though the fighting was a mile away. All we knew was that a battle was on. A lot of the fancy, rich folk in town were Confed'ret sympathizers who decided to escape southward to Dixie. Some of 'em didn't come back for years; some never returned. The brave (I smirked) families who went south were the Goffs, Reverend Thomas—who was the slave-owning Presbyterian pastor—the Crawfords who ran the store, and Mr. Rowan who served as constable and deputy sheriff for over thirty years, and who also operated a hat factory. They all left like the Devil was on their heels.

One of my friends, Kezziah, told me a funny story one day. When her master, Mr. Crawford, heard the Yankees was planning to invade Beverly, he hitched Griz, his old gray horse, to their biggest wagon. After seating his family in the front end of the wagon, he placed all their clothes, food, and my friend in the rear. Everything went along nicely until ten miles down the road. In Huttonsville he was told, "You guys gotta go quickly. The Yankees are right on your heels, riding as fast as they can." Hearing that, Ol' Mr. Crawford he began a-runnin' that horse at such a high rate of speed that by the time they reached the town of Mingo twenty miles south, every stitch of clothing and every bite of food had bounced outta the wagon. Nothing remained, except for Kezziah, who was lying flat on the wagon bed, holding on to its sides with a death grip. The story goes that her dark chocolate face done turned white with fear!

Some of my kids fell out on the grass laughing at that vision. I imagine they wouldn't be so giddy if it happened to them.

Late that evening many Confederates who had been in the battle arrived in Beverly to get some supper. The following morning, they retreated southward.

The next day at about eleven a.m. the Union troops advanced, followed by numerous regiments in handsome uniforms. They flew banners, kept exact step to the beautiful march. Many of them were well-drilled—crack regiments in fact. Some were Germans—like the Stalnaker ancestors—having had their military training in Europe. It was claimed that about 12,000 men were under the command of Union General McClellan.

After the Battle of Rich Mountain, the Federals used the huge house of Colonel David Goff for a hospital for their wounded soldiers. They used Mr. Collett's house as a hospital for the Confederate wounded and sick. The eleven who died at the Battle of Rich Mountain were buried in back of his house. After the war, the remains of those rebels were removed and buried with their comrades on Mount Iser. The Goff house continued to be used throughout the war, which accounted for its escaping destruction.

One of my friends told me a story about Mr. Collett, who was reported to the Yankees as being a big-time Rebel.[49] They went to his home and made a mess of everything. First, they took the feather ticks from the beds, ripped 'em open and dumped all the feathers on the floor."

Cornelia's daughter, Viola, raised her hand, "'Scuse me, Grandma," in a little voice. She waited for my nod to continue. "What's a feather tick? Isn't that a kind of bug?"

"No, it's a cotton bag filled with feathers that's sewn shut, kind of like a quilt. People placed them on top of the bed to keep themselves warm at night." Viola nodded that she understood.

Those Yankees didn't stop with feathers, though. They also went into the yard and gathered up all of Mr. Collett's beehives, carried them into the house, then dumped them—bees, honey, and hives—into the feathers. Now you can imagine what a huge mess that was! But that's not all. Then they went outside and set fire to the property, burning it to the ground. It was just terrible.

"Oooh!" The children squirmed at the picture of burnt bees and sticky honey.

"How do you know all that stuff, Grandma?" interrupted one of the children.

"I keep telling y'all. We slaves listened when our masters be talking with the friends. We wasn't as dumb as they thought we was.

We acted that way sometimes to make our lives easier. But we learned by listening. Keep that in mind for your own lives, d'you hear me?"

"Yes, ma'am!" the youngsters replied in unison.

Since Massa John was the County Clerk, we all stayed put inside Beverly, trying to live our lives as normally as we could. I continued doing the laundry and a little cooking, taking care of Missus Labana's every need, like a good housemaid, as well as watching my four children. We tried to keep the kitchen garden going, but as soon as anything grew, the soldiers came along and plucked it for their meals. We got smart and started growing some plants inside our house in pots. The littlest kids laughed with delight at the chickens we hid in the back room, so we could have fresh eggs every day.

❦

"Some of those loud Rebs who talked big and bad were not brave at all. One of the Stalnaker boys was hiding in his featherbed to keep from being drafted into the army. Each time he thought there was a serious danger of being caught, he would have his wife make up the featherbed with him inside so the soldiers couldn't find him. "What do you think about that? Was he being brave or a coward?" I asked my audience.

"A coward!" they shouted. My educated son, Joseph added, "A belligerent ignoramus."

"If you was his wife or children, would you respect him?"

"No way!"

"Would you do the same thing if you didn't want to go to war?"

My audience responded all kinds of ways, agreeing, shaking their heads, booing, laughing, thinking, or describing other options they would take.

"Children, don't ever forget that war is a mighty terrible thing. Many people die, including innocent women, children, and animals."

"There wasn't enough food during wartime because most of the men who plowed the fields was gone fighting. Many soldiers and residents were almost starving."

"How starving were they?" the children shouted, as a kind of call and response game that we often played during story time.

"Well, by the time they came to a place called 'The Corner,' the men were so hungry and tired, they were willing to eat anything they could find. Before anyone knew it, one of the soldiers ran into the town tannery…"

"What's a tannery, Grandma?"

"That's a place where they turn dead animal hides into leather. It smells something awful in there. Just imagine pee pee, rotting flesh, and smelly, stagnant water all at the same time. Well, the soldier didn't care. He cut several ox tails off some of the hides that were going to be worked into leather. Fortunately, the hides were from recently killed oxen. As soon as the order was given to make camp, the soldier cleaned the stinky tails and placed them in a large iron kettle with water to cook. They later added rice to this mixture and some weeds they found in the ground. The soldiers were served oxtail soup for supper."

"Oh yuck!" one child exclaimed, horrified at the thought of eating smelly soup.

"Whatchu talking about young'un? Oxtail soup sounds really good to me!" My son Edward spoke up. "Um hmm, add some dandelion greens, salt and herbs, cook the tasty fat off them tails. Yummy. Sometimes ya gotta do what ya gotta do and learn to like it. You'll find that out when you get a little older." He winked.[50] I agreed.

Soldiers from both sides of the war would come into town and make a clean sweep of the stores, taking every item that wasn't glued down. A few men were seen parading down the streets with great pieces of colorful fabric under their arms, the beautiful cloth trailing along behind their uniforms in the dirty slush and snow. A couple of soldiers were seen with several hats on their heads, and one fellow carried about three dozen silk umbrellas which he gave away for the asking.[51]

"That's silly, Grandma. If soldiers can't use the hats and umbrellas, why did they steal them in the first place?" My smart granddaughter Edna asked.

"Very good question, m'dear," I responded, proud her parents taught her the difference between right and wrong.

You know, I gotta bunch more stories that I'll tell you tomorrow night if the warm weather holds. Go use the outhouse if you need to, then wash your hands. I made a sheet cake with lemon frosting earlier today, and believe you me, it's one of my best efforts." As we sat around licking our fingers from the sweet cake, the kids kept talking about my stories and asking intelligent questions. It was important to me that the children learn about my life as a slave as well as the horrors of war, mostly so they would never let the country fall back into that madness ever again.

More War Stories

Fried green tomatoes, smothered chicken'n gravy, cool mint tea, apple pie. Daughter Ella outdid herself tonight, as my happy stomach bears witness. I set my empty plate in the soapy sink water, then made my way outside. The ball of flame had dropped to the horizon, turning the sky deep orange, lightening to tangerine, peach mixing with light blue, blending to violet to navy at the top of our sky view. It was story time.

"Once upon a time in Ol' Virginny…" my family and neighbors spoke the well-known words in unison from their blankets and chairs on the grass. My ample bottom found itself in the comfy seat of my well-worn rocking chair, positioned on the slatted whitewashed porch of my shotgun house, situated at 134 Vine Street in Barnesville, Ohio. The year was 1905.

I began tonight's tale with: My Massa, John Earle, married into the Stalnaker family in 1838. They was one of the first pioneer families to move into the area around Beverly. Both families came from Frederick, Virginia. I knew a bunch of 'em very well since I spent my first twelve years living with the Stalnakers. Anyway, two brothers, Hamilton and Warwick Stalnaker, owned farms next to each other, but they was totally opposite in their politics and sympathies toward the war. Hamilton was a Rebel and Warwick a died-in-the-wool Yankee. You can imagine the type of disagreements they had at their dinner table.

❧

The Rebs was waiting in the mountains, getting ready to strike. Both sides wanted control over Beverly, which sat in an important transportation position in the center of the Staunton-Parkersburg turnpike at the Tygart River. A local boy, David Hart, was a Union supporter. He led General McClellan's men through the bush, laurel, and rocks for about five miles. They made a surprise attack on the Confed'rets at Joseph Hart's farm near the pass on Rich Mountain, right at the edge of the river.[52] The Feds was successful in capturing the turnpike. They forced the Rebs to leave. Then General McClellan led his Yankee troops into Beverly, capturing that vital crossroads for the Union. It was a great victory for the Feds and helped them stay in control of the important location Beverly presented on the turnpike. Uh-oh, some of the children look bored. I'd better get them involved in the story.

❧

I asked Joseph to tell a story about his grandfather while I excused myself for a few minutes.

"Certainly, mother," he responded in his proper English.

He said, "I overheard an unbelievable story about my Uncle Archibald Earle, who was not only a prominent citizen of the town, but a very strong Rebel sympathizer as well. He desperately wanted to keep free laborers—us—working his grist mill."

"I never heard of a grist mill. What's that?" young Hasting asked.

Well, you know that farmers grow wheat and corn and barley and rye in the fields, right?" The boys nodded. "And you know that cornbread and cakes need cornmeal and flour right?" The girls nodded. Well, corn on the cob is shucked, then dried for six to eight months, then it's shelled and bagged for milling. The dried corn is poured into a hopper, which is like a box above a huge grinding stone which sits atop another huge stone. When the top stone rotates, the dried corn and grains in between the stones get cracked, then eventually become finer and finer as they make their way to the edges of the grinding stones, eventually turning into cornmeal or flour, then falling off the stones onto the floor in heaps. "Cereal grains used to be called grist. A grist mill is a place where grains are ground into flours for cooking.

"Or for making booze," offered Sylvester, under his alcoholic breath, as I returned to my seat.

Joseph ignored his comment. "Millstones usually rotate by waterpower. Massa Earle's grist mill was at the edge of Files Creek, at the far edge of Beverly. Imagine a house built at the edge of a waterway. There's an eight-foot-tall wooden wheel that has buckets on each spoke. The wheel is turned by the force of the creek, scooping water into the buckets as it turns. A sluice gate[53] controls the flow of water, which powers the grinding stones that make cornmeal and flour and such. Standing inside the mill, the floorboards shake with a thunder-like rumble as the millstones move one against the other, cracking the corn and wheat kernels. The power of this process is loud and scary and incredibly exciting. As you might guess, slaves worked all aspects of the grist mill process, raking the hot new flour all around the floor, forward and back, cooling and drying it for packing into waiting barrels. Massa's father, Archibald Sr., had eight slaves in the 1830s, but fewer and fewer as the years went on."

I returned a few minutes later and resumed my Civil War stories. There was a well-liked Union man named Mr. Chenowith—the man who built the Beverly Bridge we lived next to. One day, he was in trouble. He was going to be imprisoned at Camp Chase because he liked Yankee politics. Mr. Archibald Earle, Massa John's father, walked into Rebel headquarters cursing and saying terrible things about Mr. Chenoweth. He requested the officer to give him the prisoner because he had a personal grudge to settle with him. Mr. Archibald began hitting the prisoner, pleasing the Rebels who gathered to witness the trial, cheering. He marched the prisoner along until they came to the river near his home. Mr. Archibald drew a gun and told Mr. Chenowith to remove his coat and run for his life. After the war, we learned that Mr. Archibald faked his mean behavior. He had wanted to keep his Yankee friend from being unjustly sent to prison... or worse.[54] So you see, there were some basically good people on both sides of the war.

Speaking of the Earles, my mistress, Miz Betty Earle, many times scolded their son—named John Jr. after his daddy. She warned him many times to stop climbing the cherry tree that stood in our yard. But each day them cherries became a little riper and smelled so sweet that Lil' John kept climbing a little higher to get the ripest fruit. One day he had climbed to the tippy top of the tree. It so happened that at that very moment, the famous Rebel General, Mud Wall Jackson—cousin of Stonewall Jackson, whose sister, Laura Arnold, lived in Beverly—was coming into town. Before Lil' John could get out of the tree, a cannon shell came whizzing through the air and burst onto the road directly in front of the Earle house. BAM!

The poor boy was so shocked and frightened that he fell out of the tree. Somehow, the Lord smiled on him that day because he wasn't seriously injured. I found him on the ground and rocked his little body in my lap, screaming until help came.[55] Whew! It was mighty scary to think he coulda broken every bone in his body.

I stopped talking, sipped some tea, rubbed my eyes, then looked around. "Are you getting tired of hearing these stories? Don'cha want to play tag, or hide-and-seek instead of listening to this ol' woman?"

"No! Tell us another one! More, more!" my audience demanded.

I already knew the answer. I had them in the palm of my hand. I enjoyed and prided myself on being an excellent storyteller, using my voice and body to communicate our life experiences for the next generation.

"OK. OK!" I held my arms up in surrender, smiling at their overwhelming response. Now, as you can imagine, many slaves wanted very badly to be free and some actually ran away from their masters. The newspapers carried lots of stories of runaway slaves, but here's a funny tale about Ol' Black Jerry who ran back. Before the Civil War, a fellow named Absalom Crawford owned a slave named Jeremiah Blackstitch, also called Jerry. That boy was acting crazy as usual. One day he ran away, so Massa Crawford sold his behind to a slaver who took him to southern Virginia. The farming work was so difficult "Down South" that Negroes liked to die just thinking about being sold there. Well, Ol' Jerry ran away from that tough master and made his way back to his Beverly home. By then, his master's family had deserted their house and stayed with family in East Virginia while the war raged. Once the war was over, the Crawfords were on the turnpike coming back to Beverly. They heard a rustle in the bushes near their house. Was it a soldier? Was it a vicious animal? No. Who should step from a bush, but Ol' Black Jerry.

"Please, Massa, take me back. I promise to be good and never run away again." Mr. Crawford believed Jerry and let him come back as his servant. That's where Jerry stayed, even after slavery was abolished. He was the slave who ran back.

❧

Of most concern to the Southern sympathizers, was the Emancipation Proclamation that President Lincoln signed on January 1, 1863. You see, the South had been largely winning the war in most parts of the country. President Lincoln had to do something drastic. His advisors suggested that he free the slaves in Southern states and let them join the Union Army to help the North win the war. Who better to fight hard against the Confed'rets than Negroes who had been their property and wanted freedom?

"I still don't understand," Hastings said. "What's a 'Mancipashun Procla-what?"

"Well, it's a law that President Abraham Lincoln signed to free all the slaves in the Rebel states. It allowed them to join Union forces. Wouldn't you want to have the opportunity to fight against Confed'rets that forced you to be their slaves?"

"You know that's true!" I heard my sons uttering.

Many Northerners were abolitionists who supported Lincoln's big gamble to have Negroes fight to keep the country together.

"What's a 'bolishunist?" Clara stopped me.

An abolitionist was a person who believed that slavery was wrong. So even though there were a lot of abolitionists in what is now West Virginia, most white folks in Beverly were ready to fight against the "Northern aggression" as they called it. Confed'rets thought it was the right of each state to decide whether it would keep slavery to improve its economy or not. They wanted to save the genteel Southern way of life, forcing their human property workers to keep their owners rich and comfortable.

On June 20, 1863, West Virginia was admitted into the Union as the thirty-fifth new state. It was a day of celebration for us slaves, for it meant we was truly free in the town of Beverly.

"Wait a minute, Grandma," Herbert interrupted, as usual. "I thought you just said the 'Mancipation Proclwhatever was passed earlier that year to free the slaves."

Hmmm, he was listening. Good.

Yes, that is correct. Unfortunately, the Confed'rets didn't often choose to follow rules set by a Union President. Most of 'em kept us as slaves. Many of us didn't even know we was freed at the beginning of 1863. I heard Texas was the last state to acknowledge it. They didn't tell their slaves until June 19th, 1865. Some Negroes use the term "Juneteenth" to celebrate our freedom, instead of the Fourth of July that white people celebrate as their freedom from England.

Many owners pleaded with their slaves to stay on after West Virginia eliminated slavery in its borders on June 20, 1863. "That happened to Joseph, right?" I handed the speaking stick[56] to my eldest son.

"Yes, Mother. My owner, John B. Earle, who was also my father, begged me not to leave for Barnesville with the rest of my family during the summer of 1863. He promised to give me a cabin and acknowledge me as his son, as long as I would stay and help him run the plantation. I knew his promises would not come to pass, so I declined his generous offer to stay where he had kept us—his own children—as slaves."

Silence. I supposed the audience was thinking about what they would have done if their master had offered to give them his last name, their own place, and the power to run the plantation with him.

Joseph continued. Many former slaves said, "Heck no! Enough of this mess! We want to govern our own lives from now on." Some migrated to the Northern and Western states, like St. Louis, Missouri, or Chicago, Illinois, or Cleveland, Ohio, or Philadelphia, Pennsylvania. A few went all the way west to California to find gold. A lot of people came here to Belmont County, because there had been many abolitionist Quakers here, and it seemed to be a safe place for Negroes wanting to make a better life for ourselves.

"I never knew about all this, Grandma. They don't teach this information in school." All the school-aged children agreed.

"That's why I'm here. To teach you about our history, not just the European stuff taught in schools. Remember these stories and promise you'll pass them down to your children."

"We promise." The kids and grandkids solemnly vowed.

❦

Here's another Civil War story for you. One evening, several Confed'ret soldiers were eating dinner at Bushrod Crawford's place.

One child laughed, "What kind of name is 'Bushrod'?"

I merely smiled, shrugged my shoulders, then continued the story. Just as they sat down to eat, someone banged on the door. "The Yankees are coming! The Yankees are coming!" Everybody jumped up from the table and fled back to their own houses. The table was left as it was, food still hot, beautiful silverware waiting to be used. You see, Mr. Crawford was a prosperous merchant and a cattle dealer. He just returned from Baltimore, Maryland, where he bought some fine clothing, jewelry, and household furnishings. All those expensive items were left in the house, doors unlocked. The Crawfords left so quickly there wasn't even time for the women to put on their bonnets or wraps.[57] What do you suppose happened then?

Edward spoke first, "I imagine the soldiers did what most people would have done... miraculously found a way to get a pretty dress, hat, or jewelry for their wives," looking at his lovely Minerva. The other men nodded in agreement, dreaming about the goodies those soldiers likely "inherited" on their patrols.

"And maybe they found a fancy gun or two," Sylvester added.

Oh, that boy and his guns and drink. It's going to be the death of him.

❦

OK, boys, this tale is for you. I pointed at the youngsters. Dick Taylor was a very old black man. He said the ladies at his master's house would go for long walks every Sunday evening. They required the youngest black boys on the plantation to dress in their best clothes and walk behind each lady. The boys had to carry the women's trains—which are long pieces of fabric that looked kind of like a long tail. If one of the boys happened to drop the train onto the dirty ground, he was given a severe whuppin' when they returned home.[58]

I laughed when Clara arose from the ground, pretending to be a rich white girl with long, flowing blond hair, who was wearing a fancy dress with a long train. She pointed at Hastings and Herbert and told them to, "Pick up my train now, boys, and carry it while I walk." She sang "La-de-da-de-da" as she imagined rich people might sing, as she strutted around the yard. All the grownups laughed at this scene, but deep down, we mourned the fact that our ancestors were subjected to this type of indignity day in and day out.

※

This next one is a nasty story. Of course, all the boys' ears perked up. Adam Crawford's garden was used as a burying ground for the amputated parts of the soldiers' bodies. Even today, it's not unusual to excavate the bones of legs and arms when plowing the garden each year. People whispered that the amputated hand of one soldier buried there had a diamond ring on his finger.

※

Does anyone want to take a break from stories now? Bad timing, I know. You probably don't want to eat any of my freshly baked oatmeal cookies after that last story, right?

Ida Mae raised her hand and volunteered, "Well, I'd be happy to put the cookies on a plate and bring 'em out here for your audience."

"Hurray for Ida Mae!" Everyone applauded, quickly forgetting that last horrible story. Hastings even volunteered to help. You gotta love teamwork!

After the cookies were passed around, I resumed my stories, but with maybe more pleasant tales.

✿

"Now, don't y'all ever think the women 'round those parts weren't brave. Martha Rammell was a widow, alone in her home one evening when a soldier stuck his head in the window of her living room. What would you do if that happened?" I asked the crowd.

"Shoot 'im!" (You can guess who said that)

"Scream!"

"Run out the back door!'

"Throw hot coffee in his face!"

"Cry."

"Kick him!"

"Those are all interesting solutions," I acknowledged, but here's what happened.

The soldier shouted at Martha, "Wench, get me some food!" Well, Mrs. Rammell didn't know what the man planned to do to her, so she grabbed an axe lying close by. Just as he tried to force himself through the window, she knocked him right in his big head, which killed him.[59] And she didn't care, not one whit about it. Yes, some of them ladies in Beverly sure din't play.

✿

Another lady, Mrs. Lucinda Leonard—my master's auntie—owned and operated the Leonard Hotel. They were holding a dance for the Yankees there one night. She helped get 'em good and drunk. Her brother, Archibald Earle Jr., learned the Feds were enjoying themselves at the dance instead of paying attention. Mr. Archibald and other Confed'rets familiar with the backroads, streams and

133

bypaths, volunteered to guide the Rebels into town that very night. They attacked when the drunk Feds were asleep at the hotels and private homes in the area. The Rebels took some eight hundred prisoners that night.

My youngest son, Sylvester, gushed, "Wow! That was smart, get 'em drunk, then you jump." Everybody laughed at his rhyme.

Joseph said, "Yes, children, you can never let your guard down, especially when you're fighting for something you want. Always be aware and alert and have a plan of action. If that one doesn't work, have a second plan ready to go."

The Yankees took over Beverly for most of the war, but that didn't stop the Rebels from trying to take control, with the final raid occurring in January 1865. General Rosser, I think his name was, and 300 Rebel troops successfully surprised the Union Army before dawn. They captured almost 600 men and all of their supplies. He burned the important Beverly Bridge and marched his Yankee prisoners back to Virginia through the deep snow."

After the War, many of the deserters returned to find their homes torn down or burned. Those who had supported the Union found favor in political posts for the new state of West Virginia. Beverly, as the important seat of Randolph County, continued to rebuild, grow and prosper. Many new homes and buildings were constructed in the years following the War. But our family was long gone by then.

Chapter 12 - Getting Ahead

One bright spot in my life was knowing my oldest son, Joab, would have a better life than me. Massa's sister, Miz Nannie, treated my Joab like he was the son she never had. She'd bring him to her room during the day when Massa was gone and teach Joab to read and write. Yessir, Joab don't have to work in the fields or be a servant cleaning up peoples' slops like other slave boys.

Joab was not happy with that, though, because he wanted to play with the other children.

"Mother, I like watching Mr. Suiter, the blacksmith, place objects in the glowing red and white-hot fire, feeling the warmth on my face, smelling the ash, tasting the air sharp with the scent of metal. And all the different objects a blacksmith can make from the iron rods: hand tools for digging, points for the end of plows, hooks, and horseshoes. It just depends on how he hammers the red-hot metal on his anvil as to what shape the final product will be. It's fascinating, Mother, and I could watch him all day long. A couple of times he let me squeeze the bellows[60] to make the fire hotter. Once he let me pound on a horse-shoe he was making." Joseph looked like he was in Heaven remembering that experience.

"But instead, I'm stuck inside with Miz Nannie."

My Joab always liked making things with his hands. That's a good sign that he was motivated to learn a skill, but I tell my boy, "You do what Miz Nannie say and you learn what she want to teach you, because that gonna help you in this life. Then you kin teach the rest of us slaves. That's how we all gunna do better in the future, learning our letters and numbers." I remembered Big Peg telling me that advice and it surely made sense to me.

I be so proud when he say in his good English, "Mother, the Old Missus is just a lonely woman who doesn't have a husband or children. Some days she has me bring her tea from the cook, or take her laundry downstairs, or fetch her thread and needles so she can sew some fancy clothes for me. Other days I feel like I'm her plaything because she combs my hair or rubs my head... for luck, she says. Sometimes she puts her sore feet on my back. She says her "roomatiz"[61] will flow out from her into me, and because I'm strong it won't hurt me at all. Most days, though, we have reading classes, like "Run Spot, Run." Oh, Mother, it's so boring. I'm eight years old. I want to be out playing with the other children or helping the blacksmith. Even working in the field would be more interesting than spending my days with that old woman."

"Joab, you need to learn all that good lady is willing to teach you. You know the law say it illegal to teach us how to read and write, but she want to do it anyway. You are gettin' the benefit of learnin'. The rest of us has no chance less'n you teach us. Do you understand how important you are to all of us, son?" I searched his eyes, drilling this truth into him with my stare.

Joab still din't look happy, but he nodded. 'Sides, he a smart boy who know better than to sass his mama.

"Amen!" All the parents in the crowd replied.

Some days of the week, Joab came back to our quarters behind the big house with a book Miz Nannie wanted him to study. At night, by the light of the oil lanterns, me and some of the neighbor slaves would gather inside our quarters. Joab taught us our letters and numbers, while all of us stayed warm by the open fire. We was all so excited to be learning, especially since that forbidden fruit would help us harvest a good life for ourselves and our families in the future. Lord willing, the Union side would win the war and set us free.

Chapter 13 - Enough!

Gotta admit, I do have it pretty good in Beverly, mostly. I got more power than many slave women, for you see, I carry the keys. That means I control all the doors on the farm: the house, barns, storage, everything. Among colored women, that's real power. When his second wife, Missus Labana, got sick after her last baby, Massa John had me take over most of the duties 'round here. After his wife died in late 1862, he began treating me like a substitute mama for his young children.

The Third Missus

In between doing his day job as the Randolph County Clerk, and being the town's miller, Massa John been sniffing 'round a new woman named Elizabeth Currence. I hear tell her family was one of the first folks who settled here when Beverly became a town. She's only twenty-eight—that's twenty years younger'n him.

She already got three kids by her first husband who died early. Massa has ten young kids still living at home. They need a new white mama. He can't keep depending on a colored woman he owns to be the mama of his white kids, as well as our mulatto children. Ain't proper. People 'round here is already talkin'.

Miz Elizabeth is a pretty little thing on the outside, with her blond curls and sparkly laugh, but she's right mean on the inside. She always looks at me with a "if looks could kill you'd be way past dead" kind of hard stare. Yep, I feel it in my bones every time she comes by bringing Massa John an apple pie or some stew, "for you and your poor children," she croons. She act like his children be starving from eating my cooking.

She always be saying something negative about my kids too. "Why can't those pickaninnies play behind the house, where good white folk don't have to look at their raggedy hair and rags."

Now you need to understand that my children are dressed as nice as a slave can be with the leavings we get from Massa's kids. I sew 'em up nice with extra fabric and buttons and things. My kids do not look like the ragamuffins that Miz Elizabeth calls 'em.

No, Massa John's girlfriend and I do not get along and I try to stay outta the way when she come by the house.

I cain't really blame her for feeling this way though. My belly's big right now with Massa's fifth child. I'd prob'ly feel the same angry way as her if I was in the same high position. She might be a nice person, just not to me.

Whew! I be so tired all the time. The midwife say I be having this baby any day now, probably the beginning of April 1863.

The Last Straw

It started like any other spring day. The faint smell of gunpowder scented the morning air. The Union troops was still hunkered down in Beverly, to the disgust of many southern sympathizers.

I gave birth to my precious baby girl, Ella, a few days ago. Still feeling a bit weak in the knees, I forced myself to leave our cabin get some fresh milk from our cow in the close pasture for lunch. A cool breeze met me at the door, bringing the promise of a beautiful day.

"Gal, come on over here. Now." Massa John surprised me by coming 'round the corner of our cabin. Seem like he was waiting for me, a sly smile spreading across his face. His voice raspy, licking his lips, breath stank of liquor. I knew what that meant.

"Massa John, I gots to get milk for my children, then feed my baby girl," I responded as calmly as I could. My titties started dipping milk through my dress at the thought of my Ella waiting for me inside.

Seeing the moisture, Massa flicked his tongue at me in a nasty sort of way. It been months since he tried to bother me. I guess he's done waiting.

"What about come over here now did you not understand?" He growled in a low voice. Concern lodged in the back of my brain and began to spread throughout my body.

"You better get those feet to moving, missy," he warned.

I took a step toward him, metal milk bucket dangling from my fingers. For the briefest instant, I thought about clubbing him with it, but I knew my children and I would be the ones to suffer in the end. I kept walking toward him. Slowly. Trying to keep my balance. He grabbed my arm and started pulling me along the graveled path. Determined.

I found my voice. "Massa, pleeeese. I cain't lay with you this time. I just had a chil' and I'm mighty sore down there." The sky darkened, along with his mood.

"Wench, it's been too long. Get on over here!" Massa pointed to a dark opening which led into the horse barn. That's where he often did his business with me. This time, though, he seemed different. More insistent, more anxious, more fidgety, more scary. Mad and scary, or scary mad? All I knew is that my heart began to race. Beads of sweat appeared on my upper lip. My underarms produced the smell of fear.

I couldn't figure out why he was acting so strange. Maybe it was because Yankee soldiers took over his homeland. Maybe it was his mind slipping again, slipping into drink, into darkness. Maybe he was still missing his wife, Missus Labana, who passed six months before. Whatever it was, he was gonna take what he want, and that was me... right now.

Three dun-colored horse heads turned our way as we entered the old barn. Fresh hay, smelly dung, dark, earthy. He pulled me along. I still had the pail in my hand, fighting with my brain not to kill him with it.

"But Massa, my belly still real sore from the baby. I cain't bend over that post like usual." I never once guessed what would happen if I didn't do what he axt.

"Girl, you sassing me? You think you're better than me now, just because those Yankees filled your head with that freedom nonsense? I'll show you what happens when people disobey my orders."

Massa grab me by the shoulders and push me toward one of the empty stalls in back. My eyes grew big as saucers when he reach up and grab that big black leather whip he use to make the horses gallop faster when they be pulling the big carriage. Then Massa push me outside to stand next to the big tree. He start beating me on my back with his hand. "So, you (slap) not going (slap) to do (slap) my bidding?" Then he stopped, still, quiet, dangerous. "Last chance, gal," he said, with the calm of the grave.

Massa gather up the whip, handle in hand, his arm ready to strike like a rattlesnake.

"I cain't," I sobbed, facing away from him, not seeing the crazy blooming on his face.

Crack! The sharp snapping sound was almost more terrifying than the kiss of leather against my homespun dress. The second strike ripped through the fabric, slicing through the flesh on my back. A bolt of lightning sent white-hot daggers from my spine to my brain to the area behind my eyes. The unexpected agony caused me to wail uncontrollably, just like I did while giving birth. Another Clap! sizzled from the top of the fleshy part of my right shoulder slicing through the skin, ending under my left shoulder blade. Breath escaped my lungs while flames danced on my back.

"Massa... Maaasa, please stop!" I begged, crying, pleading, twisting from his grasp. But the Devil was in him and he kept playing that sharp fiddle back and forth across my sliced body. The whip sang on. The sting was unimaginable, indescribable, like a thousand bees stinging, like a hot iron burning, like a baby being born. The memory and scars from that day would stay with me for the rest of my life.[62]

You see, I ain't never been whupped before, not ever. Here I was a nearly thirty-year-old Negro woman, just had my fifth chil' from Massa John. Before this day, he mostly been gentle with me when he take me into the barn. I cain't believe that just cuz I wouldn't lay with him, he went outta his cotton-pickin' mind.

When Satan finally lef' his eyes Massa John come back to his normal self. He stared in horror at me at the foot of the tree in a pool of blood and dirt, my dress in tattered shreds, fear in my eyes, tears flowing down the sides of my dirty face. My fingers was still spread wide in front of my leaking titties trying to protect myself. He stared at the tree-shaped welts he left on my back; his mouth open wide, gooey spittle spraying from his thin lips. Jabbing his finger at me, "You better not tell a soul about this, or else… Oh, and by the way, Big Peg is your mama!" Then he left me to my misery.

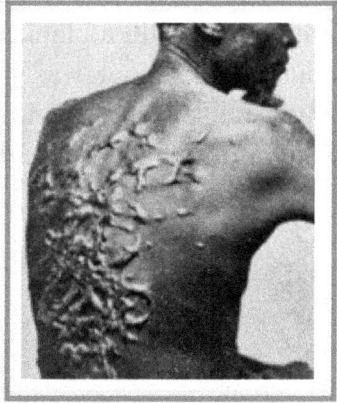

I couldn't think. I laid there for a while longer, trying to get up the energy to rise. When I could gather my strength, I walked to the horse trough where there was some fresh water. I tried to clean my face and arms, but I could barely move. I wanted to lay my whole back in that cool water to clean off the blood and straw and dirt and painful memory. Inside the barn, I rebraided my hair, trying not to burst out crying again. I found a thick horse blanket hanging from the wall and wrapped it 'round myself since my dress was ripped to shreds. I didn't want to frighten my children when I got back to my cabin. I guess I'd tell people I lost my balance and fell on some rocks or something.

What did he say at the end? Big Peg is my natural born mama?

❀

Privet bushes thick with pointy green leaves and tiny black berries bordered the red brick sidewalk. The solid green wall hid Massa John's house and property from prying eyes, but not their ears. One of my friends told me later they saw Massa's wannabe third wife, Elizabeth Currence, standing across the street from our house on that horrible day. Was she listening to me pleading and screaming as I was whipped? Was she smiling as she glimpsed her husband-to-be reentering his house? Did she walk closer to the edge of our property to see and hear more? Did she spy me going into the barn, then limpin' out with a blanket around my shoulders? At the time, all I could think about was getting back to my baby. I didn't know anyone else was watching me and I certainly had no idea that my life was going to change drastically very soon.

The Ultimatum

"It's her or me," my slave friend Kezziah told me she heard Elizabeth Currence say to her husband-to-be, in front of the courthouse where he worked. Kezziah warned me to watch out for that lady as she would most definitely be trouble for me. I already knew that, but I didn't realize that the blond wannabe would end up doing me a huge favor.

A New Beginning

A few days after the beating, my nine-year-old son, Joab, saw what Massa did to my back and he was fit to be tied. He started acting up, talking back to his daddy-owner, showing him so much disrespect that I feared for his safety.

I heard Massa John ask, "Boy, why are you sassing me so much these days?"

In his semi-educated young buck voice Joab responded, "Father, I cannot respect a man who thrashed my mama's back the way you did."

No, he did not just call Massa John "Father!"

My brave son continued, "There's no telling what more you might do in the future. I hope the Yankees win the war so my mama and brothers and sisters and me can go to a free state where there is no slavery. I want to get a job and have my own house and family someday." With his finger stabbing Massa John in the chest, Joab

142

threatened, "Don't you ever treat my mama like that again, or else!" And with that, Joab turned his back on his daddy-owner and walked away. I was so proud of my brave oldest son that I began to weep uncontrollably.

But Massa John was so angry! He sent my boy away that very day. Yes, he did. Sent him 'bout seven miles up the road to work for the Stalnakers and Whites, who was living near Leadsville.

Oh, how I missed my Joab. He would help me with the younger kids and teach us older slaves how to read and write. Joab acted mighty grown for someone so young. Now he was gone. He sent me letters that were easy enough for me to read, telling us he was learning a bit about blacksmithing and working with horses, which made me glad. He was learning skills that would help him have a better life than mine.

A couple of months after the terrible whupping incident that soured my relationship with Massa John, he took me to the barn again. I dreaded having to lay with him ever again, especially with my new baby strapped to my chest at the time. But that's not what he had in mind…

You see, it was June 21, 1863, as I recall, in the middle of Civil War fighting. My Joab been gone two months. Massa John tol' me that people in our parts of Virginia held a 'lection and voted to break away from the rest of the state. He said we now be livin' in the new State of West Virginia where slavery is not allowed.

"Wait a minute, Massa John. Does that mean I's free and my children's free too?" He nodded, unsmiling. My body began to tingle from my head to my toes, an explosion of joy about to burst outta my mouth in song. Praise Jesus! But I somehow kept quiet, with no emotion showing on my face.

Massa John say, "Margaret, you know I intend to marry Miss Elizabeth, and we both know she doesn't care for you a lick." I stood stock-still not knowing if he was going to kill me on the spot or sell me South. "She doesn't like seeing your, uh, our yellow children running around this plantation. So, we've decided that you and your children will be leaving this place. In the next two days."

143

"Where we supposed to go, Massa?" I panicked. "Beverly and Leadsville are the only homes I know."

"I think you should go to Barnesville, Ohio, about 150 miles away, on the other side of the Ohio River. It's a Quaker settlement where those darn abolitionists were stirring up so much trouble,[63] helping ungrateful slaves escape their kind masters. You and the children will be safer and happier there. Barnesville has a community of free Negroes and several small industries so your family should be able to find paid work. And your Pappy is already living there." I nodded, still in a daze about this welcome change of events.

He continued, "I've already contacted some friends of mine to help you find a place to live when you get there, but in the meantime your father has agreed to let you move in with him, according to one of my relatives who lives in Belmont County. I'll give you some money to get you started living in Ohio. You've been a good Nigra to me and my family, and I want to help you and our children."

The news was sinking in slowly, passing through my disbelieving ears into my hopeful brain. Delight, dread, depression, disbelief, dreamy distrust, then back to delight. "Massa, I don't know nothing 'bout getting to Ohio and how am I supposed to do that with five children, one of 'em just born and another only two years old with my eldest sent away?" I took a much needed breath, then pouted.

Kindly, Massa put his arm around my stiff shoulders and said, "Gal, don't worry about all that. I'll give you a buckboard and a horse and I'll help you pack what you need. I'll make sure someone helps you along the way and sets you up in your new home. We think it's best that you leave tomorrow or the next day. That will be a week or so before the full moon which will afford you starry light at night. It could take you and the children one or two weeks to get there, depending on the weather.

"I'll go with you to Stalnakers' place to pick up Joab. Maybe Hugh or George will want to go with you since they're free now too.

"You may not believe this, Margaret, but I'm going to miss all of you more than you will ever know"—Do I see tears in his eyes?—"but this is the b-best plan," he stuttered, "for all of us." With that last statement, he left me alone in the barn to think about the unthinkable: WE ARE FREE!

I could hardly believe it. I'se going to be free in a free state? Smiling as wide as the sky, twirling around with my arms stretched from one end of the barn to the other, happy as it was humanly possible to be, imagining my new life as I never could before. The future would be different. Oh, thank you Lord, and double thank Miz Elizabeth Currence for this precious gift.

My baby girl, Ella, wrapped in a blanket around my chest, started whimpering with all my commotion. I put her to my titty to quiet her while my heart soared and my brain dreamed of a blissful new existence in a free land.

PART II: FORTY-EIGHT YEARS FREE

Stories from Margaret Booker (as imagined by the author)

Figure 11: 1870 Map, showing Margaret Booker's 200-mile migration from Beverly, Randolph County, West Virginia, to Barnesville, Belmont County, Ohio, in 1864.

Chapter 14 - 150 Miles to Freedom

Sister Sister, we're really gonna miss her.
The buckboard's ready, big and steady,
The kids begin to stir.

Sister Sister, we're really gonna miss her.
Freedom papers in her hand
Will keep them safe, across the land.

Sister Sister, we're really gonna miss her.
Their clothes are packed, the food is stacked,
We'll never see them coming back.

Sister Sister, we're really gonna miss her.
The baby's on her mother's chest
Wrapped tight and safe, like she knows best.

Sister Sister, we're really gonna miss her.
Friends pray with us, what a mighty sound,
With well wishes and cakes so round.

Sister Sister, we're really gonna miss her.
To see them off with shouts of cheer,
They're leaving us in Beverly here.

Sister Sister, we're really gonna miss her.
No sadness no, just gladness glow.
Massa cries but lets his children go.

Sister Sister, we're really gonna miss her.
They leave us now, to pick up Joab,
So ready for freedom he's 'bout to explode.

Sister Sister, we're really gonna miss her.
Third week in June, sleeping under the moon,
We've got a bet they'll be there soon.

Sister Sister, we're really gonna miss her.
They'll make it through to Barnesville do.
Let's join them someday in paradise too.
Danger Abounds

❦

"Once upon a time in West Virginny…" I could now say since the new State of West Virginia was formed on June 1, 1863.

Twilight. That in-between daylight and darkness time when magic can be seen and felt. The soft glowing skylight when the sun slips below the horizon is the perfect time to tell stories.

I had a huge crowd waiting to hear tonight's tale. Folks who heard the previous horrific account had gossiped to others who confided in their friends about my history "show." I told Ella we had to make two sheet cakes this time for our guests. She voted for lemon but I wanted chocolate, so we made one of each, cutting the fluffy pan cakes into small rectangles for the crowd's enjoyment.

This special evening, I wore my prettiest going-to-church white dress with pink flowers on the bodice. My silver hair was twisted so it puffed up stylishly around my forehead, then formed a bun in back. I even wore earrings and a pearl necklace this evening. Clara fixed me some ginseng tea to give my voice strength. As I lowered myself onto my throne, I smiled at my large audience sitting in chairs they brought from their houses, or on blankets on my lawn, or standing across the street, arms crossed, waiting to be transported to another time, to another place.

I centered myself, pulling an energizing breath in through my nose down my neck into my lungs then down to my belly. Blowing the used air out of my mouth, slowing my heart rate, calming the inner flutters, I began.

Slavery was still very much in evidence during the Civil War, from 1861 to 1865. Negro slaves were frequently sent on "The National Road"[64] which opened the Ohio River Valley and the Midwest for settlement. It linked the eastern and western states in the first half of the nineteenth century. The road ran from Baltimore through Hagerstown, then Cumberland, over the Allegheny Mountains to Uniontown and Wheeling, in what is now West Virginia. The road crossed the Ohio River, then on to Zanesville, past Columbus and Springfield in Ohio, through Indianapolis and Terre Haute in Indiana, ending in Illinois.

Slaves were driven over the main road, arranged in couples and fastened to a long, thick rope or cable or chains, just like horses pulling a plow or a carriage. This may seem unbelievable to the majority of people living now, but it was a very common site in the early history of the road. Nobody was surprised to see those fettered coffles[65] of slaves. Few spoke against the practice.

The sight of human property being driven to market—like a caravan of cattle, hogs, and sheep—reinforced fears of running away from the cruel institution. Every bondsman in the Upper North of Maryland and Virginia understood the penalties of running away: being starved, flogged, branded by burning metal on the skin, fingers, or toes. Runaways could have their feet cut off. But the ultimate punishment (other than death) was to be "Sold South" where the cruelest of masters worked slaves like machines, often working them to death, without a care in the world. Runaways were often sold away from their families never to be seen or heard from again. I paused for emphasis. The smell of freedom was strong, though, and many a slave followed their nose toward the land of milk and honey—the North—where they would be free to decide how they would live their lives.

Even in the free states, though, the thought of re-enslavement loomed large. Tavern keepers frequently aided in the capture of fugitive slaves along the national road, feeling it was their duty as current or former slave owners. Yes, children, I heard many stories about runaway slaves being recaptured, and free people of color being wrongly put into slavery, as I did the mistresses' business in the town of Beverly.

The unimaginable happened. A majority of voters wanted to break away from the southern sympathizing South to join the Union cause. Congress granted statehood to "West" Virginia and, in so doing, abolished slavery in all the counties west of the Allegheny Mountains of Virginia. Was there a joyful noise heard in Beverly all the way west to Wheeling? You better believe it.

Remember, Massa John's third wife-to-be, Elizabeth Currence, wanted me and my "dirty ragged pickaninnies" as she called us, gone from her sight. Consequently, off my children and I went on June 23, 1863, with a gladness in our hearts. Every night when I say my prayers, I bless that spiteful woman for giving us a life we would have never known had we stayed in Beverly.

The Trek To Ohio

You might be asking how a mother of five could travel 'bout 150 miles from Beverly, West Virginia, across the mighty Ohio River, into Barnesville, Ohio? (Figure 11) Did we travel with other ex-slaves, or free people of color, or relatives of Massa John Earle's family, or with some man protecting us—maybe a husband by the name of Booker?

People ask me all the time how long the trip took, what we ate every day, where we slept, how we took care of our personal bidness? Did we see Indians? Did bandits try to do us harm? Did I have a road map to know which roads to take and, if so, could I read it?

Folks just cain't believe I did that trip without help. I cain't believe I did the trip at all, but my desire to be free overcame all difficulties. I love telling my kin our legacy of bravery, escaping from a slave state to a free one.

"Mother," Joseph interrupted. "We didn't escape from Beverly."

"Oh, son, the story sounds so much more important and exciting that way," I pouted. "Yes, Massa John Earle, he done give me a buckboard (Figure 12) and a horse to take on our trip in the last week of June in 1863."

You all know well by now it was the year the Emancipation Proclamation freed us slaves in southern states who were fighting against the Union. West Virginia was created to fight for the Union. After that terrible, unthinkable, unforgivable painful tree of welts on my back that Massa gave me just days after Ella was born, Massa decided I should take our children to Ohio.

I know, I know, you're saying to yourself, "There's no way a woman could take care of, or have experience with, driving horses or mules long distances, especially not with a buckboard full of kids." Well, us slave women had to do a lot of things the mistress of the house coulda never dreamed about in her whole lifetime, or the next lifetime neither.

Figure 12. The actual seat is called a buckboard. It rides on a pair of leaf springs, which are bow-shaped bands of steel just below each side of the seat. The springs cushioned the ride on rough roads, but tended to bounce, or "buck" over bumps. Some had a box behind the buckboard in which people or goods could be carried.

"Tell the truth, sister!" my female neighbors exclaimed.

"Amen!" others shouted, clapping.

We slave women had to figure it out. Whatever problems came up, we had to handle lickety-split, on the spot. Besides, it was my children who had to take care of Massa's horses anyway. They knew how much water they needed, what type of grasses they liked, how to brush 'em and care for them. Am I right? Pointing to Joseph, Ella, and George, three of my now-grown children who made the trip with me.

"Yes, ma'am!" They responded in unison.

Our future started the morning of June 23, 1863. A day which would signal the beginning of our new lives. There wasn't much room in the small old buckboard Massa gave us, but we managed to cram our few clothes, blankets, metal plates, forks and knives, jugs for storing drinking water, and pots for cooking into the wagon part of the buckboard. Slaves don't own much, so we were able to tie everything down to hooks on the side of the buckboard.

"What did you eat along the road, Grandma?" Hastings asked.

Well, we brought beef jerky, and containers of cornmeal and flour so we could make hoe cakes[66] on the way. Our friends brought us going-away cakes and containers of butter and cheese. We were told we could gather and eat acorns along the route, grinding them like the Indians did. We could also pick sassafras root to chew on, as well as collect black cherry and sweet paw-paw fruit which I was told tastes like a pear mixed with apricot.[67]

I hid the gold locket Miz Betty gave me in a slit in one of the blankets we brought along in case someone tried to rob us of our few possessions on the trip. Massa John gave me enough money to pay the turnpike tolls, shopkeepers, and whatever else was needed. I also stored the freedom papers Massa gave me in a leather purse I wore around my waist under my dress, in case we was stopped by patroller [68] along the way. Even though the Emancipation Proclamation was passed and West Virginia abolished slavery, many Southern supporters did not recognize it as law and would eagerly sell blacks folks Down South. We gladly took those freedom papers with us on our trip.

Since we nearly filled the buckboard with our few possessions, there was only room on the seat for the two youngest children, May and George whose little legs would slow down our walking progress. Baby Ella stayed glued to my chest, wrapped in a cloth, and Joab and Cornelia could walk beside the buckboard.

Our friends came out to say goodbye, bringing cakes, jerky, blackberry tea in a pot that could be used to capture clean water from a river or rain. There were so many hugs, tears, kisses, and well-wishes for a safe trip and a happy new life. I could see the hunger in their eyes, yearning to be traveling with us. Deep down, all who were left behind suspected their lives would not change one lick, even though they were theoretically free. They would continue living in the same shack, doing the same jobs for the same white people, maybe making enough money to pay their room and board. Because most had no land of their own, they would be tied to those same masters as before...

The sun was blazing hot when we said the last goodbye and finally started our journey from Massa John's house at Crawford and Main Street. His house fronted the Old Indian Seneca Trail, now part of the wider Beverly-Fairmont Turnpike. The turnpike gave access to the new railroad which had reached the nearby town of Grafton that same year (Figure 13).

I learned that a turnpike is a public or private roadway for which a fee or toll is assessed for passage. Along the road were tollhouses, like where a valley narrowed or there was only one way to cross a stream. Travelers were forced to stop because there was a long pole (or pike) across the road. The tollhouse keeper would turn the pike to let us pass through once we paid the toll. Tolls helped with the cost of road construction and maintenance. People, wagons, and animals all had different toll fees. For example, a wagon, team of horses and driver cost 25 to 55 cents. A man with one horse was six cents. Twenty sheep or hogs cost four cents.[69]

I know how to do many things exceptionally well and I'm not afraid of much. But deep down in my belly, I knew there was no way I could do the trip by myself. I couldn't read much and didn't know my numbers well. Even though Joab did have those skills, I worried that those tollkeepers coulda easily cheated me outta money. I would need someone to go with me, someone who knew how to deal with other men, knew the route, had the right amount of money, and knew where to stop each night.

I told Massa John about my concerns, so he got on his horse to ride with us to Stalnakers' to pick up Joab working nearby.

He explained that I would probably be charged thirty cents for each of the eight tolls we would pass through. He suggested hiding the money he gave me for the tolls in a pouch around my waist, inside my skirt. Massa already arranged for us to stay with my Pappy in his house on Vine Street in Barnesville. He even gave me $50 to help Pappy pay for our keep until I could get a job there. I put that money next to Miz Betty's locket for safe keeping.

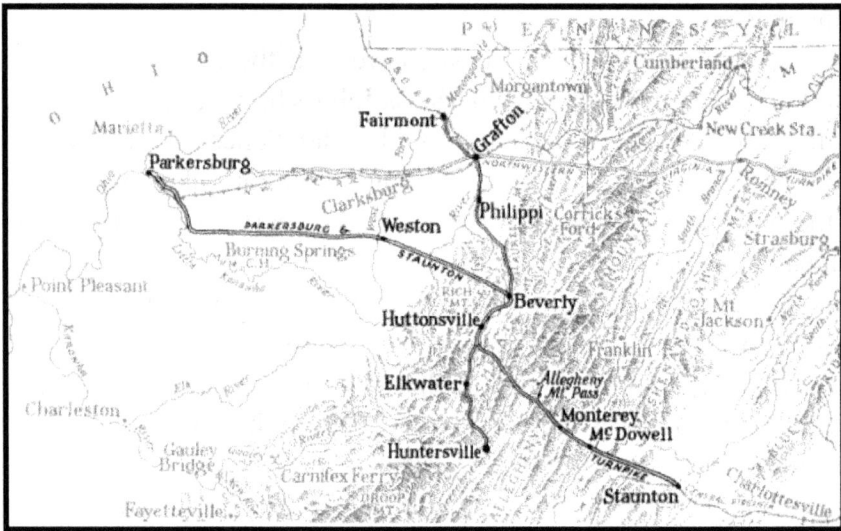

Figure 13: 1870 Map, showing the Beverly-Fairmont Turnpike route toward Martin's Ferry.

When we got to John Stalnaker's house, Hugh was grinning from ear to ear, more than happy to accompany us to Ohio. Even though I'm a capable woman, I breathed a long sigh of relief that he was going with us. When we arrived, he had a knapsack packed with the clothes and food he would carry on his back. Remember, Hugh, George and I had spent my first twelve years together so I felt safe with him, even though we hadn't seen each other much in the past eighteen years since I been with the Earles. Two hands taller than me, deep-set brown eyes, strong arms and thighs, and an ample bottom. I was surprised to feel a little quiver down there—pointing at my private parts.

"Mother!" Ella disapproved my talking this way with young children around.

Look, daughter dear, I'm just telling the truth. He was tall and chocolatey and muscular, with a great smile. Let an old woman have her tasty memories, would ya? I'm sure your brother Edward H. Booker wouldn't mind this story...

Anyway, while Hugh and me was talking about the trip ahead, Massa John said he'd go and pick up Joab hisself. Joseph, why don't you tell this part of the story since you lived it.

✎

"Certainly, Mother. Father had a different plan in mind for his firstborn mulatto son—me.

"He said, 'I want to talk seriously with you, Joab.' He never once in my life acknowledged me as his true-born son."

"Yeah, what do you want?" I nearly spat in response, not caring what he might do to me for my insolence.

"With a pleading look, Father begged, 'Please stay here and help me with the plantation. You grew up here. This is your home. You'll always have a home with me. I'll give you the cabin. You can raise your own family, work the mill with me, be your own man. You are my son after all, and I want you to stay.[70] Please...' he pleaded, crying.

"I laughed in his face, fairly spitting as I said, 'So now you call me your son now that you need me to keep working for you. Well, I'll never forget what you did to my mother. Her body was still hurting from just having your baby, and you tried to force her to...'"

"I know, I know." Father interrupted. "Listen, I still can't believe I did that to her. I… I was crazy in that moment. It had been so long since…" John Earle was interrupted.

"No, you listen to me!" Joab shouted. "I never ever want to live with you or see you ever again. The 'tree' of lashes you marked my mama's back with will always be with her. If I gave into your request it would be like I beat her too. She's done too much for me and way too much for you to betray her like that. There is something you can do, though, to make up for beating her and kicking us out of your home simply because your new young blond wife-to-be is jealous of Mother."

"A haggard look had overtaken Father's face, but he asked, 'What can I do, son, to get you to stay and help me run this place?'

"I grinned, believing I had the upper hand. 'Simple. You can give us enough money so we can live a more comfortable life, like that you provide for your full-white children. And I don't mean that little bit of money you likely gave Mother to pay for this trip to Barnesville. I mean that you can set us up in a nice house, not the shack you call a cabin you had us living in here. If you do that for us, I will allow you to visit once in a while and see your precious mulatto children that you now say you love so much."

❧

"Wow!" exclaimed the listeners, all eyes wide with shock at Joab, uh, Joseph's boldness.

"What did Massa John say to that?" someone asked.

"Well, Mother? Did our father set you up in a nice house?"

Hmmm, what should I say? Joseph is still so angry, forty years after the fact.

I replied, "It's not a palace, but I must admit we are living in a much better place than the slave shack back home. And Massa John did ensure we had a place waiting for us in Pappy's house. My oh my, I never did ask if it was Massa John who paid off the mortgage. Massa's nephew living in Barnesville did find a family I could work for during the first year we were here. Massa did send a little money for Christmas presents for a few years, but he never did visit us or write to us. None of your half brothers or sisters by Miz Betty, or Missus Labana, or certainly not Miz Elizabeth Currence ever visited or wrote to us. So, I would have to admit that Massa did do some nice things for us. But after he died in 1881, the Christmas money stopped and as far as I know, he didn't leave us anything in his Will."

❧

Herbert whined, "But what about the trip? What actually happened? Did you see any bears? Any pirates? Did anyone get sick? Did a snake bite you? Were fat rats crawling on your legs at night? Did you see any Indians? Did soldiers bother you? Did you get lost? What happened, Grandma?" He ended his tirade arms akimbo, fingers splayed wide, daring me to avoid answering him this time.

I smiled at my grandson's impatience. It meant he was so interested that he wanted to become part of my story. I finally made Herbert happy.

A-hem, I cleared my throat. Along the way to Barnesville, Hugh showed us the best places to fill the jug with clean water, which plants were safe to eat and which were poisonous. He kept us feeling safe. Honestly, looking back on our adventure, the trek to Barnesville ended up being easier than I originally feared. Since he was a man, Hugh had more opportunities than me to travel on his own, to meet all kinds of people, to learn the ways of white men, and to hear stories about stations along the Underground Railroad. He had a pretty good idea about what to expect on our trip, where to stop at night, how to pay tolls, and how to get decent food. Plus, he was good company. Real good company if you know what I mean… I winked at the women in attendance.

"Mother!" daughter Ella scolded me again, and I chuckled at her purity. It was true, though, the man knew what he was doing.

That's how Ella got her younger brother Edward, born the year following our trek to Ohio.

A daffy smile painted my lips red as I continued my story. Hugh and I slept under the stars, while our children crowded under the buckboard on leaves we spread on the ground. It was summertime, so it wasn't cold. We snuggled all night, looking up at the endless stars and the nearly full moon, imagining our future in paradise. Ah, those were lovely evenings indeed...

The twittering of birds and the slight scent of skunk woke us from our evening dreams of flying through the air to our new home. Night animals like lynx and fox and rat scurried to get their last prey before we humans disrupted their hunting. The familiar smell of wood fires greeted our noses, as the homes near the route, or travelers like us, started their day.

Beams of orange light shone through spaces between the dark tree branches, like the Lord's fingers reaching out from his white-hot sun to personally touch each of us. "Wake up now, my children, to a beautiful new day," I squatted under the buckboard, whispering into their ears.

Overall, the trip from Beverly to Barnesville went well.

Nobody went hungry. Every day we made a game of finding cherries, paw-paw, and nuts along the route. We chewed stiff beef jerky from our pack and sassafras root dug along the way. I made hoe cakes from corn meal and flour over the morning fire. We had plenty to eat because Hugh and Joab caught fish from the rivers and creeks, and there was plenty of dry wood and brush to make a fire for cooking wherever we stopped.

Nobody was bored. We sang church hymns and made up silly songs. We talked about what our new lives would be like. We spoke of the friends and family we left behind. We raced to see who could get to the next tree the fastest. For the most part, the kids only asked, "Are we almost there yet?" about twenty-five times a day. Many snickered from the audience, knowing all too well how impatient children can be.

Nobody was affected too much by the war going on around us. Sure, we heard Boom! Crack! Pow! in the far mountains, and when we saw soldiers on the road, we pulled the horse and buckboard out of their way and waited quietly until they left. In general, though, we felt pretty safe.

Nobody got sick on the journey, and we made good progress every day because Hugh could carry one of the little ones if their legs got tired. Our feet were exceptionally sore, though, walking up to twenty miles each day.

Nobody robbed us or tried to mess with our money in any way. Hugh was a big man and he walked and talked with confidence. People felt comfortable around him when he smiled. Nobody asked for our freedom papers. The tolls got paid with little problem, and some of the stationmasters even gave us directions to the next toll booth.[71]

Nobody complained about the weather. Massa John was right when he suggested we leave in June when there would be more sun, less rain, fewer muddy roads, and more stars in the night sky. We were lucky and didn't have but one day of rain, so we didn't worry about sleeping in mud or the wheels of the buckboard getting stuck.

"Someone was looking out for us, to be sure." I looked upward.

"Amen, sister girl," said someone from the dark.

Altogether the trip took about a week and a half, I think. Not bad at all. We basically took the first half of the same route that Pappy Ned took in 1855 when he traveled from Randolph County to the Fusion Convention in Ravenna, Ohio. (Chapter 7). We crossed the Virginia-to-Ohio state line on a ferry, holding our breath on the Wheeling, Virginia, side of the Ohio River, and celebrating when we arrived at Martin's Ferry, Ohio. We kneeled and kissed the ground. We were actually, finally, really, and forever, free people of color.

My audience stood and clapped. It was time for cake.

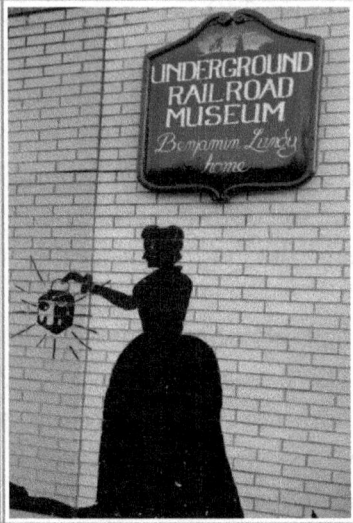

Chapter 15 - Life in Barnesville

"Once upon a time in Belmont County, Ohio. Today we are going to learn about the Underground Railroad."

My eldest daughter, Cornelia, and her husband, Joseph Anderson, had eleven kids so it was too expensive to travel with all of them on the Baltimore and Ohio (B & O) train from Pittsburgh to Barnesville (Figure 14). So today, in the middle of the 1903 August heat, Cornelia only brought her youngest girls with her, aged eighteen to seven: Grendola, Edna, Leona (like Massa John's daughter), Hazel, and Evelina (like Pappy Ned's wife Eve). Little did I know this would be the last time I would see my eldest daughter, for she would pass away in October the following year.

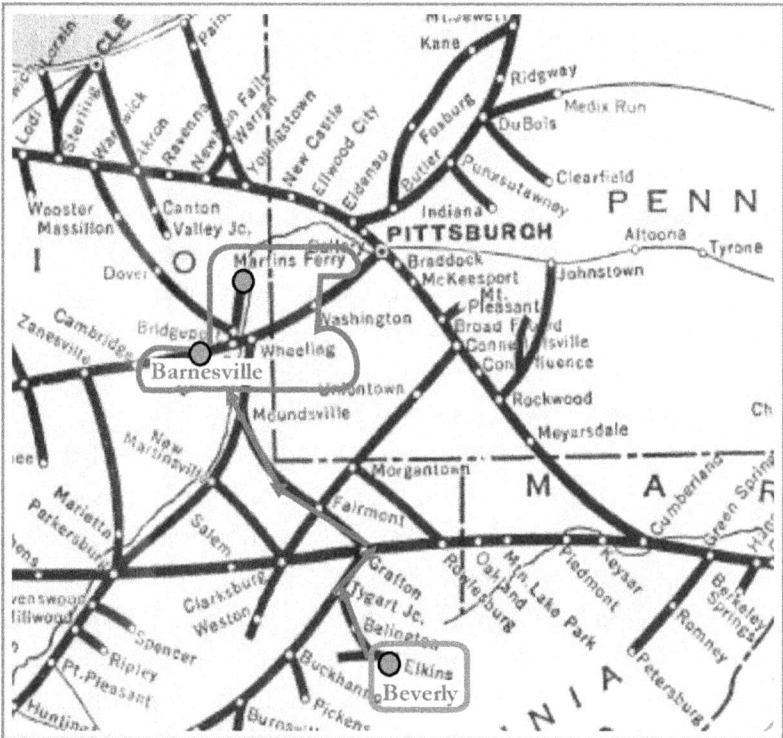

Figure 14: B&O Railroad route from Beverly, West Virginia, to Barnesville, Ohio.

I began tonight's story. Oh, if only I could have ridden the B&O Railroad from Elkins, West Virginia, directly to Barnesville. Instead, it took my children and Hugh and I a week and a half to walk here, the youngest kids riding in that bumpity buckboard. But I am lucky to have received the transportation and financial help Massa John gave me to start our new life here. I am more than grateful my Pappy let us stay in this house with him and my stepmother Eve.

I remember being at the market one day in about 1860 or so. I was picking up some fresh trout, peaches, and cornmeal for Massa's dinner and I waved at my friend Lydia Ann. She had gotten special approval from the court in 1829 to stay in Beverly, even though she had been freed by her master. She was a distinguished lady, held in the highest esteem in our small colored community.

Lydia Ann pulled me aside. Her eyes shifted back and forth over the crowd, then she whispered, "The Underground Railroad's comin' to town. Some folks is gonna want to hop on board. Uh-oh, those 'crackers' [72] are watching us. You know how they do whenever we get our heads together... they think we're trying to take over or something!"

"Miss Lydia, you got that right!" I chuckled. "As if we could ever take over," I said, with my back to her, as I pretended to squeeze a peach for ripeness. Darn. When I turned around to hear more about this railroad, she had already moved on, without giving me more details.

So, I began strolling down the stalls of vegetables, with my woven basket that I made last year from vines and grasses, ready to fill it up. I wondered if I could fit in that good-lookin' ham hanging from the metal hook in Mr. Ames' stall with the rest of my purchases. Maybe Missus Labana would like me to get some chickens for tomorrow's dinner. Hmmm, those tomatoes are early for the season. I droned on and on about nothing important.

"Grandma! Stop playing around! Tell us about the Underground Railroad! We don't care about no tomatoes. We've been wondering what that train was when you mentioned it last story time," Hastings nearly shouted at me. Then he remembered who he was talking to and apologized to his elder. Smart boy. I couldn't scold him, though, because I was playin' with him, stringing out the suspense for all it was worth. I'm old now and I gots to git what I kin git. Gotta make sure these children are really listening to my stories so they can pass them on.

I responded to Hastings' comment. "None of you ever heard of the Underground Railroad in school?" Heads shook. "That makes sense. The ones in power don't want anyone to know their white neighbors was helping slaves escape under their very noses. You see—I leaned in, speaking low and slow—this secret railroad was constructed without the sound of a hammer, pick or shovel, and could be removed from one neighborhood to another, leaving no trace that anyone except those identified with it, could find."[73]

"What? We still don't understand what you're talking about, Grandma."

I continued in my normal voice. The Underground Railroad was a network of "stations"—generally in abolitionist's houses. Those good people housed and fed runaway slaves for a night or two, sending them to the next safe house on the line, until the slave finally made it to a free state—like here in Ohio—or to freedom in Canada, the country north of the United States.

"What do you mean by 'safe house'?" Granddaughter Leona asked. Cornelia's children had not heard many of my stories because they couldn't visit but once in a blue moon. In this case, nobody had heard about this important underground road to freedom.

I continued my story. People known as "conductors" guided the runaway slaves. Hiding places included private homes, churches, and schoolhouses. These were called "stations," or "safe houses," or "depots"—the same names used for real train lines. The people operating them were called "stationmasters."

There were many well-used routes from the southern states stretching west through Ohio to Indiana and Iowa. Others headed north through Pennsylvania and into New England, or through Detroit, Michigan, on their way to Canada.[74] There were safe houses in and around Beverly too, one was thought to be in the home of Confederate General Stonewall Jackson's sister, Laura Jackson Arnold. Imagine being a runaway hidden in her attic while her famous brother—one of the best Generals the Rebels had—was eating dinner right below them?

Anyway, the Ohio Valley area where we are now was very active in Underground Railroad activities. It's been the home of many Quaker settlers, most who were passionate abolitionists and call themselves the "Society of Friends." In fact, Martin's Ferry, which we reached after crossing the Ohio River from Wheeling, West Virginia, was a major stop on the Underground Railroad. The station there was in the woods and underbrush that crowned the hills between Martin's Ferry and Burlington. It was located near colored Richard Naylor and Samuel Cooper's houses. Strangely, their depot was known and approved by white confederates and their co-workers.[75] So, my children, whether you knew it or not, you already took a ride on the Freedom Train when we left for Barnesville in 1863.

[Author's note: An Underground Railroad Museum was founded in 1993 by Dr. John Mattox in Flushing, Ohio, only fifteen miles from Margaret Booker's home in Barnesville.[76]]

"I thought you said President Lincoln already freed us in that 'Mancipation Procla-whatever," Herbert objected.

Well, during the Civil War, the southern states split from the Union and didn't care to follow rules made by a Union President. Any colored person traveling around the South before 1865 when slavery was officially outlawed everywhere, could—and sometimes were—sold back into slavery. Remember when I said Massa Stalnaker freed George and Hugh in his Will in February 1863? Well, people in Beverly treated them like they was still his family's property up until Hugh came with us to Beverly months later. During our trip here, any one of us coulda been stopped by patrollers and sold South if we hadda lost the Freedom Papers Massa John wrote for us. Every day on our trip to Ohio, I was biting my fingernails in fear that we wouldn't make it.

Cornelia, you asked why I came here to the village of Barnesville? There was jobs here for all people and Massa John had some family in Belmont County. You are Massa John's blood kin, after all. He wanted to be sure his children were in a safe place. The most important reason, though, was that my Pappy was already living in this house and he invited us to live with him. Massa John mighta given Pappy some money to house us, in addition to the horse and buckboard.

"Mother, you never told me all that. I always thought Grandpa and Eve were living with us, not the other way around," Cornelia objected.

I certainly did tell everyone, at the end of Ned's Story, remember? (Chapter 7). Oh, that's right, y'all weren't here for that tale. I'll have to tell you all about your grandpappy tomorrow morning, after you fix me breakfast. It'll be like the old days when I was doing my best to take care of you, but in reverse now.

A History Lesson

"What was Barnesville like when you first came here?" Cornelia's daughter, Grendola, asked.

I was told the area around Barnesville was settled by pioneer families, mostly Quakers, coming from Maryland, Pennsylvania, and some southern states. James Barnes started developing the town of "Barnesville" on his land in the Warren township in 1808. He first built a meeting house, then a graveyard. The town was laid out and divided into blocks of two acres each along Main Street, with separate lots of one-fourth acre each. Of the hundred or so initial parcels, Barnes reserved the corner lot at Main and Chestnut Streets for his family home. During the next years, the Barnes brothers and other Quakers, built a tannery, a brickyard, mills, and several farming and crop lands.

James Barnes opened the first store a coupla years later. It contained dry goods, groceries, hardware, holloware,[77] glassware, leather, salt, etc. On Main Street there was a cabinetmaker, several blacksmiths, a silversmith, a tinner,[78] a stonemason,[79] a tailor, a shoemaker, and a hatter. There was a nail factory, drug store, and a hotel with a stoop that extended the length of the building. Several large brick buildings housed smaller businesses, like a mercantile[80] and storerooms. By the 1830s, there were still a few one- and two-story log homes. One was used to fire tobacco before packing it into hogsheads for shipment.

"Oooh! They put tobacco inside a goopy, bloody hog's head?" Edna grimaced. "And then someone smoked the tobacco? Yuck!" she exclaimed with a look of distaste written all over her face.

"I imagine they had a reason for doing that, but it does sound gruesome, although I think a hogshead is a kind of barrel," I smiled.

Two-story frame houses and weathered board structures were popular. Fires were always a scary occurrence, for they could destroy an entire town in a short time, so less-flammable brick was becoming more popular for buildings. A little old schoolhouse was built from brick on Chestnut Street. The "Bradfield block" housed the bank. Mr. Bradfield was one of the richest people in Beverly.

There was even a tall two-story log building to dry Chinese ginseng. In fact, the gathering and shipment of the ginseng root was a noted industry in town, often as much as thirty-thousand pounds being shipped a year.[81] It makes a peppery, spicy, almost bitter tea that's good for an upset tummy. I add honey to make it delicious.

There were sixty-four houses used as dwellings, for a population of four hundred. By the turn of the century, there were ten times as many people living here, over 4,000.[82] More settlers started moving here when the railroad was built through the town, leading to more people coming and twelve different churches being built to accommodate 'em.

City folk started tearing down them original town buildings, replacing them with the Victorian style which we have to this day. Now, when you go down Main Street, you'll see flat-topped red brick buildings, large brown stone buildings with arched windows and, of course, some fancy Victorian buildings like the Bradfield Mansion.

A Barnesville for Us

The Belmont Glass Company was established a few years after I came, creating jobs for whites and coloreds. Even though we got the physically hardest and most dangerous jobs for the lowest pay, we was working and were able to buy houses and nice things for our families, like we never could before in the South.

The Watt family started a small foundry when I came here, producing plow points for farming. By the end of the decade, their business had expanded to the Watt Car and Wheel Company, producing cook stoves and mining car wheels. A few years later, they began manufacturing mining cars because coal became so important for heating homes and running engines and such.[83] This created more jobs that our strong men could work.

"How many colored people lived here when you came in 1863?" Leona asked.

Well, I did hear of a colored man, Lee Baler, who liked to worship at the Methodist Church. Unfortunately, a fellow named James Riggs moved here from Hagerstown, Maryland, and built a nail factory in town. He hated Negroes and was said to have "escorted" Lee Baler out of the church. The other church members didn't want to cross the new businessman who had created jobs for their families[84,] so they didn't stand up for poor Lee Baler. He did nothing wrong by wanting to worship in a church that was supposed to believe that all men were children of God."

"What's new?" Sylvester added a snide, but true, comment.

During the 1840s, a Methodist Reverend came to town with a few slaves. That was frowned upon in an Ohio church, so the Methodist Church became divided into North and South sympathizing members and eventually led to the African Methodist Church being established.

Another story I heard was about Sammy Williams, an old slave who came to town in the 1840s with his wife and many children. The townspeople sent the Sheriff after him, but Sammy hadn't done anything wrong, so he couldn't be arrested.

"Again, what's new?" commented Sylvester, who had seen his share of misdeeds toward colored folks, even in "The Promised Land."

I cleared my throat but did not comment on his truthful observation. "If I may continue... At first, the talkative Sammy tried to be a preacher, but he failed at that. Next, he became a stump speaker and auctioneer, but that didn't work either. He gossiped about folks, sold all sorts of junk, and ran his mouth on street corners. The townspeople became tired of his rantings, kids even stoned him to shut him up. Well, sadly, after the age of eighty-three, Sammy froze to death one night."

Silence.

Here's a positive story. A woman named Silky made her way to the black Captina Creek community in Belmont County a few miles south of Barnesville. While living there, she engaged in domestic work for a white family at fifty cents a week. When she had built up her savings to eighty dollars, she bought fifty acres and a cow to make a home of her own.

She met another former slave, a blacksmith named George Turner who had purchased his own freedom by saving up the $300 necessary to buy it. They married and had two sons and a daughter. Their daughter, Margaret, married Joseph Betts and they moved to Old Washington. After her husband died, Silky ended her days living with Margaret's family in Guernsey County. Having spent her first twenty-one years in slavery, Silky was in her early sixties when the Civil War was fought. She then spent her last twenty-one years as a full American, having made a good life for herself. That's a pretty nice story, eh?

Some nodded, others looked bored.

When we came here in 1863, there was mostly whites from Ohio, Virginia, and Pennsylvania, but some were born in Europe. There were very few black or mulatto folk, aside from us, Stewart and Angelina Betts, George and Martha Nicholson, James and Joanna Brannon, the Linns, the Myers, the Cowens, and a handful of others I can't recall right now. Most coloreds lived on Vine, South, and Chestnut Streets.

"Did anyone else from Beverly live in Barnesville?" Granddaughter Edna asked.

"Except for Pappy and Eve, not that I can recall, but the Betts, Nicholsons, and Linns came from Virginia, as did the white Gills, Odowds, and some Moores."

While he was throwing a ball into the air over and over again, Herbert asked, "What'd you all do when you came here, Grandma?"

That boy better become a good baseball player as often as he's always messing with that ball.

We stayed with Pappy at this house, right here. Back then, it looked a bit different than it does now with this white siding. It used to be a log home before Pappy bought it in 1861.

We had a big garden out back. Pappy assigned a different gardening task to each of my children. Joseph helped him with the disc harrow to till the soil where Mama Eve's garden crops would be planted. Pappy created the furrows and sections of the plot for each type of vegetable or fruit. Eve was a collector of vegetable seeds from the previous season's crops and from the store. She had several dried seeds to choose from, like mustard greens, tomatoes, green peas, cabbage, lettuce, black-eyed peas, and watermelons.

We had a separate area for a "hotbed" partially covered in straw to warm up the soil. We would sometimes start the seeds when the weather was still too cold for full planting. The children would pour buckets of water around the seeded soil. The youngest kids were responsible for watching to see when the seedlings began popping up. "Mama, mama," little May would cry. "I see something green coming outta the dirt!" We were extra careful to make sure the new sprouts did not wither, giving them more water. When they were several inches tall, we would transplant the seedlings to the regular garden which provided most of our food.

Pappy kept chickens and hogs to provide us with eggs and meat products. Three-year-olds were taught how to carefully retrieve the eggs from the warm nests and place them gently in a woven basket. Four-year-olds graduated to feeding slops to the hogs and making sure they had enough water in their pens. Everybody pulled their weight.

Six-year-olds could learn to milk our one cow, Missy, and seven-year-olds separated the cream from the milk and churned it into butter.

The girls were taught to cook, launder, and sew clothes and blankets and the boys did most of the farming chores, like everywhere else, I imagine. Looking back, I shoulda made those boys do more work so some of 'em would be more productive now.

My gaze traveled to Sylvester and George who were still living with me but not contributing much to the household. (George moved to Wheeling, West Virginia, the following year and found a woman to marry.)

In the 1870s, the strawberry industry begun by Mr. Barr a decade earlier had become famous. For many years as many as thirty thousand bushels of strawberries were harvested a season and were shipped to the big city markets. We had a whole row in the garden dedicated to strawberries out back. Everyone volunteered to pick them, but I doubt that all the ripe strawberries made it into the basket for the rest of us to eat. I gave a side glance to my children who promptly bowed their heads.

❦

Most of the streets were not paved before 1891. Flooded roads could be a problem for those of us living on the lower end of the sloped streets. In fact, the first paved streets were laid on Main Street from Lincoln Avenue to Broadway, and on Arch from Church Street. Our neighborhood was a few streets to the south, graveled, but not paved like those downtown streets a few blocks away. Muddy rain boots were left on the porch outside our front door during rainy periods.

We had to huddle with each other during the freezing winter months. We used sheets of paper from the Montgomery Ward shopping catalog to paper our walls. We wadded up old newspapers to plug up holes and spaces between the wall boards to help keep the cold air out. There was only one wood stove for cooking and heating the whole house. We stored wood under the house to keep it as dry as possible. Pappy and Eva said it was actually more pleasant and warmer having so many bodies sharing the house with them in the wintertime. That made us feel welcome and not a burden.

We Were a Working-Class Neighborhood.

Soon after arriving in Barnesville, we got to know a little about the town. Pappy and Eve took us to church that first Sunday after we arrived, over to Captina African Methodist Episcopal Church. That's where I met other folk who would become my lifelong friends. They schooled me on where the best markets were, where the kids could go to school, which white folks might be looking for a housekeeper or laundress, and other important things like that.

I was lucky that my next door neighbor, Maria Phillips, hired me right away. It was so close to home that I could keep an eye out on the kids. Plus, Cornelia was about seven and Joseph nine or ten, so they had to learn quickly how to handle the young'uns when I was away working. In a few years, Joseph and George helped Pappy working our farm that butts up to Southern Cemetery property.

Many colored women took in laundry to pay the bills. Ella and May helped me wash and hang the clothes out to dry. A long line of shirts and pants, sheets and towels flapped in the steady breeze in back of our houses, from one end of Vine Street to the other.

A few women, like my granddaughter Clara, became cooks. A lot of Negro women did housework in private homes. They were called "servants." Ella was a servant for the Crew family in 1880 when she was seventeen.

Many of the men drove wagons for hauling lumber or junk to the Transfer station. Neighbor John Lynch worked in the stone quarry and several men labored in the foundry. David Petterson had a real good job as an engineer in the paper mill. John McCourtney and William Ellis owned their own barbershops. The Columbian Hotel on Main Street employed some of us as porters and servants. Most men labored at odd jobs, called "working out."

Very few of us just sat around day after day, smoking and drinking their lives away. It was all I could do to avoid looking at George and Sylvester.

Barnesville is where we met the Myers and Walkers who intermarried with our Booker family. Many of us migrated to Mount Vernon, located in the center of Ohio. Oh, the stories we would tell about slavery days when we got together. Children today have it so easy in Ohio. We old codgers must school youngsters to what real work was like down South so they can appreciate their good fortune here, and not squander their opportunities.

Reading and Writing and 'Rithmetic

Perhaps the most important thing about being in Ohio was that my children could go to school. Getting an education was the key to having a better life. Big Peg told me that, but I already knew it. After the Civil War the Freedmen's Bureau helped build schools for colored children in the South. Quakers and black churches built schools in the North.

One of my proudest moments was escorting Joseph and Cornelia and George to their new school. All Negro parents encouraged their children to pursue an education, so few missed a day of elementary school. In the South, most colored children could only go to school six or so months out of the year during the fall and winter, having to help with planting and harvesting during the spring and summer. Kids in many northern communities could go to school for the entire nine months, because farming was not the only job opportunity in town. This greatly improved their chances to get a good education, leading to a better job and better life.

Free blacks could now urge their children to concentrate on their dreams and goals instead of the legal roadblocks white folks consistently put in our paths. Schools for colored children were generally separate and unequal from those of the whites. Hand-me-down books with missing or tattered pages came from the white schools. There was no heat in the classrooms and minimally-trained teachers. But that was not always true in Ohio towns, as my son Joseph would find out later when he moved his family to Mount Vernon, Ohio. Schools were integrated there. Joseph's daughter, Myrtle, graduated from Mt. Vernon High School in 1899, one of two colored girls in a class of thirty-five. She was expected to learn all the same subjects as the white kids, including French.

"Mais oui, grand-mère," ("But of course, grandmother.") Myrtle replied. "And I expect my children will carry on that tradition."

Until 1855, very little was done to educate colored children in Barnesville. Their first teacher was Jesse Hargrave, partly paid by the parents and partly out of public funds. In that year a school district for colored children was formed. A room was rented on Arch Street and Miss Price was the teacher. In 1868, a brick schoolhouse was erected for them about a quarter of a mile south of town. The school was over McKeever's hardware store. By 1900, there were about 150 colored students going to school there.[85]

We encouraged our children to read as much as they could and to learn how math could help them manage a farm or get a good job. Education is everything! Don't ever forget that children.

Fun Times

"Work, work, work. What did you do for fun?" Hastings interrupted again. I glared at him for a pregnant moment until he looked down at his hands.

We sometimes held Pumpkin or Harvest Festivals at the end of September. Just imagine standing alongside Main Street. The sun is bright, but the weather is chilly. Trees lining the street are starting to put on their autumn robes, changing their leafy garments from green to orange to red. In the distance, we hear the thump, thump, thumpity-thump of drums coming toward us. We soon see a line of uniformed marchers holding blaring trumpets, pounding their big drums with long sticks, twittering flutes, and strumming banjoes. The pumpkin parade is coming down Main Street toward us. We clap and cheer as the band walks by. Then come the horses pulling wagons with huge, misshapen orangey pumpkins inside. The mayor or another important person is sitting on the seat waving at us. People dressed in pumpkin-shaped hats dance around the wagons, sometimes throwing wrapped candies to the laughing children. As the parade passes, the crowd follows it to the park where there are pumpkin pie cooking and pie throwing contests, musicians, dancers, and plenty of pumpkin juice tasting. The highlight of the day is the giant pumpkin weigh-in, some of the huge orange globs weighing hundreds of pounds. Does that sound like fun?

Bored, Hastings replied in a monotone, "Sure, anything else?"

Son Sylvester added, "Fishing was always relaxing, if you got a good spot underneath the shade of a tree. Me and Edward and our friends would go to Chestnut Creek in the morning. We'd bring spools of string, worms, a knife, one metal hook, and a bucket. When we got there, we'd looked for straight sturdy branches to use as fishing poles. We'd use the knife to strip off twigs and leaves. We tied a twenty-foot long string onto the thinner end of the stick and wrapped it around a bright-colored one-inch rock. Holding the thick end of the pole in our left hand, we tossed the rock into the creek with our right. To attract a fish, we'd jerk the rod up and down, up and down, making the rock dance in the water. Believe it or not, sometimes we actually caught fish that way. Usually, though, we'd tie a worm, and maybe a colorful piece of cloth or wrapper onto the string above the rock.

"We learned to be creative and patient. When the string pulled tight it meant a fish had swallowed the rock. Game on! We'd pull the pole up and back toward the shore, hoping the rock didn't come outta the fish's mouth. Whoopin' an' hollerin', 'I got one! I got a big one!' so the others would come to watch. We'd pull the wriggling fish out of the creek and place it in the bucket filled with water. Once, I caught three fish that way. Realistically, we usually needed to use a hook to ensure the fish stayed caught, but we often only had one hook for four boys, so we had to be creative. Proudly, we'd bring our catch home to mama in the bucket, thinking she would take it and do whatever was necessary to have a fish fry for our dinner. But no, she'd give us a spoon and tell us to scrap the scales off its sides into some old newspaper. Then she'd make us pull out the bloody guts before she would clean and fry it for supper. The delicious end result was worth the trouble," Sylvester said, smacking his lips.

"Well, I caught four fish one day," younger Edward bragged.

Son George spoke up. "If it was too hot to play on the porch, we would find a shady spot under the big tree over there (pointing to the tree in the front yard). We found pieces of wood to make trucks. We made the wheels from old bottle tops from the store. Large jar tops attached together became double tires for the truck's front wheels. Smaller jar tops attached together became the back wheels. We used old screws, nails, ropes and wires to keep our trailers and tractors in tip-top shape. We built our own roads and bridges, digging trenches in the dirt under the house. We used twigs, rocks, or wood to drive our trucks through tunnels or over bridges and through rough terrain. Edward and I made a good team even though we were six years apart in age. Joseph was only interested in school and didn't play much with us."

"I guess that sounds like fun," Hastings said.

We adults enjoyed attending our Secret Societies. The colored Odd Fellows and Knights of Pythias were active and vigorous organizations which catered to brickmasons and other skilled craftsmen. Those organizations made us feel on a par with whites.

Whatever we were doing, whether it was working in the garden or fields, going to school or attending church services, we enjoyed ourselves. That's what families in our community were like.

The House of the Lord

"What church did you say you went to again, Grandma?" Maude Ellen asked, as she was bouncing her whining baby boy on her lap.

From the first Sunday we attended, I was welcomed into the Captina A.M.E. Church about five miles away. It has an interesting history and still is the rock of the colored community here.

The village of Captina, which was originally called Guinea, became a stop on the Underground Railroad. Like the Quakers in the area, free blacks directed slaves along the stations. Guinea had cross-connections to Somerton, where Dr. William Schooley helped the runaways. Stops were also located in Belmont, Quaker City and Barnesville, as I already mentioned.

Guinea was known as a safe stop where the residents were well-armed and ready to fight if they needed to. Following the end of the Civil War and slavery, Captina continued to be a farming community and the church continued to be the center of it. The historic Captina A.M.E. Church cemetery dates back to 1830 (Figure 15). Interred there are one Mexican War veteran and nine Civil War veterans. Also interred there is Underground Railroad conductor Alexander "Sandy" Harper. He owned the 300-acre property, prior to 1825 when the church was established.

The Captina cemetery stands as evidence of a once thriving African-American farming community established in the 1820s with the aid of Harper, who was the community's leader. It was the only free settlement of African Americans in Ohio, prior to the Civil War and was the first in Belmont County.[86]

Christmas was a special time too. The church selected neighborhood colored children to play the parts of Joseph and Mary, the baby Jesus, and the three wise men. They told the wonderful story of the Christ child's humble birth at a special Christmas Eve program. We lit candles at the evening service and sang hymns. The next morning, we had a special breakfast at home, then at the church.

We colored citizens from Barnesville attended Captina until the Bethel A.M.E. church was formed in 1864. It was closer to home so we usually worshipped there on Sundays and for Bible study on Wednesday nights.

The African Methodist Episcopal church was organized in 1863, with a membership of twenty-five persons. The old threshing machine factory of Henry Noris was bought by the society which fit it up as a place of worship. It is still standing on the corner of S. Street and Reeds Rolle, but the congregation had outgrown it and in 1894, a new church was erected on W. South St. It is a large structure, very conveniently arranged on the interior. It is surmounted by a belfry in which hangs the old bell which for so many years called the Methodist to worship at their church on the corner of Chestnut and church streets. When Mr. Bradfield bought the old Methodist Church, he gave the bell to the colored people and they hung it in their church. It is said to be one of the finest toned bells ever cast.

The membership of this church is about fifty with

Figure 15: Captina African Methodist Episcopal Church, Belmont County, OH.

Reverend Morton being the present pastor. The A.M.E. Sunday school was first organized at Stillwater and was moved to Barnesville in 1865. Mr. William King was the first superintendent and remained as such for thirty years. About sixty members went to that church.[87]

I taught the children to say their prayers every night, thanking the Lord for the blessings He bestowed upon this colored family. He made it possible for us to live in a safe home with quiet neighbors—the cemetery behind our backyard (smile). He ensured we have enough food to eat—the kitchen garden behind the house. The Good Lord also helped me to establish my own business.

Chapter 16 - Minding My Own Business

"Once upon a time in Belmont, Ohio... I now get to start my stories, instead of Ol' Virginny…"

At the beginning of 1863, I was nearly thirty years a slave, but by the end of that year I was a free woman in Ohio, earning my own money by working next door as a cook and house cleaner. I lived in a real home with my Pappy and stepmother Eve, taking care of just my family, not answering to anyone else except myself. I pinched myself on that first Christmas Day of freedom, marveling at how far I had come.

"Why did you want to start a laundry business?" Joseph asked.

Well, nearly all the black working women in these parts were household workers, called "maids" here. Most of 'em began domestic work as teenagers and worked until they were sixty-five or older. I had done that type of work as a slave and honestly, I was tired of it. Here, more black women worked as laundresses than in any other type of work.

Some believe laundry is the most difficult of all domestic jobs. All those new-fangled machines that made cotton into cloth meant that people could buy more clothes that had to be washed and ironed by someone... us Black women. Laundry work was the first chore women would hire someone else to perform if her family had the slightest bit of extra money. I certainly would hire others to wash and iron our clothes if I had the means.

Lots of my friends in the neighborhood have their own laundry businesses and they welcomed me to help them for a while to learn their process. There's plenty of work to go around, so they weren't scared to show me their hints and tips.

They make their own soap a little differently than we used to in Beverly. We took ashes from the hearth and through a lengthy process cooked them down with fat until the mixture was just right, then poured it into bar soap molds to harden. My neighbors taught me how to make it from lye and starch from wheat bran, using washtubs from beer barrels cut in half.

Our work begins on Monday mornings, when maids drop off clothes and linens from their employers to our house. We have to identify each bag of clothes by family so they don't get mixed up with someone else's. That means most of us laundress businesswomen had to learn to read at least a little bit. Our school-age children benefited from colored schools built after Reconstruction and they taught us to read and write.

This process continues throughout the week until the clean clothes are picked up on Saturday. Throughout the week, we would carry gallons of water from wells, pumps or hydrants for washing, boiling, and rinsing clothes. Then, after hanging the clothes to dry, we'd iron the clothes and linens, alternately using several heavy irons.92

I would clean my hearth really good then set my wood-handled irons in front of the fire. I would iron the clean, dry clothes all day long without stopping. I cooked and ironed at the same time."

Washerwomen worked long, tiring hours six days a week and we only earned from four to eight dollars a month. We had to add on clients or get help from our children—I pointed to my helpers—to make ends meet. We worked mostly in our own homes or in our neighborhoods with other women. When the weather was good, we worked outside in the shade and hung the clothes on clotheslines attached to tree trunks or tall poles in the ground. When the weather was bad, we had to hang clothes all over the house to dry, and that's difficult when your house is small and filled with people wanting to walk back and forth under the drying shirts and pants.

The good thing about living here in Barnesville is that a lot of us women were laundresses too. Since our backyards were open, we could see and talk with each other while we were doing our respective businesses in our backyards. It made the very difficult work more enjoyable to have other women who understood what we were going through.

I was the sole breadwinner for this family after Pappy and Eve died. I had to feed and clothe my children from my earnings. I had to work, whether I had a husband or other man living in the house or not. I had to cook, clean, and fix furniture to make the house a home. Of course, being a smart woman, I trained my children to do many of those chores.

"You got that right!" All the children and grands spoke up at once, laughing, slapping each other's hands.

Well, you're right, and I don't regret it. You learned how to take care of your own household, so you would be prepared for adulthood and your own places... for those of you who cared to move out on your own, that is. Looking at several of my sons, and my daughter Ella, who was living here with her four kids, I blew a kiss at Ella, saying, "I think I'm more living with her these days, as she takes such good care of me in my old age." Ella blushed with the acknowledgment of her kindness, an appreciation which I rarely voiced.

Although being laundress was nowhere near an easy job, it was my choice of occupations, for I could stay at home and watch the young children at the same time. I could control what hours I worked and how many customers I took in. Being in control of my choices was the best thing about being free.

Chapter 17 - The Last Tale

"I am an old woman now. I lived thirty years a slave, brought my children into the free State of Ohio during the middle of Civil War fighting, and made a decent life for myself and my children in Barnesville. I've seen so many incredible changes in this country during my seventy-seven trips around the sun, from 1834 to 1911, that I pinch myself to make sure this is not a dream.

I been living on Vine Street with the Southern Cemetery in my backyard for nearly fifty years. Barnesville has come a very long way during that time period. Now there are five miles of paved streets, an abundance of clean water for drinking and manufacturing purposes. There are three banks in town with total resources of two and a half million dollars. There are two building associations, two large window-glass factories, one shoe factory, half a dozen cigar factories, two planing mills, a large canning factory, six tobacco packing houses, one flour mill, and two box factories. It's also the home of the Watt Mining Car wheel plant, which is known throughout the world. The main plant of the United Dairy Company that services Ohio, West Virginia, Pennsylvania, and Maryland is here. There are clothing stores, dry goods stores, hardware stores, and numerous grocery stores that furnish the people here with everything that's needed.

Negroes can live a reasonable life in this town. Many of us own our homes because we can get decent jobs in town. Our churches and our colored organizations thrive. I bet there are over one hundred Negroes in Barnesville, most living on Franklin, Mill, South, and Vine Streets, but there are also a couple of families on Main and Henderson Street. My neighbors and longtime friends have been the Betts, Brannons, Linns, Petersons, Nicholsons, Cowans, Mabras, Myers, and Goins. Some of these families moved on to Mount Vernon and other parts of Ohio.

During my first thirty years, even though I tried my best to be a "good" slave, I always wanted more for my life. Every time I opened the window in my bedroom, I smelled pine, grass, and human desire.

I knew what I wanted: my own path in the world, my own house, my own man, my own family someday. I wanted to be able to style my hair as the fashionable ladies in town did and buy lovely silk frocks from the shops in town instead of the shapeless homespun shifts that I had to sew myself out of sacks. I wanted to dance with a handsome mate of my choosing. I wanted to form friendships with other girls my age instead of babysitting someone else's spoiled children.

Truthfully, I was jealous of those white girls. They had not a care in the world, just what dress their slave would bring them, what hairstyle their servant would give them that day, what they'd tell their cook to make them for lunch, which store to shop at, which friend to visit, and on and on. They had no real responsibilities like we had. And they seemed to know so much about the world, but I only had access to farming, cooking, and cleaning around the Beverly area. The exception was the bits and pieces of news I overheard from my owners, or the people at the market or walking the street when I was running an errand. Those fortunate girls were allowed to read books, but it was illegal to teach a slave to read or write.

Then happy twelfth birthday to me. I was so depressed on that February day in 1846, being sold for one dollar, that I wanted to crawl into a hole and die.

Clara rushed to hug me tightly. "I'm glad you didn't, Grandma, for none of us would be here if you did." She's right. I hugged her back, then everyone came up to hold me, to kiss me, expressing their thanks for the things I've done for them their entire lives, how much they respect me, how much they love me just as I am.

This outpouring of emotion destroyed my ill temper. Oh, such a weight that little girl lifted off my heart. I am indeed a lucky woman now, here, in this time and place. My story goes on.

ACKNOWLEDGMENTS

First and foremost, I'd like to express an undying appreciation to my family for listening to my constant musings about genealogy, teasing out their memories, and sometimes editing my writings. M. Lavata Williams, our remarkable family historian, is at the top of the list for never hanging up the phone on me for yet another question about our ancestors. My elusive cousin Joe Booker gave me two intriguing pieces of information to investigate about Confederate General Jubal Early and slave holder Lavinia Booker. His daughter Suzanne and her mother Karen briefly discussed what I had found and what they knew. Uncle Dale Carter and his wife, Paula, reminisced about Margaret's son, Joseph Booker. My Great-aunt Margaret Williams was a constant well of support. Her now-deceased husband, Great-uncle Charles Williams provided the DNA that is the most valuable DNA for finding the way-back relatives.

As profiled in Appendix C, the Beverly Heritage Center[88] is at the top of the list of priceless treasures which brought the history of Beverly to life with video, audio, and actual artifacts housed in four historic buildings. Larry Matt Hatton, Americorps Preservation Associate, showed me around the Center during my 2019 Genealogy visit. Dr. Chris Mielke, Medieval Historian and Executive Director of the Center became my newest best friend. During the corona virus (COVID-19) pandemic of 2020, to keep us engaged, Dr. Mielke delivered weekly online streaming presentations about the Beverly Courthouse, Staunton-Parkersburg Turnpike, and Rich Mountain Battlefield, and other interesting topics. Whenever possible, he included the experience of enslaved people, with sensitivity and insight. One of his slides—"A Woman Named Margarett"—totally changed the trajectory of my search. He never seemed to tire of my incessant questions and provided me with documents and ideas for additional study. I believe the ancestors put him in my path, for without him this book would be nothing like the finished product.

Let me also give a shout out to the remarkable work the Historic Beverly Preservation, Inc. has done to commemorate their town. Their https://www.historicbeverly.org/bevtrip.htm website is a treasure trove of history and photos which greatly helped reveal Margaret's story. Once I determined who the owner was, I could read about the history and architectural details of his house.

Professor Ric Sheffield, Peter M. Rutkoff Distinguished Teaching Professor in American Studies, at Kenyon College in Gambier, Ohio, provided crucial information about our Booker family living in Mount Vernon, Ohio. He personally knew my Great-uncle George Booker, grandson of our heroine, and of the history of the Booker's in Knox County.

My cousin, Barbara Slater Nelson, a professional genealogist specializing in the Myers and Lett clans, provided important historical information about Barnesville, Ohio. Many cousins whom I met through DNA research volunteered to look through their family records to help solidify my theories of parentage. I will continue to bolster these relationships in the future.

The Elk Grove Senior Center writing group listened to my weekly 2,000-word snippets from the book, always providing gentle ideas for improvement. Special thanks to Cynthia Hobson, Rosemary Covington and Barbara Barrett for always giving me an extra ear when needed. I was constantly refueled with inspiration from my monthly Black Women Write group who provided support in the way that only Sistahs can.

I am thankful that Jean Cooper, Metadata Librarian and Genealogical Resources Specialist at the University of Virginia Library, agreed to perform the final edits and proofing for The Mystery of Margaret Booker, as she did for my dual award-winning Finding Daisy: From the Deep South to the Promised Land.

Finally, it's the closest ones who suffer right along with us authors as we give our all to complete these works of passion. Many thanks to my boyfriend, Michael Fitzwater, for his patience during my constant musings about this book.

APPENDICES

A: The Descendant's Turn
B: Researching
C: The Research Process
D: Author's Biography
E: Journey: Beverly & Barnesville
F: Slaveowner Connections
G: Selected Timelines
H: DNA Research Plan
I: Solving Your Mystery

Appendix A - The Descendants' Turn

What is the measure of a life? Is it the amount of money made, the size of the house, the number of furnishings, the circle of friends, health, happiness? Is it the lessons learned, or family mysteries revealed? I look back with pride on my life, both slave and free. I hope you've enjoyed my story. It was told with heart and as much factual information as I could remember, channeled lovingly into my third great-granddaughter's brain every morning.

Gazing at my eight children and two dozen grandchildren, I know my legacy will continue. Now it's time to pass the Speaker Stick to my direct descendants and let them reveal their own tales. Much love to you all.

Sincerely, Margaret Booker

Kanika Marshall

Joseph Lewis Booker (1855-1952)
[The author's great-great-grandfather]

I am the eldest of Margaret Booker's children. Though I was born a slave on September 9, 1855, in Beverly, West Virginia, I never let that dictate the boundaries of my life's story.

Aside from my dear mother, the single most important person in my early life was my father's spinster sister, Nancy Earle, who taught me to read when it was illegal to do so. Even though I hated being stuck in a room with her while my friends were outside playing ball, I soon recognized the benefits of her tutelage. That academic leg up not only fostered a lifelong love of books, but it also helped me get a good job which led to buying my own house, furnishings, and beautiful clothes for my family. I expected my cultured children to read and write well too.

I am also beholden to the Stalnakers who exposed me to the rudiments of blacksmithing. Along with being an excellent reader, a knowledge of metalworking helped me get a good-paying machinist job as an adult.

There's no need to repeat the myriad of experiences we had in Beverly, or our brave trek to Barnesville, Ohio, as mother aptly described our enslaved lifestyle and voyage to freedom.

Frankly, I would love to be able to forget the first ten years of my life. But one must acknowledge that those hardships and indignities served to mold my serious personality and iron will to exceed my station at birth. Those early experiences fueled me to create a well-bred family and become successful despite that humble beginning.

Moving to Barnesville, Ohio, when I was ten years old was the best thing that could have happened to me. Attending the Captina A.M.E. Church, in Somerset Township in Belmont County, Ohio, introduced us to a whole new class of people. Many of those Negroes had always been free, living in Ohio or Pennsylvania their whole lives. They knew how to dress, how to use proper English, how to read and write and enjoy classic literature. Many owned their own homes and had decent jobs. The possibilities seemed endless and I awoke every morning with new vigor, new expectations that I would make a great life for myself. And through becoming a member of Captina A.M.E., I met a beautiful young woman named Sara Elizabeth Myers. She was sweet, shy, and the daughter of John Myers and Corintha Crewett, who were distinguished members of the church and Barnesville community. I knew I wanted her to be part of my family. We married on December 23, 1875. Can you imagine our bliss, with the whole congregation joining our joy right before the celebration of Jesus' birth? My bride in white lace, her veil totally covering her lovely face, so that when I lifted it after our vows, it was like I was seeing her for the first time. Our whole lives were in front of us.

Sara Myers Booker
(1858-1906)

Joseph Booker
(1854-1952)

We started our marriage living in a home at 423 South Street in Barnesville, next to the Mabra family. I was twenty-four, working as a porter and Sara was twenty-two, keeping house. Our family expanded over the next twelve years with the birth of Maude Ellen in 1877, Myrtle Lavata in 1881, Ada Mae in 1884, then Herbert Euclid in 1889.

Sara's father came from a long line of Myerses. Some say he descended from Philip Myers, a seven-year-old who left Mainz, Germany, arriving in Pennsylvania in 1766, then migrated to Frederick, Maryland, as a young adult. His son, also named Philip Myers, was a mulatto who lived in Hagerstown, Washington County, MD. Ironically, that's where the Williams in-laws of my daughter, Myrtle Lavata Booker, were enslaved. [Author: Their story is well-researched in my Finding Otho: The Search for Our Enslaved Williams Ancestors book.]

Life was going well, but I wanted more. The men's group at our church was a conduit for political, occupational, and religious news. We followed the Negro leaders of the time, supporting the gains we made from Reconstruction following the Civil War. We began hearing about job opportunities in Knox County, Ohio. The Mount Vernon Bridge Company was among the largest industries there, along with the Cooper company which manufactured a brand of industrial engines and compressors. Coopers was hiring all sorts of workers, although Negroes nearly always found themselves at the low end of the pay scale, even if they were performing the same jobs as whites. I was different, though. I appeared for my interview in a black suit and tie, comporting myself like a gentleman and speaking standard English. My skin tone was slightly tanned, but my thin lips and bearing did not immediately suggest my ancestors came from Africa. Perhaps that's why I was hired and eventually achieved the level of machinist and paid like other white workers.

I moved my family to Mount Vernon in 1884 to a home at 205 Pennsylvania Avenue. Our children went to the same schools as whites, so they got the same good education to which all children are entitled. To ensure they learned as much as possible, I began purchasing books for a small library in our home. I'm happy to report it grew into a respectable collection over my lifetime.

I was beginning to become involved in various organizations, such as the Thompson Conner Lodge, and being a deacon in the Wayman A.M.E. Church. This notability earned me high status in the Negro community, partially because I worked hard to get jobs for my family, neighbors, and friends. Everything was going pretty well in our lives, compared to many others. We had four healthy, well-dressed children whom we sent to voice, music, and dance lessons. Having cultured children was a must after being at the mercy of owners for hundreds of years. We had numerous friends and attended many social functions. I was able to buy my eventual house and nice things for my family.

Sadly, my Sara became ill and doctors couldn't isolate the problem before she slipped away on March 6, 1906. She was buried in Southern Cemetery in back of mother's house.

Our youngest, Herbert, was seventeen, with one more year of high school to go, active on the baseball team; in fact, Herbert later played on the all-colored Mount Vernon Giants baseball team who played Satchell Paige—the famous Negro Leagues star—at Mount Vernon Athletic Park.[89]

Daughter Maude Ellen married Lester Scott in 1910, just in time for my mother, Margaret Booker, to bless their first son before she died in 1911.

You may know how this goes, but often when an eligible married man becomes a widower, there's a line of desirable women ready to step in and help the poor man over his grief. Believe you me, many a home-cooked casserole was hand-delivered to my door from a different well-meaning lady each day of the week.

"If there's anything else I can bring you, please don't hesitate to ask," Lady A offered. At church, Lady B asked, "Won't you have supper at my place after Sunday services?" Lady C came by the house "With a peach pie for you and your motherless son." Lady D had a decanter of "Cool sweet tea made especially for you from my secret family recipe." Lady E said, "I'll be happy to iron your shirts anytime, just ask." Lady F offered, "To clean your house whenever you need it." The seventh woman of the week, Lady G, invited me to the movies on Friday, the one day a week that Negroes were allowed into the balcony of the movie theater.

Little did those ladies know that I had already set my sights on a woman I wanted to spend the rest of my life with. She was vivacious, sparkling, pretty, and as active as I was in community events.

Viola Virginia Symons/Simmons was nineteen years younger than me, but when I put on my most distinguished smile, she couldn't resist my intentions. On June 21, 1912, Reverend George Tulloss officiated at our nuptials at his home. At the time, my talented bride was a trained nurse and I was working at Cooper's as a Machine Hand.

We were well-suited to one another. Community-oriented, social, and musically inclined, the local Mount Vernon Democratic Banner often reported our goings on in their paper. We attended and gave many lawn parties which included games, refreshments, music, and dancing.

My wife and I were members of, and held positions for, numerous organizations.[90] She was involved with the Shining Light Court of Calanthe No. 43. As a key member of the Colored Women's Glee Club, Viola played the soprano character, Meerah, in the operetta, In India. Viola led some of the largest Church fundraisers. In 1916, she and her church sisters, Vera Payne, and the Simmons and Mayle siblings, raised $828 for repairing the parsonage and for redecorating the Wayman A.M.E. Church. Additionally, as Vice-Chairman, she helped organize twenty-five of our colored church members, who successfully petitioned the all-Caucasian, Red Cross to form a chapter to be known as the Wayman Chapel Auxiliary.

As President of the Community Chorus, we helped to perfect the chorus among the colored young people of the city, the initial meeting having been held at the home of Mrs. Dana Hill.

Not to toot my own horn too much, but I've been on the "Gentlemen's List" for many years. I was a Trustee and Viola was a Vice Nobel Governor for the "Household of Ruth, No. 568." I achieved the position of Worshipful Master of the Colored Masons of Vernon Lodge No. 43, F. & A. M. and was a Prelate of the Thompson Conner Lodge.

The good thing and the bad thing about being in the limelight is that everything that happens to you—good or bad—is reported in the local newspaper. My wife was carrying our second child and gave birth in Mount Vernon hospital in 1915. Our precious baby girl, Mary Elizabeth Booker, died two days later after an illness of infantile diseases. Our friends' continuous well wishes were kind gestures, of course, but they were a constant reminder of our loss.

I was proud of all my children, the first four with Sara Myers and the last with Viola.

My eldest daughter, Maude Ellen Booker was a statuesque beauty. She married Lester Guy Scott in Columbus, Ohio, in 1910, but they chose to reside in Orangeburg, New York, most of their lives. They had two sons, William and Kenneth Scott.

Daughter Ada May Booker met George Burns Keyes in his hometown of East Liverpool while she worked a live-in maid job there. They married 1904 in Mt. Vernon. George eventually had his own barber shop at 704 East Chestnut Street in Mount Vernon, Ohio. They had no children.

My third daughter, Myrtle Lavata Booker married Otho Sherman Williams in 1905 in Philadelphia, Pennsylvania, but she has respectfully requested to tell her own tale.

My spoiled son, Herbert Euclid Booker seemed to be a devil-may-care young man. Always dressed smartly, charismatic, bold, unique, handsome, the very picture of a Romeo with smoldering gray eyes and black hair. Herbert was a star baseball player in Mount Vernon. Married three times, he had no children that I knew about. He registered for World War I and World War II from his home in Chicago, Illinois, where he was a well-paid chauffeur. Charm and tips go hand in hand in that job, which was helpful for I taught him to dress and comport himself like a gentleman.

My last offspring, George Reynolds Booker, was my and Viola's only child. He had such a big personality that he insists on telling his own story. That's the Booker spiritchart your own course!

George Reynolds Booker
[The author's great-uncle and penpal in 1976]

Music was always a major component of our household, almost like a brother. I was born in 1913 and was blessed to grow up in a house full of academics, music, sports and culture. My father, Joseph, an ex-slave, and his second wife, Viola, a nurse, were my talented parents. Dad was an educated, cultured man who provided the best environment that a colored child in early twentieth century America could expect.

Like my half-brother, Herbert Booker, I could be described as gregarious, talkative, sociable, friendly, and a lover of history. A postman for twenty-eight years, I was often asked to be the Master of Ceremonies for our family reunions and for many local events. I was an avid sports enthusiast too. During my youth, to see football games on Saturdays, I used to ride my bicycle five miles to Gambier. I also loved watching the All-Negro baseball leagues play during the 1920s and 1930s, cheering my brother, Herbert, and neighbors who were playing on the Mount Vernon Giants.[91]

After high school, I worked at various jobs, including the Dowds-Rudin Company before enlisting in the US Army in 1941. I was part of the 829th Aviation Engineers, an all-black unit which was sent to repair bombed airports and build new landing strips in Liverpool, England, and France. Prior to D-Day, a 200-voice black soldier's chorus sang in the Royal Albert Hall, Glasgow, Edinburgh, as a good will gesture to the United Kingdom.

Herbert Booker

Herbert Booker

Maude Booker

Ada Booker & George Keyes

Three weeks after finishing my civic duty in the Army, I eagerly married Sarah "Geraldine" Walker in November 1945. We lived at 307 Cooper Street, in Mount Vernon, Ohio. I got a great job as a postal carrier which I proudly held for forty years.

I was an avid musician, as was my son, Joseph George Booker. He was born in 1946 and is now an amazing saxophonist. He married three times and had three children: Martin, Tonya, and Suzanne Booker.

My mother, Viola, passed away in 1952 and my remarkable father, Joseph Booker, died on November 9, 1952, at the esteemed age of ninety-seven full years of life. Most of our family was long-lived until the twenty-first century.

Myrtle Lavata Booker (1881-1972)
[The author's maternal great-grandmother]

I was born in Barnesville, Ohio, in 1881, the second child of Joseph Booker and Sara Elizabeth Myers Booker. Soon afterward, father moved us to Mount Vernon, Ohio, to take a good job at the Cooper Company as a machinist.

Father insisted that all his children had to finish four years of high school, even if they were twenty-five years old! He learned about the advantages of an education when his slave master's sister taught him to read and write. Our family was pretty well off by the turn of the century, proving that education did give us a push ahead in life. Father owned our home and filled it with nice wood furnishings. We always had beautiful clothes, not just for church, but for school too. My mother, Sara Myers, was a talented seamstress who could customize our clothing, or Father had other seamstresses create fashionable looks for us.

I graduated from Mount Vernon High School in 1899 with another Negro girl in a class of thirty-five. Even though we were groomed for more, Negro women could generally only get jobs as cooks, maids, or laundresses in Ohio. There might have been a few Negro teachers and nurses, but they were few and far between.

Father was able to secure live-in jobs for us in East Liverpool, in northeastern Ohio, located near the border with Pennsylvania. We were responsible for cooking, housecleaning, and child rearing for a couple of wealthy families.

Mount Vernon High School, Ohio. Myrtle Lavata Booker one of the two Black women in the 1899 class.

We were expected to dress accordingly, use our manners, and look pretty while performing our jobs. Both my sister and I met our future husbands at church there. Ada married George Keyes in 1904 and I wed the suave, fun-loving musician, Otho Sherman Williams92[93] in 1905 in Germantown, Philadelphia, PA.

Otho's father had been a slave in Washington County, MD, but died a landowner. Otho's mother, Alice Logan Williams took their children to Greencastle, PA, before 1900. My husband wasn't getting along with his brothers, so at the age of fifteen he packed a bag and left with a few friends to make his fortune in the world. They went to Pittsburgh, PA, for a while, working in a steel plant or other odd jobs. Then, as luck would have it, he ended up in East Liverpool, OH, as a driver, and that's where we met.

Lord knows why Otho and I wed—we were such opposites! I was raised to be reserved, prim, and proper. Laughter and hugs were not standard fair in my parents' household. Otho was carefree, social, always smiling, and always tapping his foot to an inner beat. Let's just say married life was not always harmonious. Even so, the babies came—Reba May in 1907, Pearl Lavata in 1908, Helen, stillborn, in 1910, and Otho Sherman Jr. who died shortly after birth. By then, tensions were so high that I moved our children back home to Mount Vernon with the promise that I would send my husband to jail if he didn't straighten up and start taking proper care of his family. He tried to be more responsible and registered for the war effort in 1918. I took the girls and moved back to my parent's home in Mount Vernon, Ohio.

My father got Otho a low-level job at Coopers and we moved into one of their company houses on Norton Street next to the factory. Jayne Elizabeth was born in 1920, Charles Elmer in 1924, and Robert "Bobby" Williams in 1928.

Guess what happened the following year? Our twenty-one-year-old daughter Pearl came back from her job in Dayton, with husband and baby Norma in tow in 1929. They stayed at Arthur Carter's mother, Ella Roy Carter's, house during Norma's first year of life, then moved in with us for the next fourteen years. Then in 1933, Reba came back home from her job in Columbus with baby Lavata. Babies seemed to multiply like rabbits and by 1938, sixteen people were living in our house! Pearl's family of eight was crammed into one bedroom and kitchenette on one side of the house, and the rest of us in three bedrooms, large living room, dining room, and full kitchen on the other.

Like my deceased grandmother, Margaret, I established a successful laundry business in an add-on room downstairs. Professionals in Mount Vernon would have their servants drop off bags of dirty shirts, pants, and linens at my door on Monday mornings and by Friday the clothes would be spotless and perfectly starched and pressed. I loved the ironing part best, hanging each completed shirt throughout my house so I could admire the work. My business earned $312 in 1940 [Note: $5,700 in 2020 dollars].

But children, a husband, and laundry did not occupy my entire life. I was an excellent cook, often "putting on the dog"94 for visiting pastors and other notables at our home. My stepmother, Viola Symons Booker, would organize dinners for sale to help the church and she could always count on me to cook dozens of meals for the cause.

I was an active member of the Wayman A.M.E. Church, and Church Sewing Club, meeting at least once or twice a month.

Don't let me forget to mention that I was a member of the Order of the Eastern Star.95 My father was a proud Mason96 which allowed me entrance to that esteemed community service-oriented organization.

I was often invited to operas and other top-drawer97 events by Mr. and Mrs. Newsome. I gave my eldest daughters voice lessons from one of the opera singers in town, in exchange for free laundry service.

My husband claimed, "You are the most organized person I know." He's right. Every night before I go to bed, I've already planned the next day in detail, with the amount of time needed to complete each task. I rise every morning by six a.m. to ensure that breakfast is ready and my husband's lunch bucket is packed. In the wintertime, I would get up early, remove the used ashes from the coal stove, then build a new fire in the stove, so the house was warmer when others got up. I learned all of these skills from my father, Joseph, who learned them from his organized mother, Margaret Booker. I hope my children pass those skills down to their children too.

Sixteen People Lived in the Williams' House

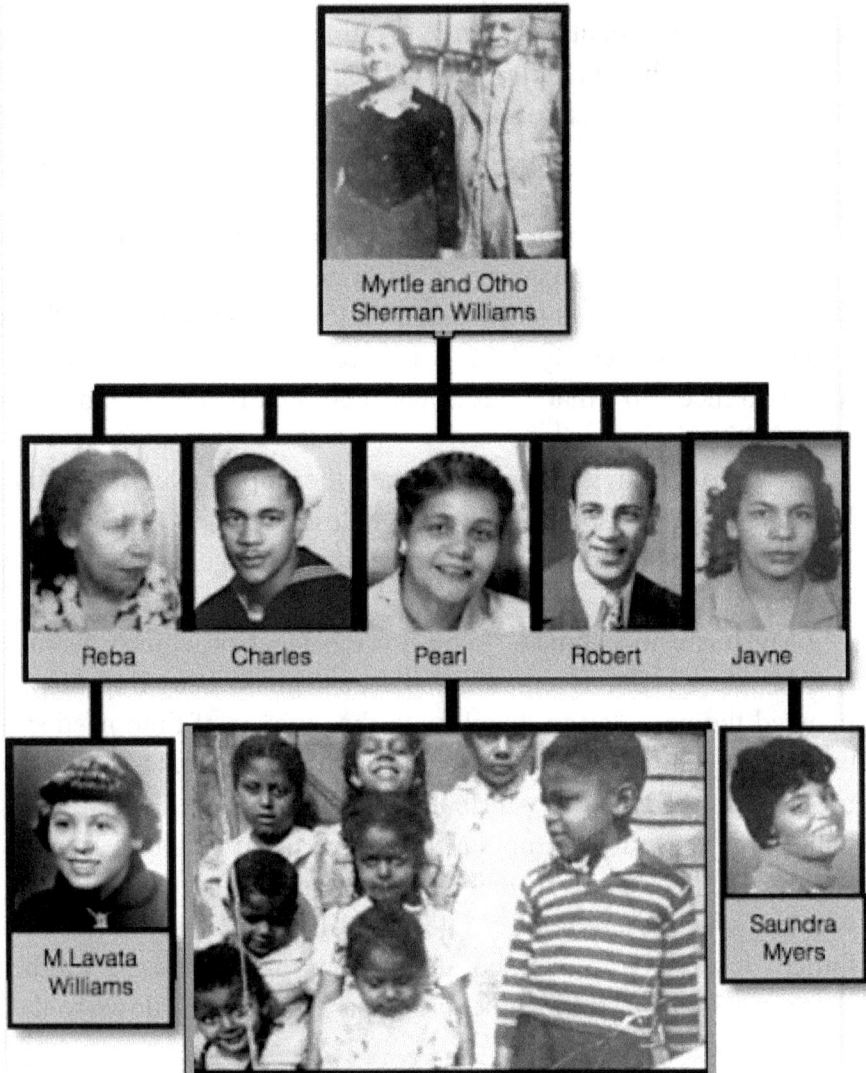

Myrtle and Otho
Sherman Williams

Reba   Charles   Pearl   Robert   Jayne

M.Lavata
Williams

Saundra
Myers

Top: Myrtle "Lavata" Williams, Sara Carter, Norma Carter
Mid: George Carter, Mary Carter, Arthur "Sonny" Carter
Bottom: Dale Carter, Elizabeth "Betty" Carter

Booker-Williams Photos from 1930s and 1940s

Pearl Lavata Carter (1908-1990)[98]

Raising seven children on a domestic employee's salary in Mount Vernon, Ohio? I never thought that would become my life's legacy! I wanted to be a secretary after I graduated from high school in 1926. I was not going to be like those other colored girls who got pregnant right away and had a bunch of babies and cleaned other peoples' houses all their lives. No, I was planning to go to business college, working in an office, taking dictation and typing up correspondence from the boss. I would be a respected professional office employee. But life doesn't always turn out as our childhood dreams expect...

At church one day in 1927, I noticed the very handsome Arthur Taft Carter looking at me with smoldering sienna brown eyes. Well, you can guess what happened next. I fell head over heels in love with him while attending Mount Vernon Business College. Nobody would hire a Negro girl as a secretary in Mount Vernon, so I found a job in Dayton, Ohio doing housework and laundry in private homes. Arthur followed me there and turned on the charm. We quickly got married and moved back to Mount Vernon with my first child, Norma, in 1929, with his mother, Ella Roy Carter. And I continued to do day's work for the rest of my life.

Arthur began disappearing for days at a time "looking for work," he said. Sara was born in 1931, then I had to move back home with my parents, Myrtle Booker and Otho Sherman Williams. I needed a safe place to stay and someone to watch my children while I worked during the day. Arthur came back for a hot minute, then Arthur "Sonny" Carter was born in 1933. My husband was usually gone after that, "finding work" but never bringing home any money. Every time he visited us, I'd be mad as a hornet but after he petted me and held me... Well, you know the rest. Mary came along in 1934, George in 1936, Dale in 1937, and Elizabeth "Betty" Carter in 1938. My parents had enough! Arthur was no longer allowed near me, since he refused to support our babies and I couldn't say no.

Thank goodness for my parents allowing the eight of us to live in their house along with them, my brothers Charles and Robert

Williams, my sister Reba and her daughter Lavata (our future family historian), and sister Jayne and her daughter Saundra. Sixteen people lived in Otho and Myrtle's row house owned by the Cooper-Bessemer company where my daddy worked with my granddaddy, Joseph Booker.

Carter Stair-Step Children, c. 1940

I had been deeply hurt by my husband and was simmering with anger toward men the rest of my long life. I was now the woman I vowed never to be, raising a pile of children on a domestic employee's meager salary. I was doing housework, light cooking, washing and ironing clothes, in addition to janitorial work at night at a dentist's office. It was hard physical labor and every evening I walked home extremely tired, sometimes struggling to put one foot in front of the other, sometimes even having to lean against a tree trunk while I caught my breath. I would return home to my large family every night only to cook and clean for them too. I have no idea why I never thought to teach my children how to have dinner ready and our house cleaned for me. I certainly had enough of them to take that burden off me!

I was exhausted every day and my health paid the price for it. Over the years, I developed diabetes leading to blindness, and I had a bad heart. My limbs ached from the constant stooping and scrubbing that came with janitorial duties. But I had no pension and needed to support myself, so day's work occupied my existence until I was in my early seventies.

I did finally get an answer to my daily prayers. My large family got a huge break when our Wayman A.M.E. Church let me rent their old two-story, brown shingle-clad house on Walnut Street for seven dollars per month. This certainly was a lot more room for us eight. There was at least one member of my Carter family living there from the late 1940s until Sonny's death in 2006.

While my life wasn't what I had dreamed, I am proud of the good citizens my union with Arthur produced, from teachers and engineers to computer specialists and artists. All were nice, hardworking people who improved the world by their presence.

Mary Ellen Carter Marshall (1934-2007)99

On Easter Sunday, April 1, 1934, I was born in Mount Vernon, Ohio, almost exactly one hundred years after my enslaved great-grandfather Otho Williams was born in Maryland in 1834, and my enslaved great-great-grandmother, Margaret Booker, was born near Beverly, West Virginia. I was the middle of seven children, primarily raised by our capable mother, Pearl Lavata Williams Carter.

I never had a father in my life. I remember meeting him only once when I was five, at Grammie Ella Carter's house—his Mother's lovely home. I remember it vividly: he gave me a nickel. That is the extent of "me and my father" memories.

My mother, on the other hand, was my hero. She worked tirelessly doing "day's work," cleaning other peoples' homes all of her life to keep food on the table for our large family. I knew at an early age that I would not be stuck in that small town, would not get married until I was twenty-one, and would not have a ton of babies that would limit my options for the future! Yes, I was driven to have a different sort of life.

Even though shy, I was athletic and very competitive at everything, especially marbles, basketball, and skating. Later in life, my competitive passions were contract bridge, tennis, and golf. This tomboy was selected to become the first black female to be in the Queen's Court in high school! Besides my mother, my junior high school art teachers, Mr. Loomis and Mrs. Lewis, shaped my life, as well as Mr. Colbert who lived in Zanesville and critiqued my artwork by mail. I was selected to be the Art Editor for the 1952 Mount Vernon High School Yearbook—the first black student selected for that role.

I happily left my hometown to marry the man of my dreams, Thomas Richard Marshall, whom I met in 1952. He was going to Ohio State Medical School when we met, quite unexpectedly, on a car ride to a skating rink in Zanesville, Ohio. After that initial encounter, we saw each other sparingly since Cleveland was 130 miles away and he had no car. We were married by a Justice of the Peace one month after my twenty-first birthday, on May 7, 1955. We moved to a furnished one-room studio apartment across from the Medical School at Ohio State University.

I became pregnant with our first child during the fall of 1956. As the due date got closer, I moved in with Tom's mother, Daisy Dooley Marshall,[100] in Cleveland, Ohio. [More in Finding Daisy: From the Deep South to the Promised Land]. Daisy was a nurse and would know exactly what to do in case Tom could not get away from school to be with me for the birth. Ironically, Tom was training to become an obstetrician and gynecologist!

My sweetheart of a father-in-law, Austin Henry Marshall,[101] was a Pullman Porter. He treated me to the most magnificent train ride from Columbus to Cleveland, treating me like I was a rich white woman who purchased an expensive ticket. He was the father I never had.

We had our first child, Kathy Marshall [the author], in 1957, in Cleveland, under the watchful eye of nurse Daisy. During the year that Kathy and I lived with my mother-in-law while Tom finished school, she diligently instructed me about how to care for an infant, myself, and a husband.

Once Tom graduated in 1958, we moved across country to Seattle, Washington, where he completed his medical internship and military obligation as a Navy Lieutenant in the Medical Corps. Our second child, Carrie Marshall, was born in Seattle in 1959. Then we moved to San Diego, California, in 1961, to complete Tom's military service requirement in the Medical Corps. From 1963 to 1964, we lived in French Camp, California, so Tom could complete his medical residency. I took classes at Delta Junior College. We had our third child, Gregory Marshall, in 1963.

One year later, Tom purchased a brand new house costing $16,000 in the Larchmont Riviera area in far eastern Sacramento. I still remember the rather horrible avocado green carpet and orange accents in the house, but having my own house was absolutely WONDERFUL, after spending some thirty-odd years without a "pot to pee in," as my mother would say.

My husband, now Dr. Thomas R. Marshall, opened his first Obstetrics and Gynecology medical practice in South Sacramento where a good proportion of African Americans lived at the time. I was his receptionist, assistant, and billing staff until he hired a wonderful woman named Myrtle to be his office manager. Then I was freed up to finish college.

By then, having worked so closely together, seeing each other twenty-four hours a day our marriage was strained beyond repair. Tom asked for a divorce in 1966, so he could marry our dancing instructor. I was not unhappy at all (smile).

My mother, Pearl, encouraged us kids to learn as much as we could in school so we would have more job opportunities in the future. I am proud to say that I was the first in my Carter family to finish college, earning an Associate of Arts degree in 1966 from Sacramento City College, then a Bachelor of Arts degree in Education at Sacramento State College in 1970. I eventually earned a master's degree in education administration in 1975. Being an elementary school teacher for a few years was fine but being a Principal in several Sacramento City schools until I retired in 1989 was much more fulfilling.

I took Auntie Mame's motto to heart: "live, Live, LIVE!" I sold our family home for $160,000 more than the purchase price and bought a 1,100 square-foot home in Sun Country for active seniors in South Sacramento. I had only worked for twenty years and had a minimal retirement check, so I needed to pay all debts before retirement.

An artist to the core, I took draw-by-mail courses as a teenager and used my artistic skills to dress windows at Ringwalt's department store. In blessed retirement, I was free to take every art class available at Cosumnes River Community College near my Sun Country home. I finally focused my energies on watercolor painting. Persuaded by my children, I established what ended up being a very successful "Mary Marshall Watercolors" art business for over ten years.

I inherited our family's organizational abilities from my mother Pearl Williams Carter, my grandmother Myrtle Booker Williams, my great-grandfather Joseph Booker, and his parents, Margaret Booker and John B. Earle.

It was not easy being a single mother, but with the cooperation of my three children, we made it work. We had no extra money, but I always provided used-once paper from school, ink pens, and pencils and crayons for artistic projects, yarn for crocheting and knitting, my old Necchi sewing machine from my mother-in-law and dollar-per-yard fabric from Hancock's Fabrics.

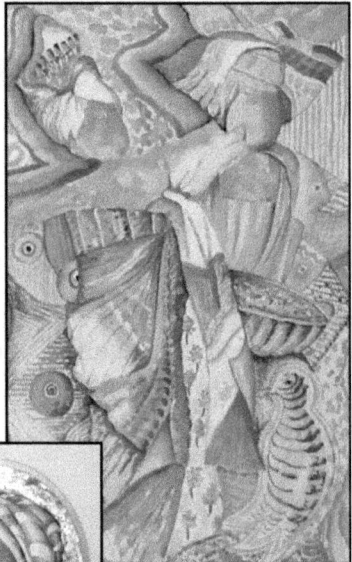

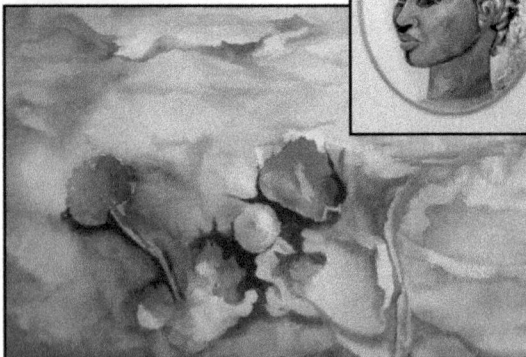

Sample of Mary Marshall Watercolors shown in the Elk Grove Artists "Art in Public Places" Program, 2006. Owned by Kathy Marshall.

My kids were taught to use their brains, imaginations, and creativity to make things happen for their lives. Our house was safe and comfortable. There was no yelling and no physical fights after my husband left. We all thrived in peace. But life is a pendulum.

In 1996, I was diagnosed with breast cancer. After surgery and chemotherapy, I was still cancer-free at the magic seven-year mark when one can assume the cancer is gone for good. Unfortunately, cancer is a deceiver. It came back with such virulence that I battled for my life for three years, reducing me to a coma by January 26, 2007. That afternoon, my daughter, Kathy, came into my room and played a video captured from my hometown in Mount Vernon, Ohio. My Aunt Reba had turned 100 years old and she was being celebrated on the evening news. The video captured her voice singing in the background as Kathy described the green trees and red brick that defines the home of my birth.

She said, "Your parents and sisters and brothers are all waiting to welcome you, Mom," I could hear her through my coma fog. That night she lay next to me in the bed, her tear-streaked face against mine whispering, "You have been the best mother, always keeping us safe and fed. You nurtured our creativity and always made us feel like we were capable of doing anything with our lives. You lead by example. We will miss you terribly, but it's time now, Mom. Time to be with your family. They're all waiting for you. We will be all right and will never forget you. I love you so much, Mom." After Kathy left that night, I relaxed, loosened my grip, slowed my breathing, and allowed morphine to take me where it wished, crossing over on January 27, 2007.

Kathy Marshall

I have so many happy, fun, but sometimes emotionally draining memories of our childhood years from our stints in Seattle, San Diego, and Stockton during the first six years of my life. Most of our childhood experiences, though, took place at 2549 Key West Way in Sacramento, California.

My sister, Carrie, and I shared a bedroom while Greg, lucky boy, slept by himself. I was an introvert and need to spend lots of time alone, in a relatively organized space. My sister was much more socially adept and prone to collecting and saving too many things in our small space. It was stressful for both of us. I stopped whining about our cramped arrangement when my mother said she and her six siblings slept in a room the same size as ours.

When Dad left us in 1966, we began to understand what frugal meant. I think it's actually a good thing to be poor of money because one is forced to cultivate creativity and problem-solving skills. Carrie and I learned how to sew our own clothes or alter clothes from the Salvation Army, and we crocheted scarves and hats for gifts. All of us could bake sweets and cook meats better than many kids. Greg taught himself how to build things, like a wooden fort in the garage rafters, a four-by-eight-foot train set that descended from a pulley system in his room.

We kids attempted to grow vegetables in our backyard garden and helped mom make ice cream and delicious cobblers from our thirty-foot peach tree. We kids played hard together—riding bikes, skating, pogoing, spreading couch cushions on the living room floor for flips and handsprings, and we worked as a team to complete our household chores before Mom came home.

Mom encouraged us to be proactive, have goals, adopt plans of action, and to implement those plans to achieve the goals. She felt she learned these skills from her Grandmother Myrtle.

As I got older, my sensitivity to racial inequalities began to bubble to the surface. I noticed there were only two pages in our history books about Black folk in America, and they were only about slavery. Didn't Black people contribute anything positive to society? The Civil Rights movement was in full force as I entered the integrated and troubled Hiram Johnson High School in 1972. There were daily uprisings and fights between the Black, White, Asian, and Hispanic students at our school.

Matthew and Ken Anderson, Romeo and Carrie Malenab, Lauren McGhee, Mary Marshall, and Isaac Anderson. Photograph by Kathy Marshall. 1991.

I graduated from high school early to get away from the madness, completing an Associate of Arts Degree from Sacramento City College in 1976. I was offered a full-time job at the California Highway Patrol the same year. My second night on the job an African-American coworker, Phyllis Matthews, shades lighter than me, asked who the white people were in my family. That started me on a quest to find out about my family lineage by writing letters to my elders in Ohio. My great-uncle George Booker and his wife Geraldine wrote back interesting stories about our Booker heritage and got me thirsting for more.

Life happened, though, before I could delve more into that topic. I met my husband to be, Kenneth Wayne Anderson, via his Aunt Phyllis, obtained a Bachelor of Arts degree, got married, bought our first house, got promoted, earned a master's degree in public administration, got promoted, had a first child whom we named Isaac after Ken's grandfather. We Buppies102 bought our dream house in the posh Pocket area of south Sacramento, had a second child—Matthew Anderson, got promoted, and started an art business called "Kanika Marshall Art."

All of a sudden the brakes squealed, locked up, then life stopped abruptly. My husband and I divorced after eighteen years together, losing our dream house, losing our family unit, seemingly losing everything. I found a smaller house and became a single mother. Then the unimaginable happened: my ex-husband was killed in 1998 by a drunk driver. I had to supplement my full-time State worker income with sales of my ceramic and steel artworks.

Isaac joined the Marines while still in high school in 2003, was assigned to Iraq for a year, then married his high school sweetheart, Jameillah Davis, in 2005. They had my first adorable, brilliant grandchild—Jazmine—in 2008, handsome grandson—Isaiah—in 2010, and second cutie-pie grandson—Jeremiah—in 2016. They have been able to travel to North Carolina, San Diego, and twice to the idyllic tropical island of Okinawa, Japan.

Jazmine, Isaac, Jameillah, Jeremiah, Isaiah Anderson, 2020, Okinawa, Japan.

Matthew Anderson, 2019, Third-Degree Black Belt, Sacramento, CA

Matthew moved away in 2014—a huge year for him. He got a full-time job with the State of California, bought a house, and attained a Bachelor of Science degree in Computer Science. He earned his first-degree black belt in 2010, second-degree in 2015, third-degree in 2019 and was the US National Taekwondo Champion in "Free Style" Taekwondo in 2015-2016, nearly making the 2016 US Olympics Team. Wow!

I officially retired from my day job in 2012 and began traveling the world, for the first time about to fulfill a lifelong fantasy. I took my first DNA test and got swallowed up in a genealogy hobby that has become my passion. I breathe, eat, and sleep genealogy, with the goal of publishing one book per year of family histories and encouraging others to do the same. This is my fourth book in four years. On track.

Carrie Marshall Malenab

I was born in Seattle, Washington, in 1959, when my dad was doing his one-year medical internship. Spending time with family and friends is my true joy, especially if there is water and a warm sandy beach nearby. My daily goal in life is to love others and honor God. I always worked hard in school. I was fortunate to earn a nearly full-ride scholarship to Pepperdine University in Malibu, California, where I had the opportunity to study in West Germany during the 1977-

Carrie and Romeo Malenab, Lauren McGhee, and E'Drece Walls, Sacramento, California, 2016

78 school year. I transferred to Scripps College in Claremont, California, and completed my Bachelor of Arts degree in International Relations in 1980.

After graduating from college, I married my high school sweetheart and worked for Volkswagen of America in Culver City, California. On December 15, 1981, I was blessed with my own angel, Lauren Elise McGhee. Unfortunately, drug abuse was a huge problem in California in the 1970s and 1980s, and very soon my husband's problem caused us to divorce. My daughter and I returned to Sacramento to live in an apartment close to my childhood home where I rededicated my life to God and restarted my life. My mother, brother, and sister were, and always have been, a wonderful support system for us.

To make additional money, I began selling Mary Kay Cosmetics and created my own sewing business, along with working full-time at McLaren Engineering. McLaren is a subcontractor for Aerojet, which is an aerospace firm. In 1985, wanting my work to have a greater impact in the world, especially with young people, I went back to school to earn my teaching credential, while continuing to work full-time, as a single parent.

I taught at Carriage Elementary and Sylvan Middle School in the San Juan School District. After eleven years, to be closer to home, I took a job at T. R. Smedberg Middle School in the Elk Grove School District. I eventually taught social science and AVID at Sheldon High School prior, to earning my master's degree in educational administration. I worked for nine years as a Vice Principal at Pleasant Grove High School, prior to retiring.

During the busy time in my life, I became an active member of the Alpha Kappa Alpha Sorority, Incorporated, the first African American Sorority dedicated to service to all mankind. I also met my real Romeo, who lived in my apartment complex. Romeo Faustino Malenab, was born in the Philippines and immigrated to California in 1977, after waiting eight years to obtain the proper immigration approvals. He served in the United States Air Force, both active and reserve. Greatly appreciating the

American Dream, he was able to purchase cars and a home in 1985 while he worked in the Operations Department of Sacramento's nuclear power plant, part of the Sacramento Metropolitan Utilities District. Romeo and I married in 1990, and Lauren and I became a part of his large, loving, Filipino family.

Twenty-eight years later, I fell in love again when I welcomed my precious grandson, E'Drece Brian Walls, into the world on October 16, 2008. Romeo and I are having a wonderful time being retired grandparents and pouring our lives into E'Drece.

Greg Marshall

At the age of thirteen, I designed and built a five-foot tall concrete safe in my mom's garage, for my coin collection. When I was fifteen, I installed a security system in her home. In my later teenage years and early twenties, I tricked out (customized) several of my Volkswagen Beetle cars. I do not know where this natural mechanical and engineering ability came from, but my sister says it may have been genetically passed down from our enslaved ancestors who were ironworkers.

Who can forget the fun times we had at my father's country home in Loomis, California? Every other weekend at Dad's house, one of our favorite chores was digging up to six-inch rocks from the entirely rocky soil around the house. This de-rocked area would eventually become the front lawn. The dug-up rocks would soon become a retaining wall around the dining room, which we helped our Renaissance Man of a father build.

In 1986, I joined the Sacramento Fire Department, being trained by my sister's husband, Ken Anderson, who was a Captain and Trainer at the Sacramento Fire Department's "Training Tower" for several years. I completed an Associate of Arts degree in Fire Science, then became an engineer, being responsible for maintaining the Light Plant truck for hazardous materials investigations and heavy rescue calls for service.

I also invented several tools for firefighters and developed my own design of portable meditative water fountains, as well as many other inventions. People call me MacGyver because I enjoy solving complex problems and making things out of ordinary objects.

When I was twenty-three, I purchased my first house in North Sacramento, and maintained several small businesses in my spare time. I was also a daredevil on my bicycle, a stuntman as a baseball shortstop, and I continued our Dad's twenty-five-year record as a bicyclist at Eppie's Great Race, which was a triathlon of running, bicycling and kayaking teams. I rode the bicycle leg on my teams.

In 1994 when I was thirty-one, I met my soulmate, Sue Walker, at a country and western dance club. She was another entrepreneur and go-getter who sold many different holistic health products. We married in 1995 and purchased my dream property in Garden Valley. Our compact, 1,200-square-foot ranch-style house was surrounded by woods and a babbling brook in the lower backyard. We had our wedding on the huge backyard deck. I was proud to say this was similar to the amazing rural hill-top property our father had for thirty years in Loomis, California.

After a few years, Sue and I both decided to retire from our respective day jobs, sell our individual properties, and purchase a Hypnotherapy School together in Auburn, California. I used my building skills to retrofit the two-story building for living quarters on the second floor, as well as the office and school rooms on the bottom floor. We successfully managed the school for a few years, but then eventually decided to divorce in 2002.

Following our divorce, I became a building contractor, rehabbing houses by performing electrical, plumbing, and other home renovations for customers. I also maintained some of my health-oriented entrepreneurial businesses, as well as continuing to stay physically fit. After a while, aches and pains encouraged my body to suggest that I trade the physically taxing activity of construction work to something more cerebral, like financial services, including life insurance. Life is good and I remain optimistic about the future.

(End of Joseph Booker's descendants)

Cornelia Booker Anderson 1856-1904
(Margaret Booker's oldest daughter)

Mama did a good job describing what our lives were like in Beverly, West Virginia. The Negro women there had the same lot, the same story, the same experiences: housework, cooking, a little gardening, taking care of the master's many babies as well as our own. Real life started happening for us in 1863 when we migrated west to Barnesville, Ohio, in that bumpy buckboard. Sending us away was the best thing my owner-daddy, John B. Earle, could have done for us. It was a breath of fresh air that we sorely needed.

Being the oldest girl, seven, I helped mama with the younger kids while she did "day work" next door for a few years, before she established her own laundry business in the house. Grandpa Edward got me a job as a live-in maid for his homeowner friends, Margaret and Benjamin Reed in Union, Fayette, Ohio. Union is where Grandpa and his wife, Eve, were living in 1860 before buying the house in Barnesville and letting us move in with them.

The Reeds were good, hardworking colored people who saw to it that I got an academic and social/cultural education while I was there. I learned how to dress and do my hair in a more fashionable way than we were allowed as slaves. The Reeds introduced me to many different people at church and other social functions. For the first time in my life, I had friends other than my family members. And that's when I met Joseph Anderson.

By 1880, we were married and living in Washington, Pennsylvania, in a cute little house on Beaux Street and Alleys adjacent, near the railroad tracks. The house was mighty crowded though. We had four children by then: Viola (6), Joseph (4), John (2), and a newborn named Frederick. Joseph's mother, Matilda, and her ten-year-old granddaughter, Daisy, were also living with us, as well as my brother-in-law, George (22), who was a hotel waiter. We had to be quite industrious to keep everyone fed and clothed.

From 1886 to 1889, my husband, Joseph F. Anderson, Sr., was a waiter. By then, we were all living a block from our previous home at 139 West Wheeling in Washington, PA.

I was so proud of my husband opening his own restaurant in 1897, located on North Main Street, living at 153 E. Walnut.[103] He was able to put a down payment on a house too, in a mostly black neighborhood at 153 East Walnut Street, a few blocks from our previous homes. Unfortunately, the business folded years later.

By 1900[104] our large family was living at 153 East Walnut Street in Washington, PA. I was forty-four by then, taking care of ten living children in the household: Joseph, Sr. (billiard room keeper), Joseph, Jr. (day laborer), Fred (porter in barber shop), Raymond (porter in drug store), Victor (school), Grendola (school), Edna (school), Leona (school), Hazel (school), and Evelina (school) Anderson. Also living with us, to help pay the mortgage, were boarders May (dressmaker) and Henry (infant) Matthews, niece Daisy Herron (servant), and Florence Hatcher (servant). All of us could read and write. All of us shared the load.

On Sundays, we either went to Wright's Chapel, Zion Methodist Church, headed by Reverend A.P. Parker, or to St. Paul's A.M.E. to hear Reverend D.S. Bentley and their magnificent choir.

Cornelia's Descendants (by the Author)

Margaret's eldest daughter, Cornelia, died in 1904, the year after her husband passed. Some of their children got married and formed their own families. Others continued living together. Most stayed put in Washington, PA, for their entire lives.

By 1940, Grendola (53), Joseph (64), Leona (48), and Evalina Anderson (42) were living together on Sumner Avenue in Washington, PA. No other documentary information was uncovered for these children from Cornelia Booker and Joseph Anderson.

Their son, George Frederick Anderson, died of congestive heart failure and senility at the age of eighty-one, in 1960. He was a retired building superintendent.

Joseph Francis Anderson Jr., a retired laborer in Washington, PA, died at eighty-seven in 1963 due to infection from gangrene to his left foot.

Hazel Anderson (21), married Albert Smith (22), in 1913. She was a housekeeper and her husband was a porter.

In 1897 (and still in 1905), Clarence Raymond Anderson, was a porter for R Price, bds, living at 153 E. Walnut. He married Lillie May Mosebay in 1910, six years after his mother, Cornelia, died. They had two children: Robert Raymond Anderson and Ethel May Anderson. Clarence died in 1955 at seventy-two, from hypertension. Ethel May Anderson married John H. Griffin in 1935 in Washington, Pennsylvania. She had twins Robert and Barbara Griffin in 1937, and a daughter, Patricia, in 1939. The DNA from the Griffin twins was captured by Judith Heald and has been used extensively in this analysis.

The Rest of Margaret Booker's Kids

George Booker (1858-?). George was born in Beverly, West Virginia, migrated to Barnesville, OH, and was living with his mother Margaret in 1870 and 1900 when he was a caterer for the railroad. The 1910 Census indicated George was a boarder on Chapline Street in Wheeling, West Virginia, working as a janitor at an office building; he was only thirty miles away from The Booker family home in Barnesville. By 1920, George had been married for seven years to Hattie Rivers. Even though he was still working as a janitor, they had purchased a home free and clear on West Chapline Street.

May Booker (1860-). Few documents were found for May Booker except for the family lore that indicated she had a son named Corkny with a man surnamed Williams. They may have settled in Brooklyn, NY.[105] In many of our generations, "May" is selected as a middle name.

Ella L. Booker (1863-). With an unknown man, Ella had a daughter in 1883, Ida Mae Booker, who married James Hamilton in 1904. They had seven children: Lind, Lloyd, Ralph, John Robert, Philip, Clyde, and Helen May "Betty" Hamilton. In 1920, Ella was listed as widowed. Ida Mae lived in Barnesville through 1940. She died in 1973 in Uniontown, Fayette County, PA.[106] Her daughter Clara, born in 1889, was still living in Margaret's Vine Street home in 1920. She seems to have had a son named William Foster who married in Detroit, Michigan, in 1950.

Edward H. Booker (1864-1919). Edward was Margaret's first child born in freedom, the year after her family migrated to Barnesville. His 1899 marriage certificate indicates his father was Hugh Booker. The author theorized that Edward's father was the same Hugh who was freed by John White Stalnaker in 1863, and that Edward's middle name was Hugh, although not confirmed in records.

William A. Booker (1869-?). William lived with Margaret until 1900, but may have gotten into mischief, ending up in the Allegheny

County, PA, workhouse in 1901. He was described as being five feet five inches tall, 160 pounds, black hair, brown eyes, mulatto. His occupation had been a teamster, but he was assigned to being a carpenter's helper. This was his first offense, listed as a "Susp. Person" who had served thirty days in prison. The only other document found was a Social Security Application Claim filed March 29, 1950 that may have been for Margaret's son.

Sylvester Booker (1871-?). Sylvester lived with Margaret off and on for a few decades in Barnesville, eventually moving to Columbus, Ohio. There, he was shot in the head and died of a head wound. Whether Sylvester had a too-close friendship with gin and tonic and stumbled in front of a car is unknown.

Appendix B – Researching Margaret's Life
[Spoiler Alerts!]

Our family historian, M. Lavata Williams, shared fascinating stories about my three times great-grandmother, Margaret Booker, at our 1983 and 2003 family reunions in Ohio. (Figure 16)

So why, after forty years of research, had I still not found documents specifying the first and last name of Margaret's owner, whether there was more than one slaveholder, who her parents were, exactly where she was born, exactly where she lived during her years in bondage, where the name Booker came from, and whether she was a cook, laundress, farm worker, or breeder?

I used a plethora of documentary evidence, social media communications[107] and DNA evidence to test my theories. Many were proven beyond a shadow of a doubt, others still require further research. I wanted to learn enough about Margaret Booker to write a convincing literary nonfiction story from her unique point of view. I wanted the reader to imagine what it was like to be thirty years a slave followed by nearly fifty years of freedom.

I developed a rigorous research plan to accomplish these goals (Appendix A). I vowed to conduct an exhaustive search of records, not just sampling online documents from my comfortable home in California. Appendix C describes my genealogy visits to West Virginia and Ohio where Margaret lived from 1834 to 1911. I read numerous books about slaves and free people of color living in both states.

To learn how to perform intermediate and advanced-level DNA analyses, I took a three-day intensive course from the Midwest African American Genealogical Institute in 2020. I was determined—crazed, really—to finally uncover the truth about my three times great-grandmother.

Thankfully, there were only a couple of hundred slaves in Randolph County, West Virginia, which made it possible for me to research almost all of them in an attempt to find my family relations.

BOOKER'S GENEALOGY
by M. Lavata Williams, 2003

After President Abraham Lincoln signed the Emancipation Proclamation on January 1, 1863, the plantation owner freed Margaret Booker and her five children, and he also gave her a buckboard and, I assume, the horse that pulled the wagon.

Four of her children—Cornelia, George, May, and Ella—resided with her on the plantation, but Joseph (born Joab) Booker, who was around ten years old, had been farmed out. Margaret and her four children climbed aboard the buckboard and drove to the plantation where her oldest child, Joab, was on loan.

Now having her five children, she left Beverly, Virginia (now West Virginia) and headed north. They traveled by day and slept under the buckboard at night. Crossing the Ohio River at Martin's Ferry, the family settled in Barnesville, Ohio, where Margaret made a living as a washwoman. She had three more children—Edward, William, and Sylvester—as a free woman.

Margaret Booker was born into slavery in February 1834 and died after 1900 in Barnesville. While a slave she was tied to a tree and horse-whipped because she refused to lay with the master, having just given birth. She died with the whip marks on her back.

Joab Booker's father was the plantation owner. His (white) wife and Margaret Booker gave birth to sons the same day. The plantation owner named the son by his wife Joseph and the one by Margaret Joab. When Grandpa Booker was freed, he changed his named to Joseph.

Figure 16: Interesting snippets of information about Margaret Booker obtained from the family elders was provided by Historian Lavata Williams at the 1983 and 2003 family reunions.

With a lucky nudge from the ancestors one Saturday morning during the fifth month of work on this project, I glimpsed unexpected hints from an online slide show given by the Beverly Heritage Center in Randolph County, WV. They shed the stark light of truth on my fevered investigative efforts and helped solidify my theories into plausible proofs.

Who Owned Margaret?

My list of research questions began with learning the name and lineage of Margaret's slaveowner. If family lore was true that the owner fathered five of her children, then he would genetically be my third great-grandfather. Margaret's grandson, George Booker, revealed in a 1976 letter to me that the slaveowner's surname was Earle. But what was his first name?

Months into this latest genealogy adventure, I found a transcribed interview from 2003 that held the long-sought secret. Great-uncle George confided to Professor Ric Sheffield of Kenyon College in Knox, Ohio, that the slaveowner's name was John Earle. I contacted Professor Sheffield, who became a fount of knowledge concerning my Booker family.

Fortunately, there was only one Earle family in all of Randolph and its adjacent counties in West Virginia. As described in Chapter 2, I was able to trace the Earle lineage to Frederick County, Virginia, back to Westmoreland, Virginia, all the way back to Sir John Earle I. He was the first of their ancestors to sail to America, coming from Somerset, England, in 1649.

DNA evidence found some relatives who descend from the same Earle line (Appendix F). This gave me some measure of confidence that we were blood-related to the Earles, thus confirming family lore. However, I would have expected more, and much stronger, DNA relationships than found.

It soon became evident that John Baylis Earle was not Margaret Booker's only owner. Serendipity—or maybe the ancestors working overtime—maneuvered me to see a digital slide entitled, "A Woman Named Margaret," from a live streaming presentation at the Beverly Heritage Center.

I learned that in 1846, John White Stalnaker' sold a twelve-year-old slave girl named Margarett to Elizabeth S. Earle who was John B. Earle's first wife and, thus, my Slave Margaret's new owner (Chapter 4). When Elizabeth died in 1851, Slave Margaret became the sole property of John B. Earle. That means my Slave Margaret was owned by John B. Earle, Elizabeth S. Earle before him, and John W. Stalnaker before her.

But there's more. John White Stalnaker's mother, Margaret Elizabeth White Stalnaker Kittle died in 1846. In Chapter 5, I imagined Slave Margaret called her Miz Margaret Elizabeth and I called her MEWSK by her initials.[108] Therefore, MEWSK probably owned my three times great-grandmother from birth, as explained in the next section. When MEWSK died in 1846, John White Stalnaker sold Slave Margaret to Miz Margaret Elizabeth's granddaughter (Appendix D), Elizabeth S. Earle, for one dollar. Heavy sigh.

The 1846 bill of sale solidified my thesis linking my Margaret to the Stalnakers and the Earles. There was derivative evidence—a typed list of slave births paperclipped to the front of the "Index of 1853 to 1883 Births" at the Randolph County Courthouse—indicating a slave named Margarett was owned by T. B. Earle; I feel the first initial was likely a typo for J. B. Earle (John B. Earle).

Therefore, I concluded that my Margaret had four slave owners during her nearly thirty years a slave: Miz Margaret Elizabeth (1834-1846), John White Stalnaker (1846), Elizabeth S. Earle (1846-1851), and John B. Earle (1851-1863).

Who Were Margaret's Parents and Siblings?

Another fortuitous finding from a Beverly Heritage Center slide show discussed the tale of "Ginger Cake Peg." According to a story by local author, Lucy Brown McCrum, in her "Recollections of Old Beverly," six-foot-tall Peg became the servant/slave of schoolteacher Jane Crouch until the end of the Civil War and afterward.

An 1832 estate transaction indicated that deceased Herbert "Richard" Kittle bequeathed a slave woman named Peg to his wife, Miz Margaret Elizabeth, and that he willed a slave girl Phebe to his daughter, Jane Kittle. A slave named Phebe is also found in the 1840 Will of Adam See, and the 1850 Slave Schedule of Adam Crawford, with a death date of 1856. I presumed Phebe was Peg's child likely born in the 1820s.

My Margaret was born in 1834. A slave girl under the age of ten was listed in John White Stalnaker's home in 1840. I mused that the girl was my Margaret only six years old. I theorized she was Peg's daughter and Phebe's sister. I believe John White Stalnaker's widowed mother, Miz Margaret Elizabeth, was living in his household with slave girl Margaret until Miz Margaret Elizabeth died in 1846, then her son sold my Margaret to Elizabeth Earle.

Court records specify that Peg was willed to Miz Margaret Elizabeth by her husband, Herbert Richard Kittle, after he died in 1831. I believe Peg consorted with a slave named Edward "Ned" Backus and had his baby in February 1834 (my Margaret). I theorize that Peg lived with baby Margaret in the John White Stalnaker household for only a few years. There is no paper trail proving my presumption, but there's plenty of circumstantial evidence that supports the contention.

Since there is no mention of a slave woman living with John White Stalnaker in 1840, I assumed Peg was living elsewhere by then. I don't know if Miz Margaret Elizabeth sold Peg to Jane Crouch or possibly freed her. Hence, the story in Chapter 4 musing that my Margaret was largely raised by Miz Margaret Elizabeth until the elderly lady died in 1846.

Since Peg is a nickname for Margaret, I believed my three times great-grandmother was named for Peg or Miz Margaret Elizabeth (Chapter 8).

I speculated that Edward "Ned" Backus—a slave of the Crouch family—was my fourth great-grandfather. The light bulb illuminated the reason why my Margaret and her children migrated in 1863 to Barnesville: maybe they went there to live with her father, Edward Backus, who was already living on Vine Street with his wife Eve. At least that's my speculation of why they were all living together in the Vine Street house in Barnesville in 1870.

As explained in "Ned's Incredible Adventure" from Chapter 7, Edward "Ned" Backus was finally freed by Abraham Crouch's Will in 1854, even though Abraham died in 1849. Sadly, Ned's wife and children were kept in bondage by the Crouch heirs. Unbelievably, he received legal and financial assistance from the magnanimous Bernard Tyler, Esquire. Ned pled his case at the Fusion Convention—a precursor to the Republican Party. On August 18, 1855, the Portage Sentinel newspaper described Edward's incredible story in welcome detail. Ned and his beloved family were blissfully reunited in Starks County, Ohio, as of the 1860 Census.

I concluded that during her nearly thirty years a slave, my Margaret was the daughter of Peg and Ned Backus, and that she was owned by Miz Margaret Elizabeth, John White Stalnaker, Elizabeth S. Earle, and John B. Earle, the latter who sent Margaret and their children to Ohio in 1863. However, there is still a niggling feeling that Eve Backus might actually be Margaret's true mother…

Were There Two Josephs?

Family lore in Figure 16 asserted that the owner's wife gave birth to a son named Joseph, on the same day that Margaret Booker's eldest mulatto son, Joab, was born in Beverly. The slaveowner was allegedly the father of both boys. Joab was said to have changed his name to Joseph after he became a free man, purportedly to be like the owner's son's name. Was that story true?

It is true that my great-great-grandfather Joseph Booker (nee Joab), was born on September 9, 1855, in Beverly, Randolph

County, Virginia. [Note: Some records indicate he was born in 1854]. According to his Social Security Application, Joseph's father was "Unknown" and his mother was listed as Margaret Booker.

It is true that a white baby named Joseph E. Earle was born in "abt 1855" and died two years later, according to a death record. He was the son of Eveline (no maiden name) and Samuel Henry Earle (1813-1874). It is true that the white toddler named Joseph Earle lived in Berkeley County, West Virginia, about 150 miles away from the mulatto Joab in Beverly. It is possible that Samuel Earle visited Beverly around Christmastime in 1854 and perhaps took some "warm comfort" one night, impregnating slave Margaret to create my second great-grandfather Joab/Joseph Booker. It's an unlikely long shot, but possible.

It is true that Samuel H. Earle was the son of Colonel Joab Early and Ruth Stovall Hairston who was a member of the Hairston family who owned 10,000 slaves on forty-five plantations throughout four southern states.109

It is true that Samuel H. Earle's uncle was the infamous General Jubal Early, avid proponent of the Lost Cause of the South.110 It is possible that General Jubal Early found his way to Beverly at some point during his Civil War forays east of the Shenandoah Valley. It is rumored he made many mulatto babies.

It is true that we have several DNA matches to Hairstons, Stovalls, and folks from Jubal Early's clan. However, those DNA relations may have been more due to an as-yet-undocumented Booker connection, as is explained in the next section.

Birth and Bill of Sale documents indicate that John Bayles Earle owned a slave named Margarett in Beverly. There is no documentation that John Earle fathered a child named Joseph. However, it is true that his second son, John B. Earle, Jr. (the tree climber in Chapter 11), was born in December 1855, three months after my Joab/Joseph's birth. More evidence points to Margaret Booker's Joab being the son of John B. Earle. However, the family lore about two Josephs may be possible if confirmatory documents surface in the future.

Conflicting information casts doubt on the veracity of the two Josephs having the same father. Therefore, I could neither corroborate nor overturn the elders' story that "the slaveowner fathered two boys who were born on the same day in 1855, one by his white wife and the other by his black slave Margaret."

Additionally, there is conflicting date information about when Margaret's family arrived in Barnesville, Ohio. Our family historian was told by the elders that Margaret's family left Beverly, West Virginia, "soon after" the Emancipation Proclamation was signed, however, the historian said Joseph was "about ten" when he was "farmed out" before the family left Beverly. Joseph's Social Security Application indicates he was born in September 1855. An extensive newspaper article about the Booker family, written by Joseph's grandson, Joe Booker, in the 1999 "Mount Vernon News Looking Glass" indicated Joseph was "freed from slavery when he was ten-years-old and that the Bookers arrived in Barnesville in 1865." However, Joseph's brother, Edward H. Booker, was born in September 1864 in Barnesville; however, the June 1870 Census indicated he was five; hence for a possible 1865 birthdate in Barnesville. For this story, I chose to imagine they left Beverly in the summer of 1863. The story would be no different if I chose 1864 as the migration date instead. I still believe Hugh and Margaret fathered Edward soon after the trek, and project that Edward's "H" middle name is Hugh.

The Derivation of the Booker Name

The Booker surname was attached to all five of Margaret's children, even though family lore and genealogical and DNA evidence (Appendix F) suggest that slaveowner John B. Earle was the likely father of Joab/Joseph, Cornelia, George, May, and Ella, all of whom were born in Beverly, West Virginia. So where did the Booker name come from?

Margaret "Backus" was listed as the mother on Edward H. Booker's, Marriage Certificate in 1899. Hugh "Booker" was named the father. Therefore, it is possible that Slave Margaret took the "Booker" surname, perhaps through an unfound marriage to Hugh, sometime after 1863 when they left West Virginia for Ohio.

A family surnamed Butcher lived next to the Old Earle Farm near the current location of Elkins, West Virginia. One of their sons was named Hugh (and Hugh was a fairly common first name amongst Beverly residents). Great Uncle Charles' closest DNA match who had Butchers in her family tree, had generations labelled "Butcher/Booker" from eastern Virginia in her family tree. Was John White Stalnaker's slave Hugh originally the slave of the next-door-neighbor Butcher family? Did he choose the surname Booker when he was freed in 1863?

A second edition will have to ferret out exactly where the Booker name came from and why we have many DNA matches to black and white Bookers from Amelia and Cumberland Counties in Virginia.

The Confounding Booker Connection

Part of the Genealogical Proof Standard requires researchers to address any confounding information and describe how it was resolved. There was no end of conflicting data on this project, from differences in dates and names, DNA connections that suggested additional family lines, as well as the example in the previous section.

Because slave women were often coerced into sexual relations by their masters, overseers, or the master's friends, there can be any number of possible genetic relationships that don't correspond to a traceable paper trail.

With that said, exciting documentary and DNA links between my family and the Samuel Henry Earle family required a lot of brainpower to unfurl. Samuel's grandmother, Mary Booker, was a member of the prominent slaveholding Booker family in Amelia and Cumberland Counties, Virginia.

Was baby Joseph E. Earle's mother, Eveline, actually a light-skinned slave born to Bookers in Cumberland? Is that why Margaret's granddaughter was named Evelina? Was Edward Backus' wife, Eve, in any way related to the white Joseph E. Earle's mother Eveline?

Was Edward Ned Backus' surname originally "Crouch" or "Booker" or "Butcher" or "Backhouse?" Did Edward choose to change his surname to Backus after he was freed by Abraham Crouch's Will in 1854? Were Abraham's other slaves—Richard, Lorza, Mae, Joshua, Brown and Lydia—kin of Edward or his wife Eve, or their children Lora Ann and Anzina111 Were any of them kin of Margaret Booker? A future research trip to the Virginia Archives and pertinent landmarks in Cumberland and Amelia Counties may help sort out the truth from the noise.

A Surprise Connection

I received a surprising email from a brilliant local genealogist friend of mine, Sharon Styles. From her home in Sacramento, California, she found my name in a list of DNA matches for her family. How exciting! After a bit of digging, I was delighted to find our common ancestor is most certainly Margaret Booker's last slaveowner, John B. Earle! His eldest son, Baylis Earle, migrated to Waco, McLennan, Texas. That's near where Sharon's family had been enslaved! Her riveting documentary, Speak My Name and I Shall Live Again, chronicled her family's efforts to find the Marlin, Texas, cemetery where her ancestors were buried. Her documentary is syndicated on the Public Broadcasting System. The icing on the cake is that Sharon also has Booker ancestors…

Is Mary S. the Key?

I craved to prove genetic descendancy from the Margaret Booker /John Earle ancestral couple. To that end, I utilized several analytical tools offered by various DNA companies. As briefly explained in Appendix F, Ancestry.com has useful family tree and DNA matching tools and a huge database. However, their monumental flaw is that they lack a chromosome browser.112 The Family Tree DNA, 23andme, and My Heritage DNA companies offer a chromosome browser, triangulation,113 and clustering114 tools to help find relatives who match overlapping segments of specific chromosome. I employed all of those devices in this research.

In the spring of 2020, 23andme began offering a "Predicted Tree" which estimates which of our DNA relatives descend from specific ancestral couples. I used my DNA results and that of my maternal Uncle Dale Carter, as we are known direct descendants of Margaret and John Earle. (Figure 27) There's another direct descendant, my distant cousin J. B., but I've been unable to reach him to obtain access to his full DNA results on 23andme.

I was thrilled to find one woman, Mary S., who 23andme predicted descends from the Margaret & John Earle ancestral couple. Mary S. matches Dale on chromosomes 1, 5, and 6, for a total of 55 centimorgans,115 indicating she is probably a third cousin once-removed, sharing a second great-grandparent with Uncle Dale. Her 23andme account indicates her maternal grandfather was born in Minnesota and that her family surnames included Myers. Bingo! Two of Margaret's sons, Joseph and Edward, married into the Myers family in Barnesville, Ohio.

I tried without success to contact Mary S. for more information about her family. Persevering—as all genealogists must do—I looked at every bit of information on every online platform I could find, such as: other DNA companies, Facebook, and Google. Only about three percent of Mary's genome is from Sub-Saharan Africa, 96.5 percent is from Europe. I found seven people in the 23andme database who match both Mary S. and Dale. Appendix F reveals a few of the steps I took to feel comfortable in affirming that various DNA tools genetically connected numerous Earle, Kittle, Crouch, and Stalnaker lines to my family.

The Second Edition

My goal was to produce a first edition book which provided enough evidence to substantiate Margaret's owner, her parents, where she was born, where she lived, what tasks she performed during and after slavery, and how she got the Booker surname. I wanted to write this book from Margaret's point of view, weaving factual information into an interesting and credible story that anyone could understand and enjoy.

Ultimately, I want to trace our lineage back as far as possible. Using DNA and slave manifest data, which is becoming more available to the masses, it may be possible to have my "Kunta Kinte"[116] moment in the future. I dream of learning about specific families in specific places in Africa and Europe where I may visit the land of my ancestors. And I'm still holding out for proof of that Native American connection my great-uncle George Booker and my paternal grandmother, Daisy Dooley Marshall, swore we had.

I am happy to have developed a credible theory of Margaret's parentage—Edward "Ned" Backus and Big Peg, but I would like to find more documentary evidence to prove that relationship and find out more about their roots. With each book, I strive to identify at least one more generation in our family tree.

The "Loose Ends" portion of Chapter 7 is more fodder for a second edition book. In 1770, Samuel Noah Earle III issued a Will in Frederick County, Virginia, which bequeathed one negro man named "Ned" to his son. Was the bequeathed Ned my Edward "Ned" Backus' father who fathered a son in 1791? Or was my fourth great-grandfather, Edward "Ned" Backus, originally surnamed Booker, as posited in Chapter 7? Was he and/or his parents born in Amelia or Cumberland County, Virginia, as the property of the

Richard Booker family, then sold to the Crouch family who migrated to Randolph County, Virginia, before 1800?

Was Edward's wife, Eve, connected to the Early-Hairston clan, as discussed earlier in this chapter? Or were Eve's parents always enslaved by the Crouches who came from Augusta County, Virginia, to Huttonsville in Randolph County, VA, in the 1770s? Who were Eve's parents? What is her story? Was Eve Margaret's real mother?

Was any of my family owned by the Crouches and the Earles who lived in Frederick County, Virginia, before twenty-two-year-old Archibald Earle migrated from Frederick County to Beverly in 1810?

Did some of the Kittle family migrate from New York to Frederick County, Virginia, becoming acquainted with the Earle family in the 1700s before moving to Randolph County, VA? Did the Kittles own my ancestors before migrating to Randolph County, VA?

The 1860 Census indicated Edward and Eve Backus were living in Union, Starks County, Ohio, with a daughter named Laura Ann Sophia and Angina Elizabeth, who were mentioned in the Portage Sentinel newspaper article. Was daughter Sophie Backus named for a slave-owning family member with the name Sophie, like Sophia Stalnaker? Was Angina named for John Earle's Aunt?

The 1860 Census reported that Adam E. and Sophia Backus were children living with Edward and Eve. However, there was no mention of a son in the Portage Sentinel news story. There was a daughter named Angina Elizabeth; was "Adam E" a typo in the Census? If real, why was he not mentioned in the paper as being a child of the Backuses? Was he a private who fought in the 99th Regiment of the US Colored Infantry in the US Colored Troops, his plaque C-99 on the African American War Memorial in Washington DC?

Finally, I wish to further investigate how the DNA sibling summation technique may be used to unequivocally state whether or not my Booker family is genetically tied to the Earles, Stalnakers,

Kittles, Crouches, Earlys, Bookers, and/or other families from Virginia and West Virginia.

Each new bit of information produces a greater thirst to know more. I hear the ancestors shouting, "You go, girl! Tell our stories so we will live on forever!"

The ancestors are smiling!

Appendix C - The Research Process

During my sixtieth trip around the sun, I panicked. Starting a new decade often brings up conflicting thoughts and emotions, as well as concerns about mortality. My mind became fraught with the fear that if I died tomorrow, my forty years of collecting family history information would be thrown away by my children. They don't know what to do with my boxes, binders, and folders of historical data. I had to somehow bring those census records, transcribed interviews, photographs, DNA results, and memories into interesting storybooks that my family would cherish, but how? I felt like I was drowning in a sea of tangled, unanswered questions, with no hope of providing sound answers.

The ancestors would wake me every morning at five a.m., pushing me to get up and whispering, "Write our stories. Write our stories NOW!" I fretted every day until I noticed an advertisement on Facebook from the Genealogists' Writing Room. They were offering a free webinar117 which would teach African Americans how to write our own stories, instead of letting others write our history for us. Bingo! That was exactly what I needed. I tuned into the webinar on October 1, 2016, and learned two things that finally got me headed on the right track:

"Start today by writing what you already know about one of your ancestors, not all of your family lines at once." They encouraged us to start writing a book today with whatever documents, interviews, and partially written stories we've already gathered. I had hundreds of documents in my computer, boxes, file folders, and binders. Could I really start writing a book today?

"Understand and accept that you may never be able to answer all of your questions, but that's OK. Write about what you tried to reveal, what you did find, and what you weren't able to prove. Simply indicate that the goals you did not achieve in this first edition book will be revisited in a second edition in the future. But write the first edition NOW!"

For an extreme Type A person like me, that was the perfect advice. It meant I could select one person to write about, develop research questions clarifying what I wanted to discover about that person, and gather documents, interviews, and memories I'd already collected. Once I understood I could start writing a first edition book, the disjointed cogs in my brain shifted into gear.

I began to think of writing a book like any other assignment I had during my three decades at the California Highway Patrol where I had been a researcher, analyst, and technical writer. To meet their challenging three-day turnaround deadlines, I developed a quick-start process for handling all types of assignments. I even taught my efficient quick-start system to six hundred analysts. So why not utilize the same process for writing a genealogy book? Why not start imagining my ancestors as being my bosses? I would never tell a CHP Commander that I couldn't do an assignment because I didn't know how. I had to figure it out and get it done within the allotted time period.

I could, should, and would adopt the same methodology for publishing genealogy books. With my new insight, I immediately understood how to proceed. I'm going to share my quick-start secrets with you right now. First, start with the end in mind. That means determine what the end product will be, like a paperback book, letter, blog, documentary, or photo book, for example. I wanted to write a paperback book that would be sold online, in bookstores and from my website. Additionally, I would mail books to the research libraries and archives where my family lived.

The second step is to develop a framework, like an outline, by opening a new word processing document and structuring the pages to look like the genre you are writing. For example, the first page of a family history-type book would be the Title page, listing the book title and author name. The next page could be a Copyright page, the third a Dedication page, followed by a Table of Contents, Introduction, Acknowledgments, a Timeline of Events, and maybe a Family Tree. I normally create ten empty Chapters to get me started, followed by a Conclusion page, Bibliography, Appendices, and End Notes pages. My book template is ready to be filled with words and images.

The third step is to determine who the book would be about. I pretend that I have a magic wand which allows me to interview any one of my relatives, past or present, for twenty-four hours. Then I ask myself the following questions. WHO would that one person be? WHY did I choose that person? WHERE did he or she live? What do I already KNOW about that person? WHAT do I want to find out about him or her? The next image contains my responses which provided an outline for this book.

"SO WHAT?" As one of my genealogy gurus, Dr. Shelley Murphy, likes to ask about the data we gather. It means, "What would I do with that survey information?"

The "WHO" refers to the protagonist, the heroine or hero the book is about. I prefer to mention WHO (my ancestor's name) on the Book Title and Introduction pages.

The "WHY" is the inspiration for the book, could be discussed in the Introduction and the first chapter, to set the stage for the story.

The "What I already KNOW" information might be presented in the second chapter.

The "WHERE" will be various chapters describing the locations where Margaret lived, how blacks were treated there, what the opportunities for enslaved and free were, etc.

The "WHAT" is the meat and potatoes—my goals for this book—what I'm seeking to learn about Margaret Booker. Each of those "What" questions could become separate chapters in the book.

I wrote an Introduction right away, indicating this book would be about my great-great-great-grandmother, Margaret Booker, why I chose her, and what my goals were. I wanted to prove with documents and DNA testing who her parents and slaveowner were, what her life was like as a slave and a free woman. Writing an Introduction at the beginning of the process and reviewing it periodically would keep me on track to finish writing, edit, publish/print it, and get it into the hands of my family, bookstores, genealogists, and the research libraries where Margaret lived.

Quick-Start Process for
The Mystery of Margaret Booker

WHO is the book about? Margaret Booker.

WHY write about that person? Since 1976, I've had exciting tidbits about her life, but I want to know the specifics.

WHERE did person live? Beverly, West Virginia, and Barnesville, Ohio.

What do you already KNOW about the person? (Background)
• She was born in about 1834.
• She's my great-great-great-grandmother.
• She lived in Beverly, WV.
• The slaveowner's surname was Earle.
• Her children were fathered by the slaveowner.
• Her son Joab/Joseph was my great-great-grandfather.
• The slavemaster gave her a buckboard in 1863 and told her to go to Ohio.
• She lived on Vine Street in Barnesville, OH.
• She had a laundry business in Barnesville, OH.
• She died in 1911.
• The 1870-1910 Censuses indicate who lived with her.

WHAT do you want to learn about the person? (Goals)
• The slaveowner's full name and his family history.
• Was there more than one slaveowner?
• Exactly (house) where did Margaret live?
• Was Margaret born in Beverly?
• Who were her parents and siblings?
• Was she a cook, laundress, farm worker, or *breeder*?
• Who were Edward and Eve Backus?
• Who fathered her children?
• What is the derivation of her Booker surname?
• How did she travel from West Virginia to Ohio during the Civil War?
• How did she live once free in Ohio?
• What happened to her children?
• Can DNA prove familial connections with Europeans and Africans?

One book per year is the mandate from my ancestor bosses and I don't intend to let them down. (Anyway, they won't let me sleep until I finish the job.)

Review, Ruminate, Review Again!

Imbued with my comfortable plan of action and book template ready to accept my research and elegant prose, a sense of can-do flowed through me. It felt like a meditative golden sun flowing into the top of my cranium, carrying its warm glow of energy and creative ideas to my receptive synapses. The road stretched languidly in front of me, paved and smooth, from the capital of California to Barnesville in central-east Ohio, to central-east West Virginia to my goal: a published book about Margaret Booker's life.

In my mind's eye, the documents and memories I had been collecting for decades about Margaret Booker, and new-found DNA relationships, would waltz and meld into a fascinating story of Margaret's resistance, her persistence, her resilience in becoming a businesswoman after her first thirty years a slave. I hoped my efforts to reveal Margaret's story would be rewarded this time with the truth, the whole truth, and nothing but the truth.

Sadly, preior to 2019, I had found no more information than what our maternal historian, Myrtle Lavata Williams, had collected for our 1983 family reunion. It's embarrassing to admit that we have no documented information about the Booker's lives before they migrated to Ohio in 1863. We didn't know exactly where they lived, nor what they did as slaves. We didn't even know whether their life journey actually began elsewhere, maybe farther east into Virginia.

Another compounding problem was that Randolph County where Margaret lived, had broken off from pro-Confederate Virginia, becoming West Virginia in June 1863. This means some records prior to the state split are in Harrison County and others are located in Randolph County, West Virginia files.

Another hindrance was gender. As my author friend, Robin Roberts Harris, mused in her book, *My Grandmother Rode a Horse*, "What about the women? They have names but finding them within their families is difficult. Women were ignored, their stories hidden behind the patrilineal family tree. Secondarily, they were only important because of the children they produced."

This was indeed the frustrating truth I experienced with my second book, Finding Otho: The Search for Our Enslaved Williams Ancestors. It was nearly impossible to find information about the lives of my female ancestorsenslaved great-great-grandmother, Alice Logan Williams, and my great-great-great-grandmother, Margaret Williams. I had a new plan of action for this book.

My first step was to place every scrap of paper I had collected about the Bookers since 1976 onto the floor in my "research room" (my son's former bedroom). This included documents kept in three-ring binders, thrown in boxes, nestled in file folders, or handwritten in notebooks. I organized the papers into piles by family surname, then by person within each family unit, then chronologically by date. I printed many of the documents that had heretofore only been in my laptop and added them to the appropriate stack on the floor. I transcribed videos and audio recordings and printed them out too, sorting them into the appropriate pile.

Using a spreadsheet program on my computer, I created timelines of events from those piles, for each of my known Booker and Earle family members. The timelines documented birth, marriage, and death dates; precisely where they lived; and newspaper articles about them; as well as notable events happening in America during their lives.

For the umpteenth time, I interviewed our family historian, Lavata Williams, about the Booker-oriented conversations she had with the elders four decades earlier.

As the weeks flew by, I filled out the book template chapters with narrative, dialog, and images, while I gathered additional documents. Answers began to slowly materialize as I carefully scrutinized the facts. DNA from our eldest elders' and various cousins became an important ally in suggesting solutions to my questions of blood lineage. I kept fine-tuning my manuscript, then shared the chapters with one of my writing groups and others, seeking their input to refine The Mystery of Margaret Booker. I even solicited input from my online social media Facebook and other friends in choosing a title and cover for this book.

Appendix D - Author's Biography

For twenty-seven years, my goal had been to share the strength and majesty of ancient cultures via beautiful, spiritual sculptures and clay pottery I hand-sculpted for my Kanika African Sculptures business, in my private art studio near Sacramento, California. Clay was the foundation of my artwork, but glass and vivid textiles, leather, shells, beads, and recycled welded steel enhanced the art.

Living the sixtieth year of my life in 2016, I realized the forty years I had spent collecting family history research data would be lost if I suddenly passed away. I needed to compile that collection of interviews, vital records and other documents, into stories my relatives would not only understand, but enjoy. I felt the urge to ensure our contributions would enhance the American historical record, by donating my books to the Library of Congress, local libraries and historical societies in the lands where my ancestors toiled as slaves.

After publishing my first book, The Ancestors Are Smiling! in 2017, I began to receive requests to speak about my genealogical journey at various genealogy, African American, art, and school groups. Finding Otho: The Search for Our Enslaved Williams Ancestors was published in 2018 and earned a Book Award from the Northern California Publishers and Authors organization, as well as the Afro-American Genealogical and Historical Society (AAHGS). My goal to publish one book a year was met in 2019, with Finding Daisy: From the Deep South to the Promised Land. That book earned one Book Award from AAHGS and a Phillis Wheatley Book Award from the Sons and Daughters of the US Middle Passage. The Marshall Legacy (2021) and Finding Marshalls: A Genealogy Trip with a Black and White Twist (2022) were about my paternal lines. Ken Anderson: "Alias Special K" was an homage to my husband's brilliant but short life (2021).

I also published short stories in three Anthologies: (1) "Finally a Priority" in Northern California Publishers and Authors (NCPA) Destination: The World Anthology, Vol. 1; (2) "A Nickel for Your

Thoughts, Dad" in Daddy Issues: Black Women Speaking Truth and Healing Wounds; (3) "Wolf Song" in the NCPA's Birds of a Feather.

My mission is to encourage you, the reader, to write your family stories, by leaving a printed legacy of your family's footprint on the world. I hope the ideas in Appendix G—Solving Your Mystery—help you share your family stories.

Appendix E - Beverly & Barnesville

Flying over the edge of the historic Chesapeake Bay, I gazed down at where some of the earliest American colonies began. I arrived at the Baltimore-Washington International Thurgood Marshall Airport in early October 2019. The airport was aptly named for the first African American Supreme Court judge who played a pivotal role in American history. I had traveled to Maryland to accept an international book award from the Afro- American Historical and Genealogical Society for my Finding Otho: The Search for Our Enslaved Williams Ancestors book. Why not make a little side trip to West Virginia to research our Booker family line?

I rented a sleek, black Ford Fiesta which would be my chariot from Baltimore westward to Hagerstown, Maryland. I planned to visit with two friends I had met while on my previous trip to Washington County which resulted in the Finding Otho book. That first evening, I dined with Jane Neff, who not only volunteered to drive me anywhere I wanted to go during my 2017 trip, but also helped me gain access to several key places that had impacted my family in the 1800s.

The next morning, I wanted to take more photographs of Slave Rock in Boonsboro, visit the Antietam Battlefield, and glimpse the land my second great-grandfather, Otho Williams, had purchased in 1869. I wanted to imprint the sights, sounds, smells, and ancestral spirits into my memory. Up and down, round and round, were rocky hillocks of damp green carpets, sprinkled with fallen red and orange leaves. It was an autumnal beauty hard to forget.

I could not dawdle. I had a ten a.m. appointment at the Antietam Iron Works in Sharpsburg. I had promised to deliver a copy of Finding Otho to the owner, Wayne McCrossin, who had been so welcoming to me on my previous genealogy trip. My trusty smart phone on the ready, I captured incredible views of the Antietam Iron Works complex, including the fifty-foot furnace smokestacks, as I approached my destination. After parking in their small lot next to Harper's Ferry Road, I made my way around the largest masonry structure. It served from 1763 until the Civil War as the main office, general store, kitchen, house, and post office for the Iron Works. Perky yellow and orange marigolds, velvety sage-green rabbit's ear, lavender lilacs, and various pink and red azaleas bordered both sides of the mossy, weathered brick walkway leading to the door. Those very bricks may have felt the weight of my three times great-grandfather, Prince Williams, when he worked there in 1812. I still get goose bumps imagining that I could have been walking in his footsteps at that very moment.

Wayne—still a tall drink of water—was as charming as ever. After an hour of chitchat about our lives, Wayne and his friendly daughter were more than generous, sending me on my way with three books about the area, chocolates, zucchini bread, and an invitation to stay with them anytime in the future. Now that's what I call Southern hospitality!

Jumping back into my little Fiesta, I fiddled with the in-car GPS118 to determine the best route to get to my destination in West Virginia. I didn't realize it at the time, but the switchbacks and many route changes, sometimes every half-mile, would approximate how difficult it may have been to reach Beverly before the Staunton-Parkersburg Turnpike was completed in 1845.

Starting from Sharpsburg, I drove on curvy, one-lane roads north through Funkstown, where Prince Williams purchased property in 1842 and secured his wife's freedom so she could live for the rest of her life on his property. I continued northward through Hagerstown where my Finding Otho and The Ancestors Are Smiling! books grace shelves in the Western Maryland Room library and Washington County Historical Society.

Passing Fort Frederick, I silently applauded former slave Nathan Williams who purchased the downtrodden property for $7,000 in 1860. He not only maintained but enhanced the property for fifty years. I still fume that the National Park Service destroyed the Williams' home to make room for a parking lot.

My camera captured amazing views of majestic trees wearing their colorful frocks in the glory that is the Cumberland Mountains and the Shenandoah Valley in autumn. Misty blue smoke hovered over the Appalachian and Allegheny Mountains in the distance. I traveled along many different roads, switchbacks, elevations, and declinations. I even drove a short time on U.S. 50, which extends cross-country to my home in Sacramento, California.

Being a forest girl, I had to stop many times along the way to rejoice in the thick woodland on both sides of the road. Nature was at her best with the sound of birds, bounding deer, rushing creeks, and the earthy, herbally smell of fall foliage. Bold yellows, oranges, reds, and deep greens and browns abounded everywhere. My trusty video camera held outside the car window captured the technicolor magic for a lifetime of memories.

The Genealogy Room

The first breath of morning was scented with pine, the silence pierced only with twittering bird call and response. Angry clouds suited in gray portended the coming of a cold rain. After forty-three years imagining this moment, I had awakened in Randolph County, Virginia, in a comfortable hotel room, in the county seat of Elkins, only seven miles away from Beverly, West Virginia. That day would potentially open a vista to the truth about Margaret Booker's nearly thirty years a slave in that county.

The first drops of rain kissed the windshield as I loaded my computer bag, camera, phone, notebook, and wallet into the car after a hearty breakfast. I planned to do research at the Public Library in Elkins. Entering the one-story, red brick building, I noticed a cozy room to the right of the receptionist's desk. The homey, handwritten "Genealogy Room" sign in that entryway told me I was in the right place. Still leery about who I could confide in regarding my slavery-related purpose, I entered the genealogy research area without having to speak with anyone.

The room was petite, maybe twelve by ten-feet in size, with floor-to-ceiling books packed on three sides of the room. There were two shelves peppered with books written by Pearl S. Buck. I assumed that famous author of "The Good Earth" must have been a local girl.

Darn! There was no apparent organization to the books that I could tell. Tomes were neither sorted by topic nor author. I had to look at every single book in that room. It was tedious work, but ultimately beneficial, for it gave me an idea of what was important in West Virginia during the 1800s: mining and salt manufacturing in the Kanawha Valley, and both of those industries only thrived because of slave labor.

I also found texts which appeared to be original Census records that included slave ages and genders. I found original records that compiled birth, marriage, and death records. There were even some handwritten ledgers that mentioned slaves by name. All that information was online, but it was special to touch copies of original documents. The little library also held biographies of West Virginia families, including the Earle family who family lore connected to my ancestors.

Red-eyed, I left the library at noon for a much needed lunch break. Then the adventure so long anticipated would come to fruition later that afternoon. I was going to Beverly.

Where The Ancestors Rest

By the time I finished eating a taco from a drive-through in Elkins, the sky had turned varying shades of gray. Don't tell anyone, but hoping to capture precious moments of discovery, I positioned my digital camera on the dashboard of the car before the sky began to cry. A twist of the slim rod next to the steering wheel caused the long wiper arm to swing its wide arc back and forth, as though it was saying goodbye to the drops it shoved off the windshield.

About fifteen minutes from Elkins, a sweeping right turn led me into the town of Beverly, which is nestled in the Tygarts River Valley of Randolph County. There was so much traffic on the narrow main road into town: logging trucks, cars, and every other type of vehicle on the road at the same time. Glimpsing a tiny sign for the Chenowith/Beverly Cemetery, I turned onto the lane, and parked the car halfway around the back side. I couldn't help but marvel at the beauty of willowy yellowy-green foliage and cedar and pine trees bordering the cemetery. I took lots of pictures looking for familiar names such as Earle or Early (I found none), Buckey, and Booker (I found none). At that time, in October 2019, I wasn't aware of the intermarriages between families whose names would become as important as my own in the future.

The next stop was the museum Aunt Lavata believed would provide answers to my questions. The historic town of Beverly is located on Routes 291 and 250 in the Tygarts Valley of Randolph County. I saw a large American flag and a mobile home-type building with a sign that said, "Welcome to Beverly."

I parked, got out of the car, and went inside the diminutive building. In a tight, eight-foot by ten-foot space, a big quilt that announced "Beverly" hung on one wall, and some pictures of old-time Beverly on the wall opposite it. At the twelve-inch wide glass reception window, I briefly described why was there. The worker said I was in the wrong place. Evidently, I was where people pay their bills. A police dispatcher was in the tiny back office. Another woman handed me a two-inch binder containing a lot of town history. I sat down in a plastic white chair and started browsing.

There was one bit of information that jumped out at me. A man named Archibald Earle bought two acres of land all around the cemetery. I began to wonder if that meant his plantation or farmhouse was near that area. Would that mean my family lived near the cemetery? I had no idea at that moment.

The Beverly Heritage Center

After getting directions from the City Hall dispatcher, I braved heavy showers and got back into the car as quickly as possible. I drove across a main thruway to the Beverly Heritage Center, parked, then made a mad dash over the flagstone pathway. Inside, there was an amiable fellow named Matt.

I explained, "I'm here to see if I can find any information about my third great-grandmother, Margaret Booker, who had been a slave right here in Beverly. I think her slavemaster's last name was Earle or Early. Do you know anything about the African American population here, then or now?"

Matt exclaimed, "It's such a coincidence that you're here now because the curator, Chris, and I have been planning to open up a new exhibit in the spring of 2020. It will be about the African-American population that lived in Beverly between 1880 and 1920." I couldn't believe my luck! The ancestors were working overtime for me today.

Pointing in a direction just beyond the jail, which was kitty-corner to the Historic Center, he said, "Over there is the area where we think African-Americans lived until the 1920s." I went to the steamy windows trying to see through the heavy rain toward the direction he pointed. Beyond the jail was a rather flat pasture devoid of buildings, populated with some low bushes and unkempt green grasses. Beyond that were old houses, and some low, weathered, dilapidated gray shacks. Is that where the black folks lived?

Matt said four historic buildings were moved to the square at Court Street in the center of Beverly. The Heritage Center tells the story of Rich Mountain and the First Campaign of the Civil War, the pivotal role of the Staunton-Parkersburg Turnpike, and provides glimpses of daily life in a small rural county seat through the nineteenth century. As I went through each of the rooms full of artifacts, and written and audio information, I began imagining what life was like for whites and blacks 150 years ago. The Historic Beverly website (http://www.historicbeverly.org) is a marvelous repository, bringing to life the history of this rural area.

The first building in the Center was all about Beverly military men in the first World War. I didn't see any black people represented there, so I quickly went to the next room. The second building was all about transportation, starting with the construction of the turnpike, then railroads, then automobiles. I took tons of pictures and video to commemorate what I saw and heard and felt.

The third space was the former court room. The warm tone of the wooden furnishings and floor, photos from the 1800s, gavel and all, made the scene come to life. The interactive components recreated actual court cases, including that of Lydia Ann, a slave who petitioned the court to allow her continued residence in Randolph County as a free woman of color. The laws of the Commonwealth of Virginia at the time stated that if any slave was given their freedom, they must leave the state within a year or be re-enslaved. Lydia Ann won her plea and was allowed to stay.

25 June, 1838

LYDIA ANN: "Two Months ago, I petitioned the court to continue my residence in Randolph County as a free woman of color. As you all are well aware, the laws of the Commonwealth of Virginia state that if any slave is given their freedom, they must leave this state. Honorable Judges of the court, this County is my home. I beseech you to let me stay here."

JUDGE: "It is the opinion of all nine Justices of the Peace here in Randolph County in the Commonwealth of Virginia that – as you are a woman of good character – we unanimously grant you your request to remain in the aforesaid County and State."

I later learned that, as of 1835, the population of Beverly was 184, including sixteen slaves and two free African Americans.119 Was one of those enslaved people my third great-grandmother, Margaret Booker, who was born around 1834? If so, whose slave was she and who were her parents and siblings?

Another room covered the Civil War, complete with bullets and firearms. Prior to the War there was a volunteer company in Beverly, composed of the young townsmen armed with flintlock muskets.

Another room was all about recreation, cooking implements, a printing press, and a huge weaving loom. The last room was a gift store with books, glasses, canned foods, sewn goods, etc. I ended up buying a blood-red T-shirt with "Beverly Heritage Center, West Virginia" proudly on the front.

As I left that charming tribute to local history, large puddles forced me to jump and dodge across the lane to the Historic Beverly Antique Mall. It is 4,000 square feet of space which was originally the David Goff house, with parts as old as 1795. The house was conscripted to become the Beverly Union Hospital during the Civil War. There were five rooms downstairs crammed with antiques.

In the second room, underneath the fireplace, were the cutest little irons. My great-grandma Myrtle Booker immediately came to mind. She had a laundry business in her home in Mount Vernon, Ohio. She took in dirty clothes and linens from the white professionals in town, washed them in a large metal tub, and pinned them onto clotheslines outside. When the weather was bad, clothes would hang inside the house to dry before she worked her magic with the iron and heavy starch. Great-grandma loved ironing and took immense pride in her work. Her daughter, Reba, regaled us with stories of how painstakingly her mother heated one iron in the wide fireplace, while she

Iron from Beverly Antique Mall.

used a second hot iron and starch to press each garment into stiff perfection. Myrtle would hang the pressed shirts on hangers throughout the downstairs rooms, admiring her work with a satisfied grin. I later learned my three times great-grandmother, Margaret, had a laundry business in Barnesville, Ohio. I had to buy an iron in their honor from the hometown of our ancestors. The iron had a thick wooden handle, which is an important feature so you don't burn your hands as you are handling it. Five dollars for an heirloom? A bargain!

Upstairs was crammed with handcrafted items that were made or used by the inhabitants of Beverly, such as linens, blankets, clothes, jewelry, hats, lampshades, cabinet handles, furniture, etc. I left the antique shop after purchasing the iron and three books about the local area—including Civil War Legends of Rich Mountain and Beverly, West Virginia, by Mary G. Ward.

I drove toward Fountain Drive, to see if there were any old buildings left which might have housed a small black population. On one side of the road were very old, decrepit outbuildings. Did any slaves, or their freed descendants, live in those worn buildings over a century ago?

Secrets in the Randolph County Courthouse

I awoke at six thirty on my third morning in West Virginia, thinking in bed about the day's itinerary. It would be a long stretch, spending the morning at the courthouse, and four or more hours driving to eastern Maryland. Finally rising at eight a.m., I showered, washed my hair, packed, then breakfasted at eight forty-five, checked out, hopped into my car with my backpack and computer bag. Driving only four minutes from the hotel, I arrived at the venerable old building that is the Randolph County Court Administration Offices. It took me a while to find parking, but that gave me the opportunity to drive around the charming tree-shaded, older neighborhood and take numerous pictures and video of the homes.

When I got into the County Clerk's office, the cordial office manager showed me around the various file rooms. The first held rows and rows of land deeds, wills (after 1900) and fiduciary books. The second had births, deaths, marriages, and land plats. The manager shocked me by saying I couldn't take photos of the documents I wanted to record! However, they would gladly make any needed copies, for one dollar per page. Thank you very much. Darn! She didn't say I couldn't photograph the entire room, though, so I snapped a few pictures of the deed room as soon as she left.

There was an attractive, middle-aged, silver-haired man poring over a deed volume, right in the middle of the photographic scene I wanted to take. When I assured him I did not include him in my picture, he curtly replied, "I appreciate that."

Enough preliminaries—it was time to get to work. Because I dawdled that morning at the hotel, I only had a few hours left for courtroom research before I needed to get on the road for the lengthy trip to eastern Maryland.

I reentered the second room, which provided a round table for my exclusive use. I took out my "Bookers" binder of documents, a notebook, pencil, and my Apple laptop. I kept my phone by my side, wishing I were brave enough to snap pictures of the few pertinent documents found there. I spent about forty-five minutes gathering birth and death records, and writing slave-related information in my notebook, instead of getting the dollar-per-page printed copies.

It felt like I was looking for a needle in the haystack. I didn't know for sure who Margaret's slaveowner was, even though oral history said it was someone with the surname of Earle (or Early). Thankfully, Beverly was a rather small town, so I was able to scrutinize every record I could find for every Earle who lived in Randolph County between 1833 and 1864. That was the period Margaret Booker may have lived in Randolph County, WV.

There were so few people identified as slaves or free blacks. On the one hand it was discouraging not to find records. On the other it meant to me that enslaving people was not the norm in the town in which my family lived. It could signal the population there was more pro-Union, rather than pro-Confederate as I found during my previous Maryland, Alabama, and Mississippi genealogy trips.

Opening a heavy white volume labeled "Index of Births 1853-1883," paper-clipped to the front of the Table of Contents, was an odd piece of paper labelled, "List of Slaves and Their Owners." (Figure 21) What? Would I really be able to find my enslaved relatives that easily?

Shaking my head, No, that can't be possible. Midway down the page was someone named Margarett, listed as being the slave of T.B. Earle. She couldn't be my Margaret, could she? For a split second, I jumped out of my seat, suppressing a "Whoop-Whoop!" of joyful abandon. OMG![120]

Why can't I ever seem to enjoy a victory for more than two seconds? The next moment my logical brain discounted this possible find because my Margaret was born well before 1853, in around 1835. Could someone have mis-transcribed her actual birthdate on that paper? If so, this document would be a measure of confirmation that Margaret was in Beverly, and she was the property of the Earle family, at least as of 1853.

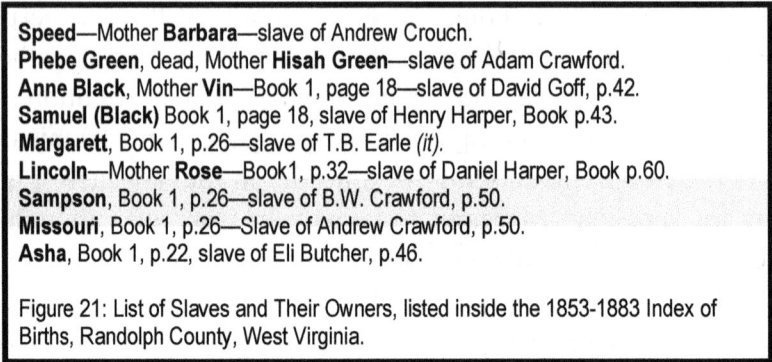

Speed—Mother **Barbara**—slave of Andrew Crouch.
Phebe Green, dead, Mother **Hisah Green**—slave of Adam Crawford.
Anne Black, Mother **Vin**—Book 1, page 18—slave of David Goff, p.42.
Samuel (Black) Book 1, page 18, slave of Henry Harper, Book p.43.
Margarett, Book 1, p.26—slave of T.B. Earle *(it)*.
Lincoln—Mother **Rose**—Book1, p.32—slave of Daniel Harper, Book p.60.
Sampson, Book 1, p.26—slave of B.W. Crawford, p.50.
Missouri, Book 1, p.26—Slave of Andrew Crawford, p.50.
Asha, Book 1, p.22, slave of Eli Butcher, p.46.

Figure 21: List of Slaves and Their Owners, listed inside the 1853-1883 Index of Births, Randolph County, West Virginia.

If the document was correct, who was T.B. Earle and was he related to the Archibald Earle I had read about the previous day at the Beverly City Hall? Cautious optimism was superseded with an urgency to look through as many books as possible in the courthouse before noon, when I had to get on the road for the four-hour drive to eastern Maryland. Back to that intriguing "Index of Births" in Figure 21. I looked for the referenced Book 1, page 26, to get more detail on primary evidence of Margarett's slave birth, but no slave births were listed anywhere in Book 1—one step forward, three-quarters of a step back. The ancestors were teasing me. Sigh.

Something is better than nothing, though, and I was now armed with more slaveowner surnames besides Earle and Booker to consider: Crouch, Crawford, Goff, Harper, and Butcher (hmm, was Butcher the correct spelling, instead of Booker?). Because owners sometimes traded or borrowed their slaves, I needed to research all slaveowner records in that small town.

I reviewed every handwritten birth, marriage, and death record in the 1830 to 1865 time period in the courthouse's Vital Records room. Then I walked back into the first room where deeds and wills were kept. I retrieved the Index of Land Deeds and began looking for deeds involving Earles and the other slaveowner names I had just found.

I must have looked perplexed to the man I saw earlier when I photographed the room upon my arrival. He spoke to me kindly this time, mentioning the oldest deeds were downstairs in the basement. He offered to show me where the door key and electronic pass-card were located at the Clerk's desk. The good Samaritan proceeded to walk me toward the elevator. With a twinge of suspicion, I decided to follow without letting my Stranger Danger radar go awry. We entered the elevator and went down into the basement. I was glad when the doors opened. I am not an elevator fan, especially when there are strangers standing next to me.

The Elkins Courthouse basement was no comparison to its counterpart that I visited during my Macon, Noxubee County, Mississippi, genealogy adventure six months earlier. In Macon, one could become lost forever in the dark, dank, musty, floor-to-ceiling repository of deliciously ancient documents. You might see a room like that in a Charles Dickens book. My friend and cousin, professional genealogist Sharon Morgan, creator of the "Our Black Ancestry" Facebook page, spent many weeks organizing the treasures in the Macon basement. In fact, she pulled up stakes and moved there so she could be closer to the home of our ancestors, and ensure their documented past was preserved for posterity. Treasures were in every nook and cranny there, but one had to look for them in the dimness of a single, naked light bulb.

The Elkins Courthouse basement was clean, light, bright, and organized. Large volumes were arranged neatly on rows and rows of six-foot tall shelving units, spaced evenly throughout the thirty-foot long room. A small army-green table under the chest-high windows was perfect for laying out documents. I found a few pertinent land records, but not many.

There was not much more of interest upstairs, except some plat maps that indicated who bought which land parcels. I had hoped the Will Index would shed light on the inventories of the Beverly slaveowners, but the Courthouse only seemed to have wills issued after 1900 (I must not have looked in the right place, as they were online). I needed pre-1865, slavery-era information. The office manager tersely said they had no manumission documents, nor were there any bills of sale. I'm not sure I believed her, but I guess I was done there.

I set my Maps App for "TownePlace in College Park, Maryland," turned on the windshield wipers and headlamps, my seatbelt, then proceeded to drive on my merry way in the autumn rain. It was already one p.m., and I strove to beat the Maryland commuter traffic, arriving before five p.m. The following night I was honored to accept an incredible book award from the Afro-American Historical and Genealogical Society for my Finding Otho: The Search for Our Enslaved Williams Ancestors book. This was part of the annual three-day AAHGS Conference which supplied me with more techniques for finding my Booker roots.

The Journey to Barnesville

I was invited to a surprise birthday party in Cleveland, Ohio, in October 2018. Always the multitasker, I decided to spend a few days visiting my mother's only living sibling—Uncle Dale Carter—and our esteemed family historian, M. Lavata Williams, before the party. I had always wanted to visit Barnesville, Ohio, the town where so many of my ancestors earned a fresh start at life. We piled into my rental car on a cold, crisp October morning. I kept my tape recorder on, recording my elders' memories, as we drove the one hundred miles from Columbus to Barnesville in Belmont County, Ohio.

The Welcome to Barnesville sign prompted me to take a picture of Uncle Dale and Cousin Lavata.

The sun peeked out momentarily when we parked at the Southern Cemetery. We scoured the gentle hills for family names. My two times great-grandfather, Joseph Booker, and his wife, Sara Myers Booker, were interred there, as well as other Myers, Goins, Carters, and a few Earlys.

I yearned to find Margaret Booker's home, but at the time I couldn't remember the address which appeared in the Census records. Being the driver, I couldn't research as I drove up and down the somewhat hilly streets. Instead, I held my camera out my open window and videotaped the entire length of Vine Street and the adjacent streets, hoping I had captured Margaret's home for viewing once I returned to California. We noted that very few of what we assumed were original wood-sided log cabins still existed.

Most homes had been renovated, replaced with mobile homes, or torn down and rebuilt. Thankfully, Google Maps captured the mobile-home-looking structure at 134 Vine Street. Lo and behold, I learned Margaret's home backed up to the back side of the Southern Cemetery! Hence, the spirit-filled beginning to Chapter 1.

The sky was darkening appreciably as we traveled a few blocks to downtown Barnesville, driving up and down Main Street, my video camera still recording the sites of the town. We decided to park by the venerable Bradfield Bank Building and explore. Brrr! The temperatures dropped considerably once the sun hid behind dark clowns. It was so cold my wimpy California girl teeth began chattering. Lavata attempted to recall what the elders had told her about Barnesville in 1982 after they requested her to put on the family's first reunion to explain to everybody how we were related. We stopped at a travel agency, or was it City Hall or the Tourist Office? We inquired about the African American population that used to live there one hundred years earlier. While there were a couple of books written by locals—which I skimmed for any mention of black folk—the employees couldn't help us much.

Back on the sidewalk, raindrops began slowly as we hightailed it back to the car several blocks away. Wet and cold but excited, we made our way back to the car and attempted to find the Captina African Methodist Episcopal Church and Cemetery in Somerset, Belmont County, Ohio. My smart phone's GPS program could not find it, so we stopped at an old gas station and a cafe for directions. Although it was only five miles away from Margaret's house, it took us a while to get there.

Family historian, M. Lavata Williams, and the author's maternal Uncle Dale Carter.

Frankly, it was ominous when we finally parked the car. Dark, dank, cold, wet, closed in by tall, dark, wet trees. The spirits roamed. I could feel them all around me, pushing their boney fingers into my shoulder, trying to determine if I was real. Thankfully, in 2017, the Belmont County Chapter of the Ohio Genealogical Society and Mark Morton of Gravestone Guardians of Ohio, with a grant from the Belmont County Tourism Council, began restoring the historic Captina African Methodist Episcopal Church cemetery which dates back to 1830.121 Once my eyes adjusted to the pall of the waning afternoon, I appreciated how beautifully restored the cemetery was. The headstones looked like new, the lush lawn mown, the evergreen trees magnificent in stature, protecting this jewel of memories from harm.

We surveyed the headstones for our family members: Philip Singleton Myers and his wife Elizabeth Simmons, and Underground Railroad conductor Alexander Sandy Harper. Myers, Letts, and other concerned descendants of those African Americans who moved there so long ago worked to get approval for an Ohio Historical Marker for this cemetery. The ancestors are smiling!

OHIO HISTORICAL MARKER

CAPTINA AFRICAN METHODIST EPISCOPAL CEMETERY

This cemetery stands as evidence of a once thriving African American farming community established in the 1820s. With the aid of community leader, Alexander "Sandy" Harper (c.1804-1889), Captina, originally called Guinea, became a stop on the Underground Railroad, a national network, shrouded in secrecy, of volunteers who directed slaves northward. Harper is buried in this cemetery, along with Benjamin Oliver McMichael (1860-1941), an educator who taught for twelve years in Captina/Flatrock at a segregated schoolhouse. There are 113 known burials in the cemetery, including nine Civil War veterans. At this site in 1825, an African Methodist Episcopal Church was established to serve the community. Many of its members left Captina to work in cities, but the church continued services until 1962. The building then fell into disrepair and collapsed during a windstorm in 1978.

OHIO BICENTENNIAL COMMISSION, THE LONGABERGER COMPANY
MYERS-HAMILTON REUNION COMMITTEE
THE OHIO HISTORICAL SOCIETY
2002

8-7

265

Appendix F - Owner Co

HOW THE STALNAKERS, WHITES, KITTLES AND EARLES ARE CONNECTED - Who Was Margaret's Father?

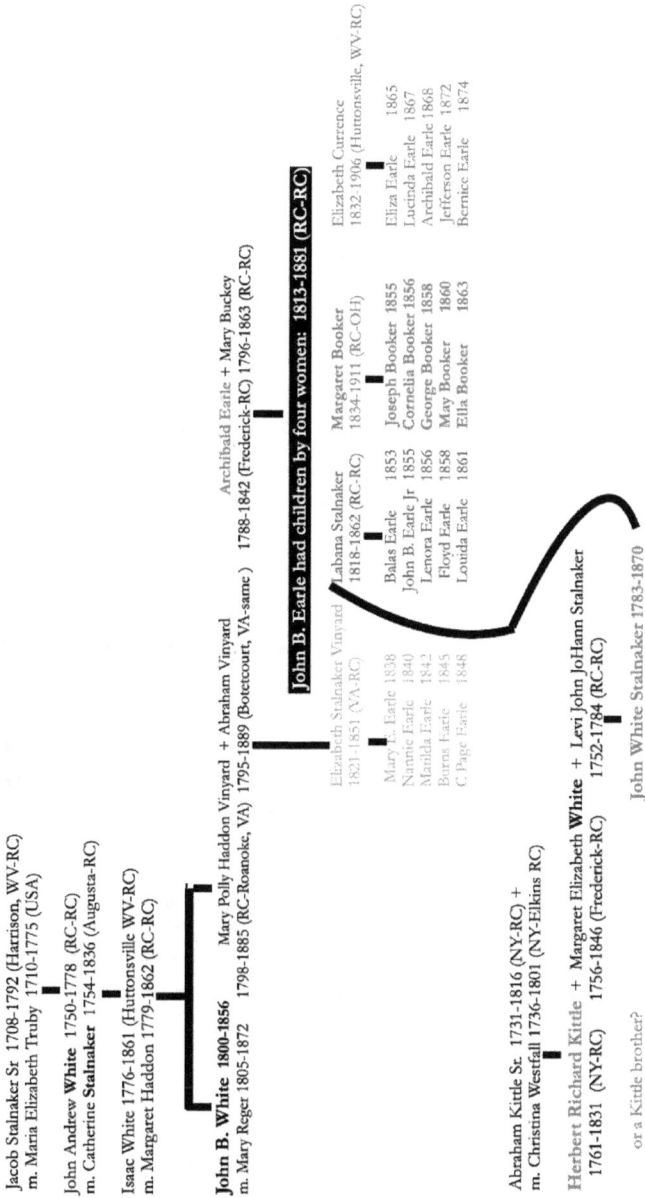

Jacob Stalnaker Sr 1708-1792 (Harrison, WV-RC)
m. Maria Elizabeth Truby 1710-1775 (USA)

John Andrew **White** 1750-1778 (RC-RC)
m. Catherine **Stalnaker** 1754-1836 (Augusta-RC)

Isaac White 1776-1861 (Huttonsville WV-RC)
m. Margaret Haddon 1779-1862 (RC-RC)

John B. White 1800-1856   Mary Polly Haddon Vinyard + Abraham Vinyard   Archibald Earle + Mary Buckey
m. Mary Reger 1805-1872   1798-1885 (RC-Roanoke, VA) 1795-1889 (Botetcourt, VA-same)   1788-1842 (Frederick-RC) 1796-1863 (RC-RC)

John B. Earle had children by four women: 1813-1881 (RC-RC)

Elizabeth Stalnaker Vinyard	Labana Stalnaker	Margaret Booker		Elizabeth Currence
1821-1851 (VA-RC)	1818-1862 (RC-RC)	1834-1911 (RC-OH)		1832 1906 (Huttonsville, WV-RC)
Mary L. Earle 1838	Balas Earle 1853	Joseph Booker 1855		Eliza Earle 1865
Nannie Earle 1840	John B. Earle Jr 1855	Cornelia Booker 1856		Lucinda Earle 1867
Matilda Earle 1842	Lenora Earle 1856	George Booker 1858		Archibald Earle 1868
Burnis Earle 1845	Floyd Earle 1858	May Booker 1860		Jefferson Earle 1872
C. Page Earle 1848	Louida Earle 1861	Ella Booker 1863		Bernice Earle 1874

Abraham Kittle Sr. 1731-1816 (NY-RC) +
m. Christina Westfall 1736-1801 (NY-Elkins RC)

Herbert Richard Kittle + Margaret Elizabeth **White** + Levi John JoHann Stalnaker
1761-1831 (NY-RC)   1756-1846 (Frederick-RC)   1752-1784 (RC-RC)

or a Kittle brother?   John White Stalnaker 1783-1870

Appendix E - Selected Timeline Entries

Timeline of Pertinent Events

Name	Year	St.	County	Event	Notes / Questions	Resource Citation
John Stalnaker	1783	VA	Harrison	Birth		
Richard Kittle	1785	VA	Randolph	Married	Married Margaret Eliz. White Stalnaker	WV, Marriages Index, 1785-1971
Edward "Ned" Backus	1791	VA	?	Born	At the Crouch's farm?	1860-1870 Census
Slave Eve	1800?	VA	?	Born	At the Crouch's farm?	1860-1870 Census
John B. Earle	1813	VA	Randolph	Born	Dad Archibald Earle	1860 Census
Richard Kittle	1831	VA	Randolph	Died	Willed Peg to wife & Phebe to Jane	RC Wills, Vol1-4, 1778-1860, p. 260
Margaret Booker	1834	VA	Randolph	Born	At JW Stalnaker's?	1870-1910 Census
John B. Earle	1840	VA	Randolph	0 slaves	No slaves in 1840.	1840 Census
Elizabeth S. Earle	1846	VA	Randolph	1 slave	John Stalnaker sold Margaret for $1	Oaths and Licenses Book
Mary Buckey Earle	1850	VA	Randolph	5 Slaves	Next to JW Stalnaker	1850 Census
John B. Earle	1850	VA	Randolph	1 Slave	One slave	1850 Slave Schedule
John B. Earle	1850	VA	Augusta	Insane	Family living with John Whites	1850 Census, Augusta & RC, VA.
Elizabeth S. Earle	1851	VA	Randolph	Wife died	Earle Cemetery, Bev.	US Findagrave Index, 1600-Current
John B. Earle	1852	VA	Randolph	Married 2nd	Lebanoe Stalnaker	WV Marriages Index, 1785-1971
Edward Backus	1854	VA	Randolph	Freed in Will	Abraham Crouch died	RC Wills, Vol 3, p. 466
Joab/Joseph Booker	1855	VA	Randolph	Birth	& white Joseph born? Author's 2x great-grandpa	Family lore
John B Earle	1860	VA	Randolph	Status	Miller, Clerk1861-1868	1860 Census.
John B Earle	1860	VA	Randolph	Slaves	Margaret & kids	1860 Slave Sched.
Lebanoe Stalnaker	1862	VA	Randolph	Wife died	Earle Cemetery, Bev	US Findagrave
Emancipation Proclamation	1863	VA	Randolph	Freedom	Freed slaves rebel states.	Proclamation 95
John W. Stalnaker	1863	VA	Randolph	Will Freed slaves	Hugh and George (Booker?)	RC Wills, Vol 5-7, 1863-1913, p. 69-70
West Virginia	1863	WV	Randolph	Statehood	Slavery abolished	Willey Amendment
Margaret Booker	1863	OH	RC to Belmont	To Ohio with 5 kids	Trekked on a buckboard	Family lore
John B. Earle	1863	WV	Randolph	Married 3rd	Elizabeth Currence	?
Margaret Booker	1870	OH	Belmont	Living w/ Edward & Eve	134 Vine Street, Barnesville	1870 Census
Myrtle Booker	1881	OH	Knox	Born	Author's great-grandma	SS Death Index
Pearl Williams	1908	PA	Philadelphia	Born	Author's grandma	1910 Census
Margaret Booker	1911	OH	Belmont	Died	Where buried?	1983 Family Reunion
Mary Carter	1934	OH	Knox		Author's mother	1940 Census

Appendix G - DNA Research Results
Proving Family Lore Using DNA and Traditional Genealogy

Some pieces of this puzzle came together in a few months after scouring census, historical accounts, and estate probate, land, and court records. There were only sixteen out of 184 total population who were enslaved in Beverly in 1830, and around 200 total slaves in the county during the decade of Margaret's birth. I developed an extensive database of ALL slaves in and around Randolph County I encountered in my research of the 1780s through 1900.

A 2003 interview with Margaret's grandson, George Booker, named her slave owner[122] as John Earle. (Appendix A) In the fifth month of research, the Beverly Heritage Center historian found a game-changing bill of sale,[123] dated 1846, involving "A Woman Named Margarett" (Chapter 4) and a slave owner named John Stalnaker who sold her for one dollar to Elizabeth S. Earle, indicating Margaret had at least two owners. A list of slave births said Margarett was the slave of **J. B. Earle** (Appendix C).

Another Beverly Heritage Center streaming presentation clued me to the possibility that Ginger Cake Peg, a slave of Richard Kittle, could have been Margaret's mother. (Chapter 8)

There was documentary evidence, or at least strong suggestion pointing to familial connections with Earles, Stalnakers, Crouches and Kittles. But could those slaveowners also be genetically tied to my family? I hoped DNA testing would corroborate the paper trail of potential Caucasian ancestors, perhaps leading to confirmed progenitors who fought in the American Revolution, as well as leads to their (our?) ancestral migration from Europe.

I endeavored to follow the Genealogical Proof Standard[124] by conducting an exhaustive research, providing complete and accurate source citations, analyzing and correlating all evidence, resolving conflicting evidence, and constructing a soundly reasoned, coherently written conclusion. DNA testing introduced the need to also adhere to the Genetic Genealogy Standards[125] for obtaining, using, and sharing genetic genealogy test results. The bones of my process and results follow.

My hypothesis was that John Earle was the slaveowner and father of Joseph Lewis/Louis Booker who was the eldest son of Earle's slave Margaret. I believe John Earle also fathered four additional children by Margaret: Cornelia, May, George, and Ella—all of whom adopted the surname Booker. I theorized that Margaret's mother was a slave named Peg and her father was Edward "Ned" Backus. I mused that Edward may have been fathered by a Crouch or Booker/Boucher/Backhouse man, that Peg's father was Richard Kittle and her mother an unknown slave.

I also think that a Stalnaker may have fathered the servant slaves Hugh and George (Booker?) who lived with John White Stalnaker from the 1830s until he freed them in February 1863, giving them (on paper) part of his estate.

To validate these hypotheses, I analyzed autosomal, Y-DNA, and mtDNA test kits from these fourteen maternal family members who descend from Margaret Booker (Figure 22).

---

1. Our eldest elder as of 2017, Great-uncle Charles Williams: Ancestry.
2. Charles' son, Bob: Ancestry, FTDNA.
3. Second cousin, once-removed Joe Booker: Ancestry, 23andme.
4. My first-cousin once-removed, Family Historian Lavata Williams: Ancestry.
5. Mom's only living sibling, Uncle Dale Carter: Ancestry, 23andme.
6. My sister Carrie: Ancestry.
7. Carrie's daughter, Lauren: Ancestry.
8. My brother Greg: Ancestry, FTDNA.
9. First cousin Julie: Ancestry.
10. First cousin Pam: Ancestry.
11. First cousin, once-removed, Brandon: 23andme.
12. Third-cousin Alaunda: Ancestry.
13. My son Matthew: Ancestry, FTDNA.
14. Author, Kathy Marshall: Ancestry, 23andme, FTDNA, My Heritage.

Figure 22: Author's family members who DNA tested. Many autosomal results were uploaded to FTDNA, MyHeritage, LivingDNA, and GEDmatch.

Our family DNA results from Ancestry and 23andme were uploaded to the Family Tree DNA, MyHeritage, LivingDNA testing companies, as well as to GEDmatch.[126] The primary objective was to validate whether Earle, Kittle, Stalnaker and/or Crouch descendants share DNA with Margaret Booker's descendants. Unfortunately, I failed to convince Joseph Booker's male descendants to submit to Y-DNA testing, which would have validated whether the Earles and our male Bookers were from the same line of Earle fathers. However, I feel the autosomal results in this appendix more than validate our genetic relationship.

I participated in a three-day intermediate-to-advanced DNA class with the Midwest African American Genealogical Institute,[127] helping me develop a robust DNA research plan and analyze results.

The Research Plan

1. Build the Booker and Earle family trees up, out and down using confirmatory census; court, probate and land records; newspapers; historical and biographical books; maps; and other documents. Record Earles back to their arrival in America in the late 1600s. *Result: Found many documents which seemed to confirm my theories.*

2. Using a combination of autosomal tests from Ancestry, 23andme and Family Tree DNA (FTDNA), DNA test as many willing maternal family members as possible, targeting all of the eldest elders and a sampling of first, second and third cousins, Kathy and her siblings and son. See Figure 23.

3. Create a pedigree chart for Margaret Booker & John Earle descendants. Figure 24.

4. Build a spreadsheet of testers whose DNA matches my family in the Booker/Kittle/Crouch/Stalnaker tag groups. Include most recent common ancestor, centimorgans, segments, chromosome, and notes. Use Ancestry ThruLines, then match surnames in 23andme and FTDNA *Almost 200 deep matches were analyzed.*

5. Create an X-DNA Inheritance Chart to capture possible X-DNA Margaret's daughters may have inherited from John Earle. *Result: No X-DNA descendants were found.*

6. To prove paternity beyond a shadow of a doubt, search for living direct-line descendants of John Earle, obtaining a paternal Y-haplogroup test for them via FTDNA or 23andme. *Result: I was unable to convince Joseph Booker's male descendants to Y-DNA test.*

7. Import shared match data into DNA Painter to obtain a visual map of chromosomal relativity. Download match data from 23andme to provide ethnicity data for each chromosome, indicating which parts of the world populated various portions of chromosomes.

8. Use GEDmatch to auto-cluster DNA matches and determine what the common ancestor is among each cluster.

9. Restate the hypothesis, methodology, summarize the findings, and state whether the hypothesis was proven true or false.

Ancestry.com Results

I used Ancestry's "DNA Matching" tools to ferret out various DNA relatives who had Earle, Stalnaker, Crouch, and Kittle surnames, and/or Beverly, Randolph County, in their family trees. The impressive number of Ancestry.com members who are genetic matches to Margaret Booker's descendants is shown in Figure 23.

DNA Matches to Booker Descendants Who Tested with Ancestry.com			
Surname	**Lavata Williams**	**Dale Carter**	**Charles Williams**
Booker	189	61	41
Common Ancestors	98	57	100+
Crouch	84	27	28
Earle	86	18	98
Early	5	25	33
Hairston	14	11	15
Kittle	37	9	19
Marteney	9	10	20
Myers	100+	100+	100+
Stalnaker	12	7	12
Number of People Who Match Booker Descendants by Location:			
Barnesville	3	9	19
Beverly, WV	16	12	24
Randolph, WV	69	38	98

Figure 23: Number of Ancestry.com members who match Margaret Booker descendants. This lends credence to biological connections.

Ancestry's "ThruLines" estimates who your ancestors might be and tries to locate your relatives. As always, there is a danger of conflated information mis-attributed to online trees, like me using circumstantial evidence to temporarily attribute Samuel H. Early as my third great-grandfather. However, Figure 24 could help corroborate my theory that Slave Peg, who is perhaps my fourth great-grandmother, may be genetically related to her owner, Herbert Richard Kittle's, family. The administrator of A.P. and E.P.'s DNA kits confirmed they are descendants from the Richard Kittle and Christina Westfall ancestral couple.

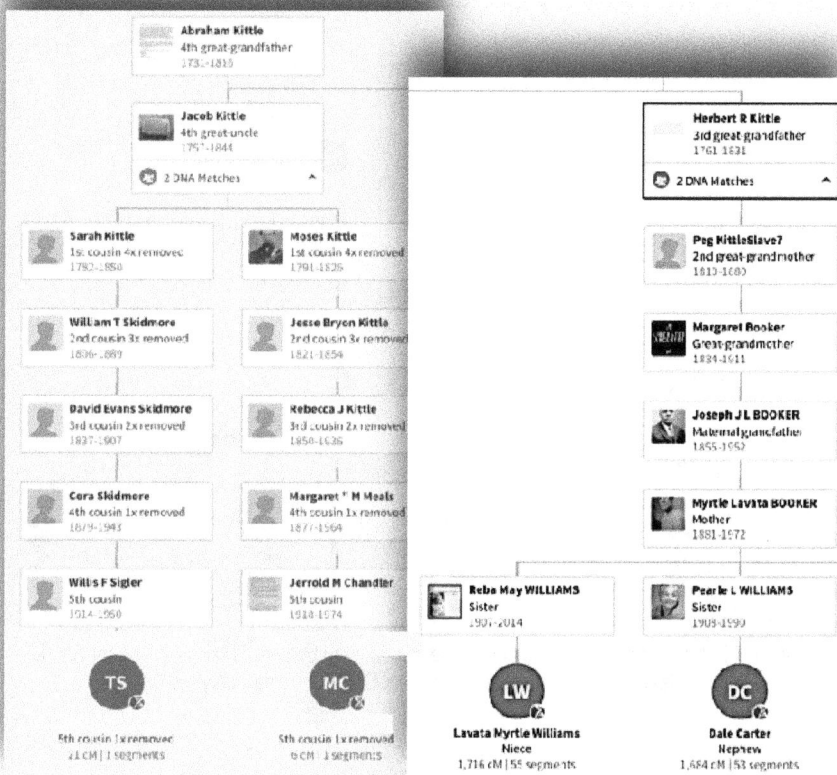

Figure 24: Ancestry's ThruLines estimate of how Uncle Dale Carter and Cousin Lavata Williams may be related to Abraham Kittle, father of Peg's owner/father?

A major flaw with the Ancestry system is that they do not offer a chromosome browser to help customers determine which chromosome segments groups of matches share, indicating a possible common ancestor. I must rely on other testing systems.

ThruLines helped visualize the relationships between Margaret Booker, her daughter Cornelia and her twin great-grandchildren, Barbara S. (bstewart) and Robert G. whose DNA results were a Godsend in many of the following DNA analyses, along with that of our historian, Lavata Williams (Figure 25).

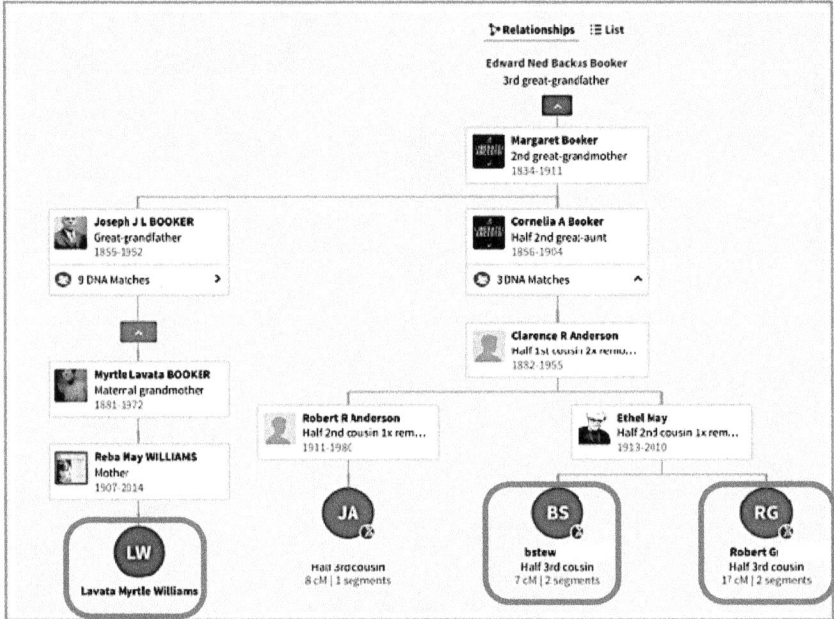

Figure 25: Ancestry's ThruLines charts the relationship between Margaret Booker and two of her children's descendants who provided critical DNA for these analyses.

23andme DNA Results

23andme has a chromosome browser that compares one or more matches to see how much DNA the user shares in common with them. Figure 26 illustrates that five people overlap Uncle Dale Carter on chromosome #5, indicating they may have a common ancestor. Mary shares 55 centimorgans with Dale, indicating she is likely Dale's third cousin once-removed. That means they may share a great-great-grandparent in common. That is consistent with 23andme's prediction that Mary and Dale both descend from Margaret Booker & John Earle.

Further research revealed that Mary, Bonita, Jessica, Letia, and Heidi all have the Myers surname in their family trees and they all have connections to Barnesville, Belmont, County, Ohio. One might conclude that the first portion of chromosome #5 is related to our Myers lineage. So what? Two of Margaret Booker's sons, Joseph and Edward married into the Myers family in Barnesville, which might account for our Booker family's strong tie to Myers.

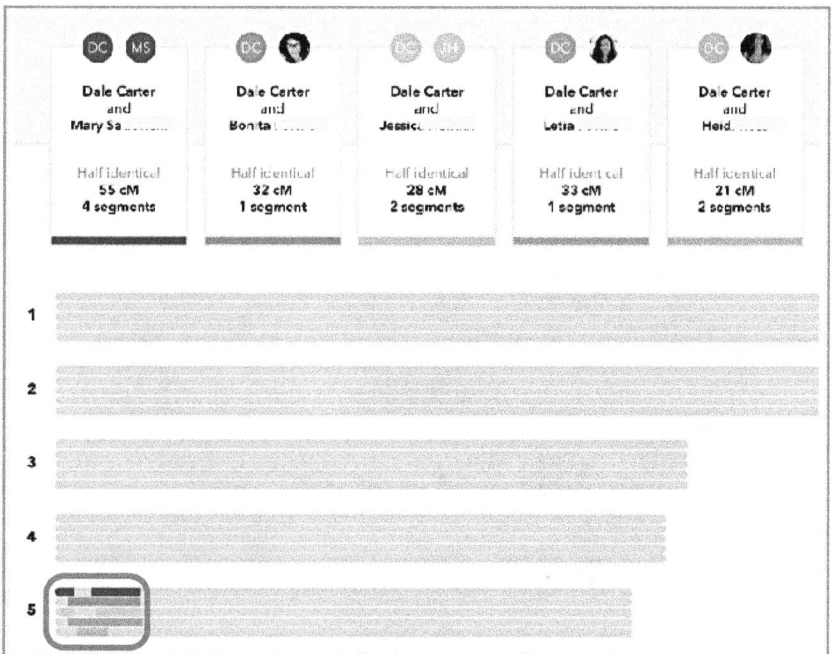

Figure 26: Five people match Uncle Dale Carter on similar segments in chromosome #5. They all have Myers surnames and Belmont County, Ohio, in their family trees. The same type of overlapping DNA segments are need for the Booker family line.

While 23andme lacks an option to record a traditional family tree, it offers a "Predicted Tree," estimating which DNA matches descend from specific ancestral couples. Figure 27 indicates that Mary S. likely descends from Edward Booker and Minerva Myers whereas the author, Kathy Marshall, descends from Joseph Booker to Myrtle Booker to Pearl Williams to Mary Carter. Thus, the matches in Figure 26 actually probably descend from Margaret Booker and her second husband who was likely Hugh Booker.

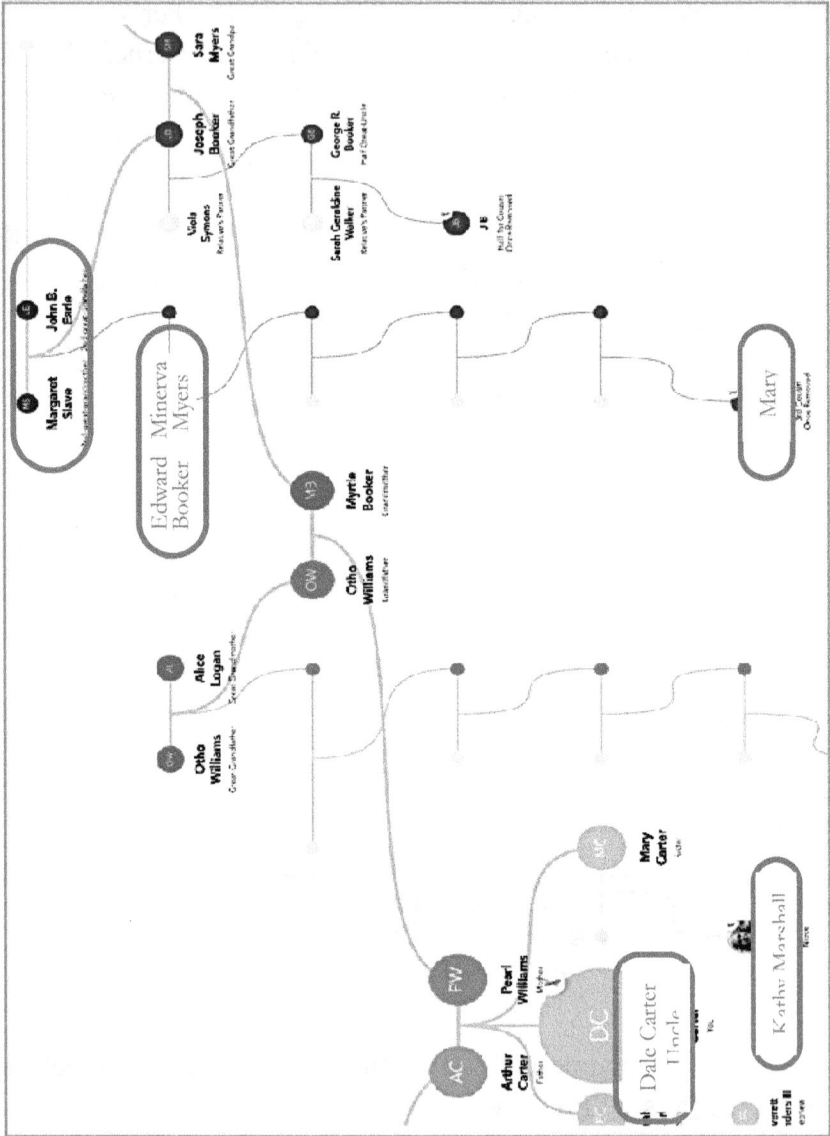

Figure 27: 23andme Predicted Tree for Dale Carter estimated that Mary S__ descended from the Margaret Booker-John Earle ancestral couple.

I need to find a descendant from the Margaret Booker & John Earle ancestral couple who can prove a biological connection via a specific chromosomal segment.

GEDmatch Comparisons

Using the DNA of Margaret Booker & John Earle's twin great-great-grandchildren, Barbara (*Barb) and Robert G. (*Griff), we determined the twins overlap five known descendants from the ancestral couple on two segments on chromosome 1. Great-Uncle CEWilliams and his son, *BWill, also matched the twins on Chromosomes 13 and 19, as shown in Figure 28.

While CEWilliams and Lavata Williams match each other on chromosome 10, they do not match the twins on the same segments, so chromosome 10 will not be included in this analysis. So what? What do all of these charts and graphs mean? How do they help us determine whether we genetically descend from the Earles, Stalnakers, Kittles or Crouches? One may predict that other DNA testers who match exactly on the same segments in chromosomes 1, 13, and 19, may also descend from the Margaret-John Earle ancestral couple, since their great-great-grandchildren match present day family on those same genetic segments.

Downloading all DNA matches from 23andme and sorting the start and stop positions for chromosomes 1, 13, and 19, I noted all the people who overlap on those same segments for they might also be descendants of the ancestral couple. The only way to know for sure is to examine their family trees to note whether they have comparable surnames and locations to those of the ancestral couple. This was an incredibly difficult and many months long task fraught with many downs but few ups.

It is important to understand that it may be impossible to determine DNA connections since it was a common practice for slavemasters to let their acquaintances slip into the slave quarters to choose some "warm comfort" at night, i.e., a slave woman. So even though we latter day genealogists may prove who the slavemaster was, it may be impossible to definitively determine how some genetic relationships happened.

DNA lent some credence to my hypothesis that the descendants of Margaret Booker and John Earle may trace their family to Esaias Earle in Frederick and Samuel Noah in Westmoreland, Virginia. Ancestry ThruLines show eleven 8-to-23 centimorgan matches to Samuel Earle. DNA analysis suggests we may share an Earle lineage back to Somerset England (Figure 29). But this is NOT proof of those connections. Evidentiary documents are required to be sure.

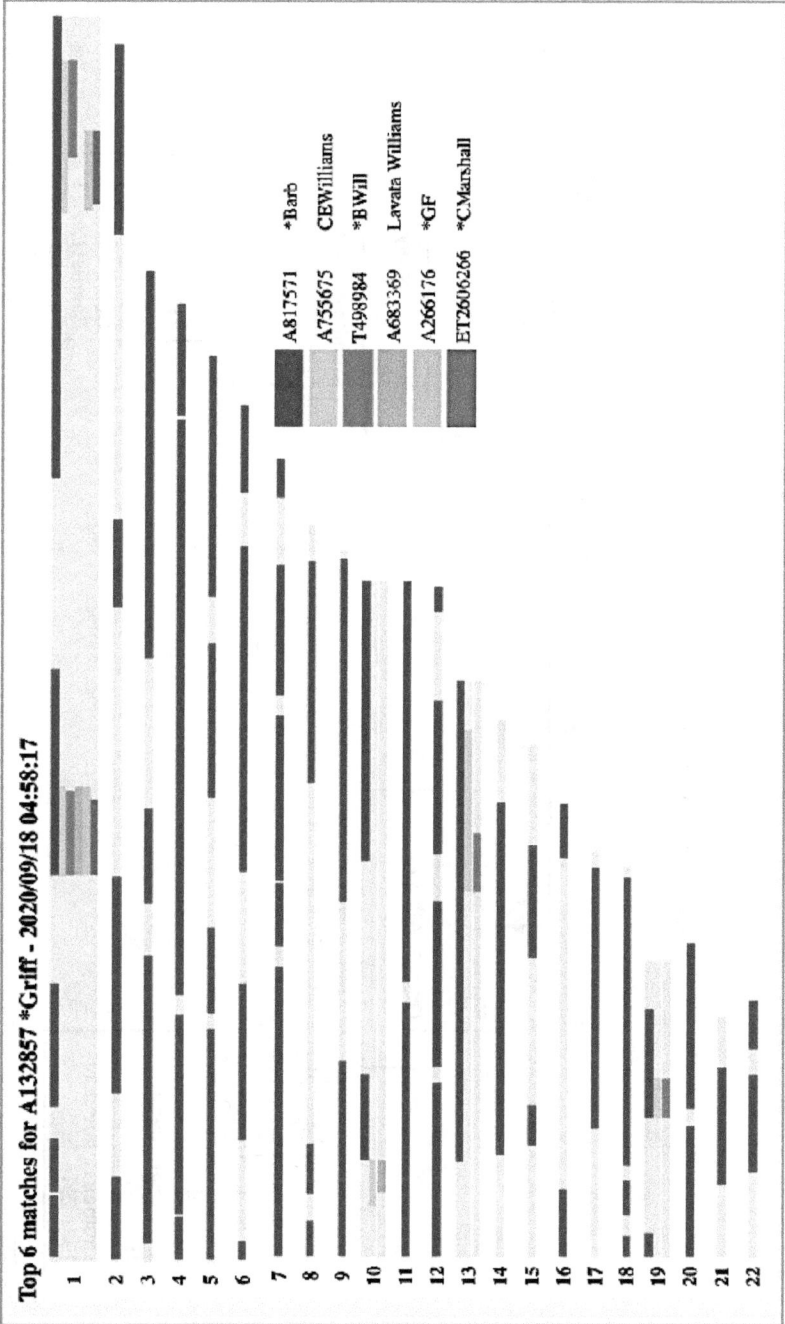

Figure 28: Chromosome browser from GEDmatch.com, comparing Griffin twins Robert and Barbara to five other known descendants of Margaret Booker and John Earle.

279

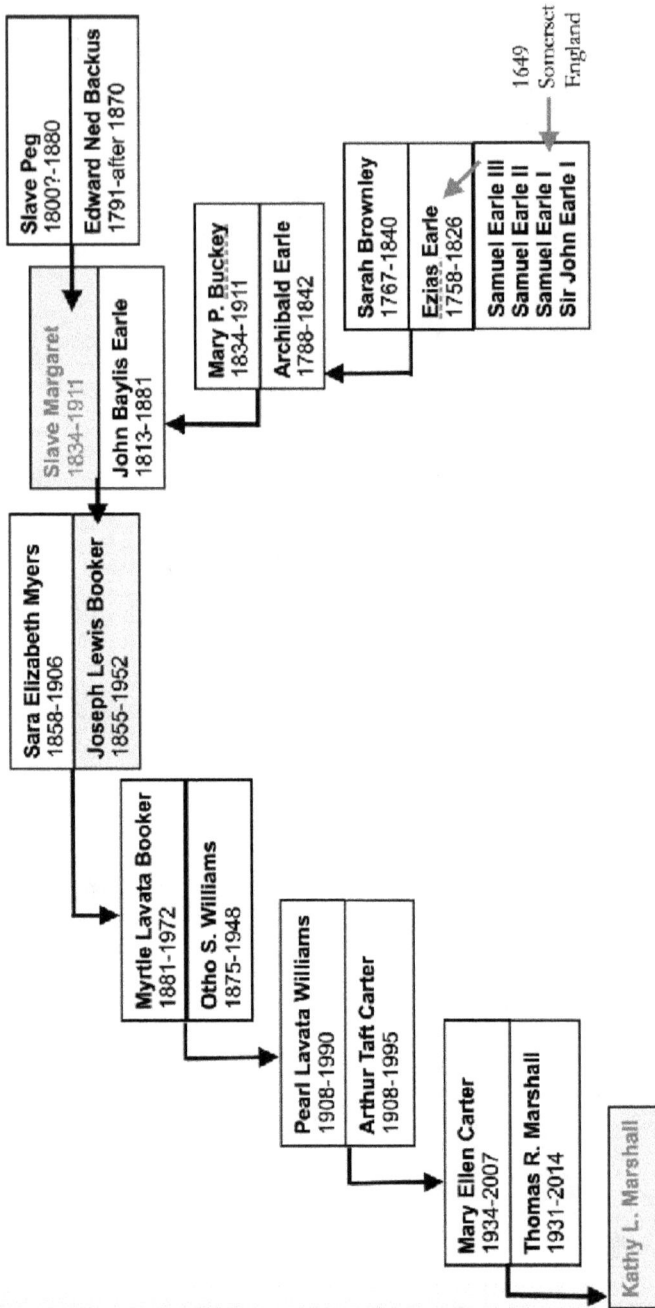

Kathy Marshall's Lineage Back to England

Slave Peg
1800?-1880

Edward Ned Backus
1791-after 1870

Slave Margaret
1834-1911

John Baylis Earle
1813-1881

Mary P. Buckey
1834-1911

Archibald Earle
1788-1842

Sarah Brownley
1767-1840

Ezias Earle
1758-1826

Samuel Earle III
Samuel Earle II
Samuel Earle I
Sir John Earle I

1649
Somerset
England

Sara Elizabeth Myers
1858-1906

Joseph Lewis Booker
1855-1952

Myrtle Lavata Booker
1881-1972

Otho S. Williams
1875-1948

Pearl Lavata Williams
1908-1990

Arthur Taft Carter
1908-1995

Mary Ellen Carter
1934-2007

Thomas R. Marshall
1931-2014

Kathy L. Marshall

Figure 29: Pedigree Chart of Kathy Marshall's Booker-Earle Lineage from England.

280

Appendix H - Solving Your Mystery

I have been researching the lives of my African American family for four decades, creating the requisite genealogy binders full of vital records, censuses, and other documents for six of my family lines, including the Williams, Bookers, Marshalls, Dooley, Carters, and Myers family lines.

An alarming thought entered my head in May 2016 when I began my sixtieth year of life. There are only three people older than me in my mother's family and three older in my father's. Soon I may be the matriarch of the family. If I don't write a book about my ancestors, who will? Now is the time to commemorate the lives of those enslaved and free people who have gone before me, and of those of us still living who are their proud descendants. I have a burning desire to ensure that my family is remembered in a tangible, written way.

After a gentle push from my spirited ancestors, I began writing The Ancestors Are Smiling! on October 1, 2016 and published it in July 2017. The next fifteen months were spent solving the mystery of my enslaved relatives in Finding Otho: The Search for Our Enslaved Williams Ancestors. Then came Finding Daisy: From the Deep South to the Promised Land in 2019.

There are a number of reasons why I was finally able to accomplish this momentous goal successfully. I had heard most of the following how-to tips numerous times over the years, but this time I finally actually did what was suggested.

Please note that the following ideas are only one way to write a book about your family, but they are steps that worked well for me. Will any or all of them work for you? Give them a try. See if they will help you to get started (and finished) with your book.

I think the first step is to decide which ONE person you'd like to focus your book on (WHO). WHY is that person important to you? What do you already KNOW about that person? WHERE did s/he live? WHAT more do you want to know about that person?

Those questions will help you to compose a focused First Edition book. Are you ready to write your book? Read on.

Planning to Write Your Book

Adopt an ATTITUDE THAT YOU MUST PUBLISH THE BOOK, before all else. Your mantra must be: "I live and breathe to publish a book about my family." Otherwise, any mundane activity will divert you from your goal to leave a written legacy for your family.

FOCUS ON ONE specific family line, or one person, or one specific aspect of the family, for example, a specific enslaved ancestor from one of your family lines. WHY is that person so important that you want to write about their life? WHERE did that person live? What do you already KNOW about that person? WHAT more do you want to learn about that person? This preliminary survey helps you determine how to focus your book.

Determine the SCOPE (extent) of the book. I wanted to find my third great-grandparents and their slaveholder, write about their lives, then publish this book. What, specifically, do you want your book to be about?

Develop a LIST OF QUESTIONS you want to answer (e.g., who were my third great-grandparents, what jobs did they do, where did they live, who were their slave masters?).

Understand that you may not be able to answer all your questions but accept that it is OK. Write about the steps you DID take and present what you did and did not find in your book. Indicate that you may resume your inquiry in the second edition when more information becomes available but do print the first edition and distribute it to your family.

Decide on the AUDIENCE for your book (e.g., children, family, genealogists, the public).

Developing the Book Framework

Decide on a computer WORD PROCESSING PROGRAM for your book, such as Microsoft Word or Apple Pages.

Open a NEW DOCUMENT and NAME IT (e.g., My Family Book) and SAVE it to a folder on your computer.

Be sure to SAVE your word processing manuscript every hour or so and BACK UP your book file every day (e.g., keep a copy on the Internet cloud or on a portable backup drive).

Develop a BOOK OUTLINE in your new word document, like the following:

Title of your book on the first page.

Copyright on the second page (copyright.gov).

Dedication on the third page.

Filler on the fourth page: add a picture, or a quote, or a poem, or a Foreword from a professional.

Table of Contents (TOC): Microsoft Word and Apple Pages automatically generate the TOC with the "Styles" Function.

Acknowledgments page thanking people who helped you write your book.

Introduction that explains what the book is about. Write it early in the process, then refine it.

Timeline of historical events, if desired.

Chapters about certain characters or topics (NOTE: Start chapters in the printed book on an odd-numbered, right-side page for chapter headings in the header).

Epilogue/Conclusion/Coda/Wrap-up to summarize your efforts.

Appendices, lists of tables and maps (if appropriate).

Bibliography listing which sources you used to develop your ideas in the book.

Endnotes or Footnotes, (optional) with complete citations, using this basic format: Author, Title, (Place of publication, Publisher, Year), page number.

Refine the book layout after some of the manuscript has been written (e.g., add photographs or quotes to the first page of each chapter, if desired).

Writing Your Book

START WRITING TODAY with what you already know (e.g., your life story, parents, grandparents). Don't worry about perfect sentences—just type your thoughts and revise them later.

COPY AND PASTE into the correct chapter any documentation that has already been written. For example, a memory about your fifth birthday party would go into your chapter, your grandparents' wedding picture would go into their chapter, etc.

TYPE THE BOOK as you are conducting your research and getting stories. Include your emotions at that time when they are fresh.

Include FOOTNOTES/CITATIONS citing your information sources as you write.

RECHECK YOUR FOCUS and scope often, to remain on track with what your book is about.

Consider writing the passages as though you are telling the story directly to your audience or writing the stories from the POINT OF VIEW of your family members.

READ OUT LOUD what you have written to uncover awkward sentence structure or to notice missing words and to hear whether the text is too conversational or too technical, keeping in mind your audience.

Gathering Information

INTERVIEW YOUR ELDERS and other family members and type their stories in the book.

Do DNA TESTING NOW for yourself, your elders, and other family members. The major DNA companies are: ancestry.com, 23andMe.com, FamilyTreeDNA.com, My Heritage, and Living

DNA. For more information, check this website: https://isogg.org/wiki/List_of_DNA_testing_companies.

Gather FAMILY PHOTOGRAPHS, using your camera or smartphone to take high-resolution photos. Copy the photos to a folder on your computer. Save them as 300 dots-per-inch (dpi) resolution for printing. Label the photos with the date, place, and names of the subjects.

Read PROBATE, CENSUS, and LAND RECORDS documents pertinent to your family.

Visit family HOME SITES and CEMETERIES (search Findagrave.com), take photographs and type your findings, and YOUR FEELINGS, about visiting these places in your book.

PRINT DOCUMENTS within each family line and organize them into separately named GENEALOGY BINDERS.

Start an ONLINE FAMILY TREE (e.g., Ancestry.com, familysearch.org) with names, dates, locations, etc., and KEEP IT PUBLIC so others may connect with you and share information about your family.

Also keep FAMILY TREE DATA ON YOUR COMPUTER (e.g., Family Tree Maker).

Use ONLINE GENEALOGY SITES (e.g., Ancestry.com, familysearch.org, USGenWeb.com, WikiTree.com, newspapers.com, fold3.com, and Genetic Genealogy Tips and Techniques.

Become a member of GENEALOGY FACEBOOK PAGES and other web pages (e.g., Our Black Ancestry, Our Black Legacy, Research at the National Archives and Beyond, Black ProGen Live).

Watch free GENEALOGY HOW-TO VIDEOS from Ancestry.com or youtube.com.

Do a simple online Google search on your ancestors' names and states to see if any books or other resources contain their name. Recheck these resources often.

Take GENEALOGY COURSES and join genealogy guilds to learn the best genealogy practices. Conduct an exhaustive search.

Document accurate citations. Analyze information. Resolve conflicting evidence. Develop a reasoned written conclusion.

DEVELOP THEORIES and prove or disprove them, but do not be too rigid. Review and revise theories and update the book accordingly. Avoid obsessing on preconceived ideas from family lore.

Discuss your book ideas and theories with other authors, editors, and family, and ASK THEM TO GIVE FEEDBACK on your work in progress.

Self-Publishing Your Book

Have the book professionally COPY EDITED and PROOFREAD to ensure the manuscript is perfect before publishing.

Export your book manuscript to a .pdf FILE on your computer.

If you want to sell books, obtain an International Standard Book Number (ISBN) through bowker.com ($295 for 10 or $125 for one). Include one ISBN on the back cover of your book file.

COPYRIGHT your book (e.g., copyright.gov).

Choose a SELF-PUBLISHING WEBSITE (e.g., lulu.com or Kindle Direct Publishing: KDP.com) and read their online instructions on uploading a .pdf copy of your book. Create an online account for your book. Choose a book size and number of pages. Upload an initial .pdf of your manuscript.

Use the self-publishing website to create a BOOK COVER (front, back, and spine). Or, make your own cover on your computer, or pay someone to make one. Be sure to use the precise measurements supplied by the self-publishing service. Export your book cover to a .pdf file.

After your book manuscript is perfected, export it to a .pdf file, then UPLOAD THE MANUSCRIPT AND COVER .pdf to the self-publishing website. Make sure you review any corrections the book website suggests (like ensuring the photos are 300 dpi), make the changes, then upload the .pdf files again.

Prepare a summary of the book, for the online DESCRIPTION of your book (you may use the text on the back jacket of your book). Look at several Amazon.com memoir book examples to see what kinds of things are written in the book description. Make it pop!

Decide on a retail PRICE for your book. The book service will tell you how much revenue you will earn depending on your retail price, the book size, and number of pages.

Once the manuscript is submitted for printing, order an ADVANCE READER COPY (ARC). Carefully REVIEW the printed book, make corrections, create a new .pdf, re-upload the file, recheck the uploaded file, order another Advanced Reader Copy. When you are absolutely certain there are no errors in your manuscript submit it for FINAL PRINTING. It takes 24-72 hours for book approval and about a week to print the book(s).

If using Amazon.com's Kindle Direct Publishing, choose MARKETING CHANNELS for your book (e.g., Amazon in America and/or Europe, resellers, research channels).

MARKET your published book (e.g., Amazon.com, Facebook page, webpage, newsletter, blog, local bookstores, donate to research libraries, and/or offer to be a volunteer speaker at local networking groups and service clubs).

An Alternative, Photo Book for Genealogy

Instead of a narrative, self-published book as described in the previous steps, you could create hard-cover, photo album style books. Simply upload your high-resolution (300 dpi or more) .jpg family photos, charts, graphs, or maps to shutterfly.com or photo.walgreens.com or costco.com or other online photo book services. Get on their mailing lists to get periodic discounts. This is an easy way to commemorate your ancestors' lives, and/or to write story books of any kind.

Always Remember

Be so passionate about commemorating your ancestor's stories that you have an overwhelming need to publish your book. Be focused on writing about a specific person or family line. Create a book template and begin typing what you already know into it and type all your new findings into it. Include source citations as you enter information. These most important actions will result in the quick development of a manuscript that looks like a ready-for-printing real book. I hope these lessons I learned help you write and self-publish your own family stories. Remember, when the ancestors call, we must listen.

The Ancestors Are Smiling!

BIBLIOGRAPHY

1850 Census of Randolph County, Virginia. From Clayton Library, Houston Public Library, copied by Madeline W. Crickard, 1969.

1897 Map of Washington, Pennsylvania, http://memory.loc.gov/cgi-bin/map_item.pl where Cornelia Booker Anderson's family lived and worked from 1880s through the mid-20th Century.

Alexandria Public Library. Virginia Slave Births Index, 1853-1865. Heritage Books, Inc., 2019.

Allen, Randy. Lemuel Chenowith, 1811-1887: Bridging the Gaps. McClain Printing Company, Parsons, WV, 2006. www.mcclainprinting.com

Bennett, Bernice A. Tracing Their Steps: A Memoir. Palmyra, VA, Shortwood Press, 2019.

Bennett, Lerone, Jr. Before the Mayflower: A History of Black America. Johnson Publishing Company, Inc., Chicago, 1982.

Berry, Daina Ramey. The Price for Their Pound of Flesh. Bacon Press, Boston, MA, 2017.

Bidlack, Mary Kay. Beverly's Buildings: An Owner's Manual. Historical Beverly Preservation, 2003.

Booker, Joe G., "Rich Family History, Community Key to Man's Memories of Growing Up in Mount Vernon," Mount Vernon News Looking Glass, 1999, p. 59-64.

Bosworth, A.S. A history of Randolph County, West Virginia, from its earliest exploration and settlement to the present time. THE NEW YORK PUBLIC LIBRARY, B09665A, -ASTOR, LENOX AND TILDEN FOUNDATIONS, R 1932. Originally published in 1898 by Hu

Maxwell.
http://wvancestry.com/ReferenceMaterial/Files/History_of_Randolph_C
ounty.pdf

Bristol and America: A Record of the First Settlers in the Colonies of
North, 1654-1675. Baltimore, Genealogical Pub. Co.,1967.
https://books.google.com/books?id=rGfczR3G5ywC&printsec=frontcov
er&source=gbs_ge_summary_r&cad=0#v=onepage&q&f=false

Centennial History of Belmont County, Ohio, and Representative
Citizens edited by A. T. McKelvey, 1905. Transcribed by Carol LaRue,
pages 141-142,
http://genealogytrails.com/ohio/belmont/undergroundrailroad.html.

Cook, Roy Bird, "Battle of Bulltown," The West Virginia Review, June
1933, p. 254-56.

Cooper, Jean L. Hidden Wills: An Index of Wills Found in Central
Virginia Chancery Records Through 1870. Shortwood Press, Palmyra,
VA, 2019.

"Earle Family," in MacKenzie, George Norbury. Colonial Families of
the United States of America, Volume II. Baltimore, Genealogical
Publishing Company, 1966.

Federal Writers' Project: Slave Narrative Project, Vol. 12, Ohio,
Anderson-Williams. 1936. Manuscript/Mixed Material. Retrieved from
the Library of Congress.
<www.loc.gov/item/mesn120/>. Interviews from Sarah Woods Burke
(Image 19), James Campbell, Fleming Clark, Nancy East, Jennie Small,
Richard Toler who was enslaved in Pocahontas County, adjacent to
Randolph County. Information about Sarah Mann, who was owned by
Bookers near Richmond, VA, was also utilized.

"Former Slaves Went on Strike in 1881 Weeks before A World's Fair in
Atlanta," https://historycollection.com/former-slaves-went-on-strike-in-
1881-weeks-before-a-worlds-fair-in-atlanta/

Frank, Barbara. Princess Book II: Aggy of Zion. N.p.: Marsh Books, 2013.

"Fusion Benevolence—The Slave Case Again," Portage Sentinel, August 18, 1855. https://chroniclingamerica.loc.gov/lccn/sn83035102/1855-08-18/ed-1/seq-2/#date1=1855&index=0&rows=20&words=Backus+Edward&searchType=basic&sequence=0&state=Ohio&date2=1855&proxtext=%22Edward+Backus%22&y=0&x=0&dateFilterType=yearRange&page=1

Gruber, K. E. Slave Clothing and Adornment in Virginia. (2018, January 29). In Encyclopedia Virginia. Retrieved from: http://www.EncyclopediaVirginia.org/Slave_Clothing_and_Adornment_in_Virginia.

Hait, Michael. Genealogy at a Glance: African American Genealogy Research. Genealogical Publishing Company, 2011.

Haley, Alex. Roots: The Saga of an American Family. Doubleday & Company, Inc., Garden City, NY, 1976.

Halpern, Rick & Dal Lago, Enrico, editors. Slavery and Emancipation. 1st ed. Blackwell Publishing, MA, 2002.

Hargraves-Mawdsley, R. Bristol and America: A Record of the First Settlers in the Colonies of North America, 1654-1685. Genealogical Publishing Company, Baltimore, MD, 2010.

Harris, Robin Roberts. My Grandmother Rode a Horse. Robin Roberts Harris, 2019.

Heinegg, Paul. "Randolph County Personal Property Tax List, 1787-1829," Free African Americans.com. [Heinegg abstracted free blacks listed in these records.]

Historic American Buildings Survey (HABS No. VA-357), District of Virginia, Prepared by Thomas T. Waterman 1941

Jacobs, Harriet A. Incidents in the Life of a Slave Girl. Dover, Boston, 1861.

Kalbian, Maral S. Rural Historic Resources Survey Report of Warren County, Virginia, 1991. Virginia Department of Historic Resources, Richmond, VA, 1991.

Marshall, Kathy L. The Ancestors Are Smiling! Kanika Marshall Art and Books Publishing, Elk Grove, CA, 2017.

Marshall, Kathy L. Finding Otho: The Search for Our Enslaved Williams Ancestors. Kanika Marshall Art and Books Publishing, Elk Grove, CA, 2018.

Marshall, Kathy L. Finding Daisy: From the Deep South to the Promised Land. Kanika Marshall Art and Books Publishing, Elk Grove, CA, 2019.

Marshall, Kathy L. Mary Ellen Carter Marshall: The Life of a Hero, Educator, Mother, Artist, Citizen, Mentor and Friend. Kanika Marshall Art and Books Publishing, Elk Grove, CA, 2015.

Marshall, Mary. Reflections from a Mother's Heart: Your Life Story in Your own Words. Sacramento, CA, 1996-2007.

Martyris, Nina. "Nurse, Spy, Cook: How Harriet Tubman Found Freedom Through Food," in National Public Radio, The Salt, What's On Your Plate, April 27, 2016. https://www.npr.org/sections/thesalt/2016/04/27/475768129/nurse-spy-cook-how-harriet-tubman-found-freedom-through-food

"Members of Colored Women's Glee Club," [photograph] in The Community Within. Digital Kenyon Research, Scholarship, and Creative Exchange, ca.1920. https://digital.kenyon.edu/communitywithin/42/

Miller, Thomas Condit & Hu Maxwell. West Virginia and Its People, Volume 1. Historical Publishing Company, 1913.

Moton, Emily Brown. Emily Brown Moton. Portrayed by Etta Neal, Presented at Jamestown Presbyterian Church, Rice, Virginia, June 24, 2007.

Mount Zion survey from the "Rural Historic Resources Survey Report of Warren County, Virginia, 1991."

Maxwell, Hu. The History of Barbour County, WV; From Its Earliest Exploration and Settlement to the Present Time. The Acme Publishing Company, Morgantown, W. Va. 1899. Reprinted 1968, McClain Printing Company, Parsons, WV.

McCrum, Lucy Brown. "Recollections of Old Beverly." Randolph (WV) Enterprise, February 1930.

The National Society of The Colonial Dames of America in the State of Alabama. In Grateful Remembrance. Southern Life Publishing Services, Inc., Montgomery, AL, 2008. https://nscda.org/wp-content/uploads/2014/06/In-Grateful-Remembrance-Biographies-Of-Our-Ancestors-The-National-Society-of-The-Colonial-Dames-of-Americin-the-State-of-AlabamOCR.pdf

Negro Washerwomen: The Journal of Negro History, Vol. 15, No. 3 (Jul., 1930), pp. 269-277, Published by: The University of Chicago Press on behalf of the Association for the Study of African American Life and History, DOI: 10.2307/2713969, https://www.jstor.org/stable/2713969, Page Count: 9

Nelson, Barbara Slater. Old Settlers of Mecosta, Isabella, and Montcalm Counties in Michigan, Volume 1, A-C. Barbara Slater Nelson, Michigan, 2018, www.mibabs.tribalpages.com.

Notes on Virginia, Number 45. "Certified Historic Rehabilitation Projects in Virginia, Proposed Rehabilitations." Department of Historic Resources, Richmond, VA, p. 56, Fall 2001.

Records of Western State Hospital, 1825-2000. State Government Records Collection, The Library of Virginia, Richmond, Virginia.

Sacks, Howard and Judith. Way Up North in Dixie: A Black Family's Claim to the Confederate Anthem. Smithsonian Institution Press, Washington and London, 1993.

Spencer, Eugene. Mississippi Born - California Bound: How Jim Crow and Racism Lost to a Family Legacy. Sunshine Solutions Publishing, 2018.

Taneyhill, R. H. History of Barnesville, Ohio, originally published by The Leatherwood Printing Co., Barnesville, Ohio, March 1899. Newly produced by Forgotten Books, copyright 2016.

Ward, Mary G. Civil War Legends of Rich Mountain and Beverly, West Virginia. McClain Printing Company, Parsons, WV, 2004.

Washington, Pennsylvania City Directory: 1903, 1905, in Ancestry.com. U.S. City Directories, 1822-1995 [database on-line]. Provo, UT, USA: Ancestry.com Operations, Inc., 2011.
https://www.ancestry.com/search/collections/2469/

Wilkerson, Isabel. The Warmth of Other Suns: The Epic Story of America's Great Migration. Vintage Books, Penguin Random House LLC, New York, 2010.

Woodson, Carter G. "The Negro Washerwoman, a Vanishing Figure." The Journal of Negro History, Vol. 15, No. 3 (Jul., 1930), pp. 269-277.
https://www.jstor.org/stable/2713969

ENDNOTES

[1] The Underground Railroad was a secret system developed to aid fugitive slaves on their escape to freedom.

[2] Cooper-Bessemer machine engine factory was the first major industry in Mount Vernon, Ohio, http://www.knoxhistory.org/index.php/exhibits/industry/186-the-cooper-story.

[3] Machinist: A person who makes or repairs machinery.

[4] Barnesville is located in the central portion of Warren Township in Belmont County in central-east Ohio.

[5] High yellow/yeller: High yellow, occasionally simply yellow (dialect: yaller, yella), is a term used to describe a light-skinned person of white and black ancestry. It is also used as a slang for those thought to have "yellow undertones."

[6] The puffy, keloided skin which resembled a tree trunk and branches, was forever sketched onto Margaret's back. This was sometimes called a "tree" and was the result of a horse whip piercing the skin as a punishment for disobeying a slaveowner's order.

[7] An anvil is a heavy steel or iron block with a flat top, concave sides, and typically a pointed end, on which metal can be hammered and shaped.

[8] Norman Conquest: the time in English history when England was ruled by the Norman people from northern France. The Norman King William the Conqueror defeated the army of the English King Harold at the Battle of Hastings in 1066. It was the last time that an enemy successfully took control of Britain.

[9] A ship named *Margaret of Bristol* sailed to the Virginia colony, albeit some years before Sir John Earle's 1649 trip: https://en.wikipedia.org/wiki/William_Stone_(Maryland_governor).

[10] *Bristol and America: A Record of the First Settlers in the Colonies of North America, 1654-1685*, contains a list of more than 10,000 indentured servants who embarked from the British port of Bristol for Virginia, Maryland, New England, and other parts between 1654 and 1685, giving information on the passengers' origin and destination. Transcribed by R. Hargraves-Mawdsley, ISBN-13: 978-0806301709.

[11] Indian massacre at Bulltown:
http://www.wvculture.org/history/civilwar/bulltown02.html

[12] Ticking is a mattress's final, outer cover. Ticking encases the entire mattress to protect comfort and support layers and keep them in place.

[13] The word **drawers** was invented because underwear was drawn on. More information: http://www.localhistories.org/underwear.html

[14] A maternity corset is a tightly fitting undergarment extending from below the chest to the hips, with several adjustments for pregnant women. Image at: https://www.pinterest.com/pin/274156696036576245/.

[15] Crinoline petticoat is a stiff or structured petticoat made of horsehair ("crin") and cotton or linen used to make underskirts and as a dress lining.

[16] A **wet nurse** is a woman who breast feeds and cares for another's child. **Wet nurses** are employed if the mother dies, or if she is unable or elects not to **nurse** the child herself. **Wet**-nursed children may be known as "milk-siblings", and in some cultures the families are linked by a special relationship of milk kinship.

[17] "Touched in the head" means mentally deranged or unstable; somewhat crazy. Often used sarcastically or jocularly.

[18] Handmaid: Long ago, a handmaiden (also called a *handmaid*) often served as the personal servant or maid to the lady of the house.

[19] West Virginia recipe for spoon bread:
http://www.foodtimeline.org/statefoods.html#westvirginia.

[20] In 1827, David purchased a lot in Beverly, West Virginia and built the first commercial brick structure in the town. Over the years it served as a county courthouse, post office, meeting place, and a store. When he married his wife Rebecca, in 1824, his father-in-law gave him several slaves. He did not believe in slavery, but he used them to burn bricks and build the storehouse. The store is now a museum and on the National Historic Registry. https://www.findagrave.com/memorial/27568108/david-blackman.

[21] A bridle path, also bridleway, equestrian trail, horse riding path, ride, bridle road, or horse trail, is a path, trail or a thoroughfare that is used by people riding on horses. Trails originally created for use by horses often now serve a wider range of users, including equestrians, hikers, and cyclists.

[22] By 1835, the population of Beverly was 184 including sixteen slaves and two free African-Americans: http://www.historicbeverly.org/wordpress/beverly-a-more-complete-history-part-two-of-three/

[23] Types of men's hats in 1860: https://www.uvm.edu/landscape/dating/clothing_and_hair/1860s_hats_men.php

[24] High yellow (dialect: yaller, yella), is a term used to describe a light-skinned person of white and black ancestry.

[25] Genealogist Sharon Styles' documentary entitled, "Speak Their Names and They Live Again," is in syndication on the National Public Broadcasting System. Her family is biologically connected to author, Kathy Marshall's, third great-grandfather, John Earle.

[26] The "Compromise of 1850" was an uneasy peace admitting California to the Union as the 16th free state and, in exchange, the South was guaranteed that no federal restrictions on slavery would be placed on Utah or New Mexico. https://www.ushistory.org/us/30d.asp

[27] The Fugitive Slave Acts were a pair of federal laws that allowed for the capture and return of runaway enslaved people within the territory of the United States. Some believe some free men were illegally captured as a function of the 1850 Fugitive Slave Act: https://www.history.com/topics/black-history/fugitive-slave-acts

[28] Enslaved blacksmiths, examples at Monticello: https://www.monticello.org/slavery/the-plantation/work-on-the-monticello-plantation/blacksmithing/

[29] The Fusion Party was the original name of the Republican Party in the state of Ohio in 1854. https://en.wikipedia.org/wiki/Fusion_Party#Fusion_Party_in_Ohio_and_Indiana

[30] Kansas-Nebraska Act of 1854: In January 1854, Senator Stephen Douglas introduced a bill that divided the land west of Missouri into two territories, Kansas and Nebraska. He argued for popular sovereignty, which would allow the settlers of the new territories to decide if slavery would be legal there. https://www.senate.gov/artandhistory/history/minute/Kansas_Nebraska_Act.htm

[31] The aim of the **Know-Nothing** movement was to combat foreign influences and to uphold and promote traditional American ways.

[32] A Quaker is a member of the Religious Society of Friends, a Christian movement founded around 1650 and devoted to peaceful principles. Central to the Quakers' belief is

the doctrine of the "Inner Light," or sense of Christ's direct working in the soul. This has led them to reject both formal ministry and all set forms of worship. Generally, Quakers were opposed to slavery.

[33] Beverly-Fairmont Turnpike: https://en.wikipedia.org/wiki/List_of_turnpikes_in_Virginia_and_West_Virginia

[34] Wheeling, Virginia and the Underground Railroad: https://en.wikipedia.org/wiki/Wheeling,_West_Virginia

[35] Martin's Ferry: http://touringohio.com/northeast/belmont/martins-ferry/martins-ferry.html

[36] How far can a horse travel in a day? https://www.quora.com/In-the-days-of-horse-and-buggy-travel-how-far-was-an-average-day's-travel

[37] Gig carriage: any of several members of a class of light, open, two-wheeled, one-horse carriages, popular in France, England, and America.

[38] "Portage Sentinel, August 18, 1855, Image 2" about Edward 'Ned' Backus' Freedom: https://chroniclingamerica.loc.gov/lccn/sn83035102/1855-08-18/ed-1/seq-2/#date1=1855&index=0&rows=20&words=Backus+Edward&searchType=basic&sequence=0&state=Ohio&date2=1855&proxtext=%22Edward+Backus%22&y=0&x=0&dateFilterType=yearRange&page=1

[39] "Portage Sentinel, August 18, 1855, Image 2"

[40] The story of Peg and the Ginger Cakes, p. 154, in Lucy Brown McCrum's "Recollections of Old Beverly" published in several February 1930 editions of the "Randolph Enterprise."

[41] The story of Peg and the Ginger Cakes, p. 154, in Lucy Brown McCrum's "Recollections of Old Beverly" published in several February 1930 editions of the "Randolph Enterprise."

[42] Princess Book II: Aggy of Zion, a fictionalized story about a slave girl in the Earle households in the Shenandoah Valley, Virginia. Author Barbara Frank shed many factual events in the lives of my third-great-grandfather, John Earle's ancestral family.

[43] Robert "King" Carter gave his grandson Robert III his first slave (a girl) when the infant was three months old. By the time he came of legal age in 1749, Robert Carter III owned 6,500 acres and 100 slaves.

[44] Mount Zion survey from the "Rural Historic Resources Survey Report of Warren County, Virginia, 1991."

[45] Historic American Buildings Survey (HABS No. VA-357), District of Virginia, Prepared by Thomas T. Waterman 1941

[46] Katydids were also called long-horned grasshoppers or bush crickets, any of about 6,000 predominantly nocturnal insects that are related to crickets.

[47] Civil War sentiments pitted brother against brother: http://www.wvculture.org/history/archives/wvcivilwar.html

[48] Civil War Through Beverly in "A More Complete History of Beverly." http://www.historicbeverly.org/bevhist3.htm

[49] *Civil War Legends of Rich Mountain and Beverly, West Virginia*, Mary Genevieve Ward, published by McClain Printing Co., p. 139.

[50] *Civil War Legends of Rich Mountain and Beverly, WV*, p. 39.

[51] *Civil War Legends of Rich Mountain and Beverly, WV.*

[52] The Battle of Rich Mountain: http://www.richmountain.org/history/battleofRM.html

[53] Sluice gate is a sliding gate or other device for controlling the flow of water, especially one in a lock gate.

[54] *Civil War Legends of Rich Mountain and Beverly, WV*, p. 46

[55] Civil War Legends of Rich Mountain and Beverly, WV, p. 40

[56] Speaker stick: The Talking or Speaking stick, used in many Indigenous cultures, is an ancient and powerful "communication tool" that ensures a code of conduct of respect during meetings is followed. The person holding the stick, and only that person, is designated as having the right to speak and all others must listen quietly and respectfully.

[57] Civil War Legends of Rich Mountain and Beverly, WV, p. 34

[58] Civil War Legends of Rich Mountain and Beverly, WV, p. 54.

[59] Told by Mrs. Willa Gibbons, from Civil War Legends of Rich Mountain and Beverly, WV.

[60] Bellows is a device with an air bag that emits a stream of air when squeezed together with two handles, used for blowing air into a fire.

[61] Rheumatism is any disease marked by inflammation and pain in the joints, muscles, or fibrous tissue, especially rheumatoid arthritis.

[62] Whipped and raped. Our Booker family history reveals that Margaret rebuked the slaveowner when he tried to "take her". Margaret was pregnant again and objected to his advances. Oral history states Margaret was whipped for her denial of his advances, but for some reason the slaveowner acquiesced, gave her a buckboard (and horse), and told her to take her children to freedom.

[63] News article by Joe Booker, "Rich Family Memories," 2003

[64] National Road: https://www.legendsofamerica.com/ah-nationalroad/

[65] Coffle: a line of animals or slaves fastened or driven along together.

[66] Hoe cakes: https://www.africanbites.com/southern-johnny-cakes-hoe-cakes/

[67] Paw-Paw fruit tree produces big, almost tropical fruit that taste like a cross between a banana and a mango: https://www.npr.org/sections/thesalt/2016/04/27/475768129/nurse-spy-cook-how-harriet-tubman-found-freedom-through-food

[68] Patrollers/Slave catchers were people who returned escaped slaves to their owners in the United States before slavery was abolished at the end of the American Civil War.

[69] A toll road, also known as a turnpike or tollway or toll plaza, is a public or private road for which a fee is assessed for passage. It is a form of road pricing typically implemented to help recoup the cost of road construction and maintenance. http://www.spturnpike.org/history/default.html#Some_Turnpike_Facts.

[70] This story came from the author's Great-Uncle George Booker in a 2003 interview with Professor Ric Sheffield of Kenyon College.

[71] Tollbooth advice: Dr. Chris Mielke, Executive Director of the Beverly Heritage Center mused that travelers on the Beverly-Fairmont Turnpike, like the Staunton-Parkersburg

Turnpike, could probably asked for directions to the next toll booth. He felt it was most likely that Margaret's family followed the Beverly-Fairmont Turnpike north then west to Wheeling/Martin's Ferry, crossed the Ohio River, then finished the last miles to Barnesville.

[72] Crackers: sometimes white cracker or cracka, is a derogatory term used for white people, used especially against poor rural whites in the Southern United States.

[73] Some Recollections of the Underground Railroad, Belmont County, Ohio, Genealogy and History, http://genealogytrails.com/ohio/belmont/undergroundrailroad.html

[74] Safe house: https://www.history.com/topics/black-history/underground-railroad

[75] Some Recollections of the Underground Railroad, Belmont County, Ohio, Genealogy and History, http://genealogytrails.com/ohio/belmont/undergroundrailroad.html

[76] Underground Railroad Museum: https://www.ugrrf.org

[77] Holloware is metal tableware such as sugar bowls, creamers, coffee pots, teapots, soup tureens, hot food covers, water jugs, platters, butter pat plates, and other items that accompany dishware on a table.

[78] A tinsmith, sometimes known as a **tinner**, tinker, tinman, or tinplate worker is a person who makes and repairs things made of tin or other light metals. By extension it can also refer to the person who deals in tinware, or tin plate.

[79] A stone mason is a person who cuts, prepares, and builds with stone.

[80] A **mercantile** establishment - a place of **business** for retailing goods. outlet, retail store, sales outlet. country store, general store, trading post - a retail store serving a sparsely populated region; usually stocked with a wide variety of merchandise.

[81] Packing tobacco into hogsheads, History of Barnesville, p. 5.

[82] History of Barnesville, p. 11.

[83] Watt Car and Wheel Company: https://ohiomemory.org/digital/collection/p267401coll36/id/23836/

[84] History of Barnesville, p. 15.

[85] History of Barnesville, p. 78.

[86] Captina: https://www.barnesville-enterprise.com/news/20170222/captinafrican-methodist-episcopal-church-cemetery-restoration-remembered-during-black-history

[87] History of Barnesville, p. 73.

[88] Beverly Heritage Center: http://www.beverlyheritagecenter.org

[89] According to George Booker, in an interview with Kenyon College, in about 1930 Herbert Booker was on the Mount Vernon Giants baseball team, playing local African American and white teams, as well as regional and national teams that scheduled games while traveling the circuit. They allegedly played Satchell Paige, the famous Negro Leagues star, at Mount Vernon Athletic Park. https://digital.kenyon.edu/communitywithin/88/

[90] Joe Booker's 1999 comprehensive article in the *Mount Vernon News Looking Glass* describes the many organizations his parents lead or participated in.

[91] George Booker's 2003 interview with Professor Ric Sheffield, Kenyon College, Knox County, Ohio.

[92] The life of Otho Sherman Williams is more fully explored in Kathy Lynne Marshall's *The Ancestors are Smiling!* and *Finding Otho: The Search for Our Enslaved Williams Ancestors.*

[94] "Put on (the) dog" is an expression that means to make a display of wealth or importance, especially by dressing stylishly and flashily.
[95] Order of the Eastern Star is a Masonic appendant body open to both men and women. It was established in 1850 by lawyer and educator Rob Morris, a noted Freemason, but was only adopted and approved as an appendant body of the Masonic Fraternity in 1873.
[96] Mason: A mason is a skilled worker who builds by laying units of substantial material (such as stone or brick). A **Mason** (or **Freemason**) is a member of a fraternity known as Masonry (or Freemasonry). They enjoy sharing the values of our nation's founding fathers; men who believe in the brotherhood of man are firmly rooted in the Constitution of the United States.
[97] "Top drawer" means the highest level in rank, excellence, or importance.
[98] The life of Pearl Williams Carter is more fully explored in Kathy Lynne Marshall's *The Ancestors are Smiling!*
[99] The life of Mary Ellen Carter Marshall is more fully explored in Kathy Lynne Marshall's *The Ancestors are Smiling!*
[100] The life of Daisy Dooley Marshall is more fully explored in Kathy Lynne Marshall's *Finding Daisy: From the Deep South to the Promised Land.*
[101] The life of Austin Henry Marshall is more fully explored in Kathy Lynne Marshall's *Finding Daisy: From the Deep South to the Promised Land.*
[102] Buppies: Young urban black professional, a black yuppie.

[103] Joseph Anderson working at own restaurant on North Main Street and lived at 153 East Walnut, in Washington, PA in 1897: (City Dir, p. 38)

[104] 1900 Census, Washington County, PA.

[105] "Booker's History as of 1983" created by historian M. Lavata Williams.

[106] Social Security Death Index, 1935-2014, issue 1973-1974.

[107] Social media is computer-based technology that facilitates the sharing of ideas, thoughts, and information through the building of virtual networks and communities. This project called for assistance from several Facebook pages, including Our Black Ancestry, West Virginia African American Genealogy, and West Virginia Genealogy! Just Ask! among many others.

[108] Miz Margaret Elizabeth: There were so many white women named Margaret and Elizabeth in Beverly, I chose to abbreviate John Stalnaker's mother's name, Margaret Elizabeth White Stalnaker Kittle, as Miz Margaret Elizabeth.

[109] Hairstons: https://www.amazon.com/Hairstons-American-Family-Black-White/dp/0312253931

[110] General Jubal Early was a proponent of the "Lost Cause" of the Confederacy, or simply the Lost Cause, is an American pseudo-historical,[1][2] negationist ideology which advocates the belief that the cause of the Confederate States during the American Civil War was a just and heroic one.

[111] List of slaves from Abraham Crouches Will, dated 1849 but discharged in 1854: WV, Wills and Probate Records, 1724-1985, Randolph, Wills, Vol 1-4 1787-1860.

[112] Chromosome browsers are tools that allow you to see the unique DNA segments, or blocks of DNA on chromosomes, shared between you and either one genetic match or a set of genetic matches.

[113] In autosomal DNA testing the term triangulation is most commonly used to describe the process of reviewing the pedigree charts of clusters of shared matches/in common with matches in order to identify a common ancestor or ancestral couple. This process is sometimes also known as tree triangulation. Triangulation is also used to describe the process of identifying shared segments of DNA and trying to identify a shared ancestor or ancestral couple from whom the segment has been inherited. This process is also sometimes known as segment triangulation. Segment triangulation requires access to segment data which is not available at AncestryDNA. Segment triangulation is best used in conjunction with chromosome mapping.

[114] Cluster genealogy is a research technique employed by genealogists to learn more about an ancestor by examining records left by the ancestor's cluster. A person's cluster consists of the extended family, friends, neighbors, and other associates such as business partners.[1] Researching the lives of an ancestor's cluster leads to a more complete and more accurate picture of the ancestor's life.

[115] A centimorgan (cM) is a unit used to measure genetic linkage. A child shares about 3400 cMs with each parent.

[116] Kunta Kinte is a protagonist in Alex Haley's novel *Roots: The Saga of an American Family*. Written in 1976, Haley's novel follows Kunta Kinte from his capture by white slavers in Gambia to his life as a slave in the United States.

[117] Webinar is a seminar conducted over the Internet.

[118] The Genealogical Proof Standard is a process used by genealogists to demonstrate what the minimums are that genealogists must do for their work to be credible: https://www.familysearch.org/blog/en/genealogicalproofstandardpart1/

[119] A More Complete History of Beverly, Historic Beverly Preservation, Inc. (historicbeverly.org/bevhist3.htm)

[120] OMG! Stands for "Oh My God!"

[121] Captina A.M.E. Cemetery restored: https://www.barnesville-enterprise.com/news/20170222/captina-african-methodist-episcopal-church-cemetery-restoration-remembered-during-black-history

[122] 2003 Kenyon College interview with George Booker.

[123] In 1846, after his wife died, John Stalnaker issued a $1 Bill of Sale to Elizabeth S. Earle, wife of John B. Earle, condemning Margaret and her issue forever to Elizabeth or her heirs. Elizabeth died in 1851, leaving John B. Earle as the sole slaveowner.

[124] The Genealogical Proof Standard shows what the minimums are that a genealogist must do for his or her work to be credible. There are five elements to the Genealogical Proof Standard:
   1. Reasonably exhaustive research has been conducted.
   2. Each statement of fact has a complete and accurate source citation.
   3. The evidence is reliable and has been skillfully correlated and interpreted.
   4. Any contradictory evidence has been resolved.
   5. The conclusion has been soundly reasoned and coherently written.

[125] Genetic Genealogy Standards and ethical guidelines for genetic genealogy: https://isogg.org/wiki/Ethics,_guidelines_and_standards

[126] GEDmatch is an online service to compare autosomal DNA data files from different testing companies.

[127] Midwest African American Genealogical Institute (MAAGI) is the only African American focused event offering a total of 48 classes over 3 days with evening lectures and guided personalized instruction. http://www.maagiinstitute.org

www.ingramcontent.com/pod-product-compliance
Lightning Source LLC
Chambersburg PA
CBHW051712020426
42333CB00014B/953